Applied Cognitive Psychology

A Textbook

Applied Cognitive Psychology

A Textbook

Douglas J. Herrmann
Indiana State University

Carol Y. Yoder
Trinity University

Michael Gruneberg
Indiana State University

David G. Payne
Educational Testing Service

Psychology Press
Taylor & Francis Group

New York London

Camera ready copy for this book was provided by the authors.

First published by
Lawrence Erlbaum Associates,
10 Industrial Avenue,
Malwah, New Jersey, 07430

This edition published 2011 by Routledge

Routledge
Taylor & Francis Group
711 Third Avenue
New York, NY 10017

Routledge
Taylor & Francis Group
2 Park Square, Milton Park
Abingdon, Oxon OX14 4RN

Cover design by Kathryn Houghtaling Lacey

Library of Congress Cataloging-in-Publication Data

Applied cognitive psychology : a textbook / Douglas J. Herrmann ...
[et al.].
      p. cm.

Includes bibliographical references and index.

ISBN 0-8058-3372-2 (cloth : alk. paper)
ISBN 0-8058-3373-0 (pbk. : alk. paper)
1. Cognitive psychology—Textbooks. 2. Psychology, Applied—Textbooks. I. Hermann, Douglas J.
BF201.A67   2005
153—dc22   2004062502
                                             CIP

Dedication

We thank our teachers for their efforts to help us understand cognitive issues such as discussed here: for Doug Herrmann (WLG, J McL, RCA); Carol Yoder (RC, JE, DM); Mike Gruneberg (JB, IH, CB), and for David Payne (BK, JN, HR).

Contents

Part III   Noncognitive Factors Affecting Cognition and Application

PREFACE

The field of applied cognitive psychology represents a new emphasis within cognitive psychology. Although interesting applied research has been published over the last several decades, and more frequently in the last dozen years, there is little published about the overall progress in this new applied area. Our goal is to present the theory and methodology of cognitive psychology that may be applied to problems of the real world and to describe the current range of cognitive applications to real-world situations. The book is intended to be used either by a student who has had a course in cognitive psychology or who is concurrently studying cognitive psychology. Depending on the students' backgrounds, the book could be used with graduate students as well as with undergraduates.

The presentation of basic cognitive theory and findings is organized here in a way that students can readily apply. Because secondary school and college science courses rarely address the differences between basic and applied science, this book begins with an explanation of these differences, especially as manifested in cognitive psychology across discipline areas. Subsequently, specific chapters address specific cognitive processes, such as learning, retention, and reasoning.

The focus of both the general and specific chapters necessarily differs from the chapters in basic cognitive texts. Basic cognitive texts usually attempt to impart not only knowledge about important findings and theories but also a feel for the adversarial process of science that led to the findings and theories. Applied texts must achieve the same goals but not in the same detail because these topics are covered in the basic cognitive texts. Instead, applied texts must indicate how the findings and theories also may be usefully applied to real-life problems. Consequently, an applied textbook must provide a briefer account of basic theories and findings, while conveying the adversarial process of scientific inquiry presented in regular cognitive psychology texts.

This book identifies the rudimentary principles of basic theory (e.g., perception, comprehension, learning, retention, remembering, reasoning, problem solving, and communication) that lend themselves to application. Each of the specific chapters presents one or two case studies that describe actual applications of one or more of the principles explained in the chapter. Using this approach, the reader is exposed to a variety of applications in academia, business, medicine, law, government, and other sectors of society. Across the chapters, students learn about basic cognitive psychology, about the application process, and about cognitive applications. They also learn about many examples of effective applications, which can be considered if in years ahead they attempt or evaluate a similar application.

The book examines a range of cognitive products and services. For example, the book discusses cognitive software products that effectively teach people information in ways not possible previously. Similarly, computer systems have been marshalled to aid or manage a variety of tasks (Olson & Olson, 1999). For example, software has been developed that reminds people of medical appointments, and personal data systems have been developed that allow people to access, at any time, far more information than was possible when people could carry only written or printed information. Services are discussed that apply findings from cognitive psychology to procedures for interviewing eyewitnesses, to methods for pretesting surveys (Loftus, Fienberg, & Tanur, 1985; Turner & Martin, 1984) to techniques of cognitive improvements and to treatments that rehabilitate cognitive impairments due to head injury and neurological disorders (Baddeley, Wilson, & Watts, 1995; Parente' & Herrmann, 2003).

This book is also helpful to psychologists - regardless of background and specialization - who desire to understand the application of cognitive psychology to problems in either academia, business, industry, or government. Also, the text is useful to students and professors in upper level undergraduate or lower level graduate courses in applied or cognitive psychology (such as Applied Psychology, Applied Cognitive Psychology, Cognition, Cognitive Psychology, Cognitive Science, and Memory and Cognition).

THE PLAN OF THIS BOOK

The book consists of 2 general and 16 specific chapters. The general chapters present information on issues that pertain to the relationship between basic and applied cognitive psychology across discipline areas. The specific chapters - like typical cognitive psychology texts - address specific cognitive processes and factors that influence cognition.

Besides being the first textbook to present a review of the applications of major principles of basic cognitive psychology, this textbook is also the first cognitive textbook to familiarize students with the institutional and social factors that affect communication between basic and applied researchers and, therefore, determine the success of application efforts. In presenting applications important to many problems in society, the book also demonstrates the value of basic research in leading to these important applications.

Readers are likely to notice that the Reference section of this book is substantially larger than in other textbooks. The substantial number of references in this textbook is a consequence of its mission. First, because this textbook focuses on applied psychology, it must review many basic findings and theories, in addition to reviewing applied research, because applied research presumably emanates from basic research. To understand topics in grater detail, it will be helpful to consult the many listed citations. Basic research textbooks assume that their mission is to explain basic research only. As a result, basic research textbooks typically cite few applied research sources because applied research is assumed to be irrelevant to the development of basic research, despite that a great deal of basic research originates in an effort to solve a real-world problem. Perhaps the day will come when the authors of basic research textbooks will choose to violate current custom and address how basic research is often derived from applied research. In the meantime, textbooks on applied psychology, such as this one, cite many more sources than are usually cited in textbooks on basic research. Second, this textbook cites a substantial number of references to help readers apply cognitive psychology. Because applications are specific to a situation with certain objectives, researchers find very similar applications to be very useful in formulating the application that they want to develop. Thus, this textbook includes in a citation not only relevant basic research and an illustrative application of the basic research but also some additional applications that would be valuable to anyone who wants to create an application that is similar to the example.

Acknowledgment

The authors are grateful to our students and faculty colleagues for insightful comments on various topics in the book. We are especially grateful to the following people, who advised us in the writing of this text: Nancy Rankin, Judy Swez, Douglas Raybeck, Virgil Sheets, Michael Sarapata, Adam Hoffman, Beth Hartzler, Toni Bolinger, Cari Riggs, and Tyler Brosey. We thank Donna Herrmann for considerable help in preparing the final draft of the text. Finally, the authors are indebted especially to Jorge W. Gordon for producing the design of the layout of the complete book.

I

Fundamentals

1

Introduction to Applied Cognitive Psychology

Know what you really need to know and you
will know what you really need.
                                    - Author unknown

What is cognition? Although coming up with a simple and straightforward definition may be a bit misleading, cognition has to do with how we know. An enormous range of cognitive phenomena have been described and explained by cognitive research. Just since the turn of the century, many textbooks on cognitive psychology have been published (Anderson, 2004; Andrade, 2004; Eysenck, 2001; Galotti, 2003; Goldstein, 2004; Keane, 2005; Kellog, 2002; Matlin, 2005; Medin,Ross, & Markman, 2004; Healey, 2004; Hunt & Ellis, 2004; Kellog, 2002; Parkin, 2000; Robinson-Riegler & Robinson-Riegler, 2004; Shohov, 2005; Solso, 2001; Sternberg, 2005; Sutherland, 2003; Thompson & Madigan, 2005; Willingham, 2004). Some of the major concepts that have been explored are awareness (e.g., do we have to consciously attend to something to learn about it?), understanding (e.g., how do we comprehend and make judgments about people or events?), memory (e.g., how do we learn and retrieve information?), and skill (e.g., how do we develop expertise in reasoning or executing tasks?).

THE COGNITIVE SYSTEM

How accurately we understand what is happening in our world depends on how effective our cognitive system is. That is, are we accurately assessing what is going on in the world around us? Are we finding good solutions to problems? Components of the cognitive system carry out particular kinds of cognitive processes that allow us to use information. These cognitive components carry out a range of processes, including attention, perception, memory, reasoning, decision making, and communication.

The configuration of the components is called the system's architecture (Anderson, 1983). For example, some psychologists feel that sensory processes connect directly with long-term memory, whereas other psychologists claim that after sensory processes occur, attention and perceptual processes must actively transfer information into long-term memory. Disagreements about how components function together constitute the primary arguments about the cognitive architecture of the mind. Throughout time, even ancient philosophers such as Plato and Aristotle, have speculated about the blueprint of the mind.

Models

When psychologists specify cognitive components and their interrelationships, they create a model of the mind. Psychologists attempt to develop models of the mind in the same way that automotive engineers make models of potentially new concept cars before they are built. Many different models of cognition have been constructed (Atkinson & Shiffrin, 1968; Conway, 1997).

One model of cognitive processing is presented in the form of the brain. This model might shade locations of the brain involved in particular cognitive processes, such as attention or memory. Fig. 1.1 shows a brain model of cognition where current research indicates that different cognitive functions are localized.

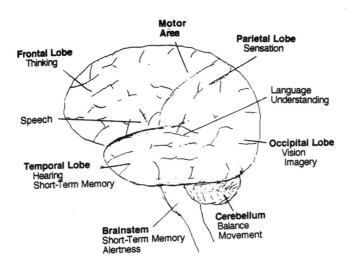

FIG. 1.1 The localization of cognitive functioning and response modes in the brain.

Another kind of model is conceptual. This kind of model is often presented in the form of a flowchart with different boxes representing certain components that execute particular cognitive process (e.g., like perception or learning) and lines connecting the boxes to show the sequence of processes in the mind. Conceptual models are usually not concerned with where in the brain cognitive processes occur. Instead these models are used to identify components of cognitive processes (such as for perception and brief memory storage) and how these components are or are not connected with each other (Norman, 1998).

However, it should be noted that many aspects of the cognitive system have been localized in the brain (e.g., sensory system, perception, attention, learning). When people engage in a range of cognitive performances, active brain areas can be pinpointed with imaging technologies. However, there are some cognitive components whose precise location in the brain are uncertain or seem to be localized in multiple areas depending on the cognitive task that is used. For example, the processes involved in the localization of comprehension, remembering, reasoning, problem solving, decision making, and aspects of communication seem to be distributed in different cortical areas. The relatively new neuroimaging techniques (e.g., functional magnetic resonance imaging) are proving to be very helpful in localizing cognitive functions because they allow professionals to view images of the brain at work (Cabeza & Kingstrone, 2002). Decisions about proposed components of models are based on experimentation (Teasdale et al., 1995; Tulving, 1983), correlational studies among measures of cognitive performance (Herrmann et al., 2001; Nyberg, 1994; Schacter, 2001), and studies of people with various types of brain damage (Schacter & Gilsky, 1986; Squire, 1987).

Levels of Cognition. Scholars as far back as Aristotle and Plato recognized that cognitive processes vary in the level of abstraction they require. Some mental processes enable us to know something new, such as when we sense, perceive, or encode something unfamiliar to us. Other mental processes, such as comprehension, learning, or remembering, allow us to access a memory from the past. Other mental processes, such as problem solving and decision making, require us to integrate many different cognitive processes to come to a solution.

Levels of Component Functioning.- If cognitive processes occur at different levels, then the components that generate these processes occur at different levels as well:

-**Lower level input systems:** sensory system, perception system, encoding system.
-**Intermediate level systems:** storage and access systems: comprehension system, registration system (learning), remembering.
-**High level systems (discovery and coordination of knowledge):** reasoning, problem solving, decision making, communication.

What we know about cognition has been discovered through experimentation, observational studies, correlational studies, and various types of interviews. The discipline of cognitive psychology has grown and matured from refinements in an ever increasing body of literature that investigates basic cognitive processes as well as real world applications of that knowledge.

WHAT APPLIED COGNITIVE PSYCHOLOGY IS

In a nutshell, applied cognitive psychology is a discipline focused on creating and refining products, services, and procedures based on principles of human cognitive processes (Berry, 1995; Davies & Pressley, 1993; Ellis & Jones, 1994; Logie & Bruce, 1990; Long, 1995). There are a number of factors that affect how well researchers can develop effective products and services.

First, to be effective at creating useful applications, applied researchers need to be well informed about basic processes and cognitive mechanisms. Having a good grasp of current understandings of the cognitive system and its various components (e.g., perception, attention, memory) is critical.

Second, besides having a thorough understanding of these components, it is also important to recognize how these components are affected by noncognitive modes. Noncognitive modes are parts of the overall bio-psycho-social system that are not normally considered cognitive but can and do influence cognitive functioning. Noncognitive modes include a person's physical state, emotional state, motivation, and social contexts.

Third, to create effective applications it is necessary to be pragmatic, practical, and flexible in how one approaches different problems. Often, effective applications call for creative approaches to conceptualizing and solving problems. It is essential that applied researchers fully understand the system, machine, and process they are trying to improve. Finally, applied researchers cannot allow themselves to get too tangled up in details and subtleties of cognitive processes unless it particularly affects the application they are trying to develop. Keeping a sharp focus on the goal is critical.

The field of applied cognitive psychology is growing rapidly. This developing area is making important contributions to a wide range of practical applications and at the same time is providing a new way to look at human behavior. How people process information in the real world is often markedly different from how they do similar tasks in a laboratory in part because everyday cognitive performances are experienced as more meaningful and personal compared to those typically accessed in the lab. Research in applied cognitive psychology, along with human factors, cognitive ergonomics, and cognitive engineering, reveals that the traditional approach of cognitive psychology is no longer sufficient to provide a complete account of human cognition (Canas, 2003; Harris, D; Payne & Blackwell, 1997). Because getting a sense of how applied cognitive psychology began may be helpful, we next describe some of the people and events that set the stage.

THE FOUNDING OF APPLIED COGNITIVE PSYCHOLOGY

The basic applied relationship was advanced nearly four centuries ago by the philosopher Francis Bacon (1620/1905). Bacon distinguished between the intellectual and practical understanding of nature while also assuming that these two kinds of understanding are interdependent.

Bacon (1620/1905) held that basic research has the responsibility of identifying the fundamental principles of nature (Adams, Smelser, & Trieman, 1982a, 1982b; Butterfield, 1957; deWolff, 1993; Hall & Hall, 1964; Pedhazur & Schmelkin, 1991; Wolfe, 1959). These principles describe how classes of variables, when independently manipulated, produce changes in other dependent variables (Platt, 1964). For example, current testing in an Air Force research lab is concerned with the problem of cognitive performance under conditions of deprivation common at the outset of war. Their research finds a 25% decline in cognitive functioning during wartime flying conditions. A variety of environmental variables (e.g., temperature, lighting) and person variables (e.g., individual difference, drug response) have been manipulated to improve pilot performance under sleep deprivation conditions.

When Wilhelm Wundt founded scientific psychology in the late 1800s, he advised psychologists to investigate basic psychology before trying to apply psychology (Boring, 1950). Nevertheless, in just a few decades, a Wundt student, Hugo Munsterberg conducted a number of applied research projects and worked hard to persuade others that applied psychology was possible (Fagan & VandenBos, 1993; Hergenhahn, 1986). For example, one of his best-known works, *On the Witness Stand* (Munsterberg, 1908), focused on why children may not make good witnesses in court.

Like Bacon, Munsterberg (1913) believed that "The knowledge of nature and the mastery of nature have always belonged together" (p. 6). Unlike Wundt, his teacher, Munsterberg urged psychologists not to avoid applied research until basic research had solved all of the most important critical issues. He noted that "if the psychologists were to refrain from practical application until the theoretical results of their laboratories need no supplement, the time for applied psychology would never come" (p. 7). Munsterberg (1908; shown in Fig 1.2) believed that "Applied psychology [would] become an independent experimental science which stands related to ordinary experimental psychology as engineering to physics" (p. 9). Munsterberg is often described as the founder of applied psychology (Munsterberg 1908, 1913, 1914; see M. Munsterberg's biography of H. Munsterberg). After Munsterberg died in 1916, interest in applied cognitive psychology went underground because behaviorism became the dominant way of looking at psychological issues, an approach that lasted until the 1950s.

FIG. 1.2.
Hugo Munsterberg (1863-1916), founder of applied psychology and pioneer in applied cognitive psychology.

Nevertheless, there were a few proponents of applied psychology in this period. Hollingsworth and Poffenberger (1929) published a textbook titled Applied Psychology, which advanced the relationship between basic and applied science set forth by Bacon and, much later, Munsterberg. In an aside concerning the use of differentiating between applied and basic science, Hollingsworth and Poffenberger commented that " every scientific discovery has the possibility of leading to some practical applications, so that sooner or later it will determine a course of events in the future and for practical life" (p. 9). Also in this period, Frederick Bartlett (1932/1995) argued that natural procedures should be used to investigate memory. Using verbal prose materials, Bartlett's study of memory and comprehension focused on the constructive nature of memory and how we create schemas to organize and remember information in meaningful ways. His research demonstrated that memory is influenced by our experience and our culture.

The advent of World War II (1940-1945) and its challenges stimulated applied cognitive research. Problems with the technology of that era (e.g., airplanes, radio) led psychologists to revisit the cognitive principles in product design and other applications (Lachman, Lachman, & Butterfield, 1979; Miller, Galanter, & Pribram, 1960). One psychologist who was especially successful in applying psychology at that time was Donald Broadbent. He investigated and solved problems concerned with aircraft instrumentation that he had encountered as a pilot in the war. As a pilot, Broadbent had been acutely aware of the confusing similarity of some of the gauges, which encouraged perceptual and attentional errors. Applying his understanding of cognitive processes to this real-life problem resulted in cockpit instrumentation changes designed to improve human performance.

Broadbent's (1958) experiences as a pilot also led him to make important contributions to understanding the process of attention. During the war, radio communication relied on a single radio frequency, where multiple messages might be delivered simultaneously. The simultaneous messages forced the listener to selectively attend to the appropriate information. Broadbent investigated this situation with what became known as a dichotic listening task. In this task, different messages were played in each ear through earphones. How people responded to the dichotic listening task made it clear that attention enables people to filter out and ignore irrelevant information. In short, several areas of Broadbent's work were shaped by real-world problems that led to creative applications of cognitive psychology.

In the 1950s, applied cognitive research turned to questions having to do with learning and language (Baars, 1986). In both research areas, dissatisfaction had grown with the stimulus-response approach of behaviorists. Also, artificial intelligence researchers showed that it was possible to program computers to simulate human processes such as learning (Gluck & Myers, 2000; Russell & Norvig, 2003). The idea that the mind functions something like a computer was compelling; this idea influenced the development of theories of cognition from the early 1960s into the present (Lachman et al., 1979).

In 1967, Ulric Neisser published a textbook titled *Cognitive Psychology*. This book provided the first coherent review of the cognitive psychological research conducted during and after World War II. Many psychologists read this book and many professors made this book required reading for their students at various colleges and universities. Because this book was the first to review this new field, modern cognitive psychology is often dated with the publication of Neisser's textbook (see also Neisser, 1976).

As basic cognitive research grew and matured, modern applied cognitive research became increasingly common (Baddeley, 1981; Baddeley & Wilkins, 1984; Berger, Pezdek, & Banks, 1987; Gillan & Schvaneveldt, 1999; Hoffman, 1997; Hoffman & Deffenbacher, 1992). Gradually more and more psychologists made a plea for broader approaches to cognitive research (Schacter, 1984; Solomon, Goethals, Kelley, & Stephens, 1986; Wyer & Srull, 1986). Many basic researchers became interested in determining whether their findings actually did anticipate how people responded in the real world (see Nickerson, 1997).

Many others pushed for research that is ecologically valid (i.e., research that evaluates whether basic research findings obtained in the laboratory could be reproduced in natural environments; Cohen, 1989; Hutchins, 1995; Neisser, 1982; Winograd, Fivush, & Hirst, 1996; Payne, 2001, and Neuschatz, Payne, Lampinen, & Toglia, 2001). More applied researchers sought to develop practical uses of basic research (e.g., Baddeley, 1990; Conrad, 1997; Neath & Surprenant, 2003; Payne, Klin, Lampinen, Neuschatz, & Lindsay, 1999; Squire, 1992; Tulving & Craik, 2000).

Two conferences that were especially important to developing the applied cognitive field focused on practical uses of scientific knowledge about memory. The first international Practical Aspects of Memory Conference was held in 1978, and the second was held in 1987, both in Wales. The conferences covered a variety of "innovative" areas, such as eyewitness memory, face recognition, metamemory, autobiographical memory, prospective remembering, maintenance of knowledge, memory for action events, rehabilitation, and educational aspects of memory. According to many, the proceedings of these conferences provided the state-of-the-art account of the research and issues in the field of applied memory (Gruneberg, Morris, & Sykes, 1988).

Although many people viewed research on the practicalities of memory in everyday life as valuable, controversy emerged between basic and applied memory researchers. This controversy was ignited by Neisser's (1978) keynote paper at the first Practical Aspects of Memory Conference, in which he questioned the usefulness of basic research in a very polemic fashion that amused some researchers but clearly irritated others.

In 1988, a second Practical Aspects of Memory Conference was convened. In the next year, Banaji and Crowder (1989) published an article that criticized the views that Neisser had advanced at the first conference, claiming that applied research revealed little or nothing about the basic principles of memory.

Subsequently, Elizabeth Loftus (1991) organized a special issue in the American Psychologist to address the controversy. However, the collection of articles (by Bahrick, Bruce, Conway, Klatsky, Loftus, Morton, Roediger, Tulving, Ceci, and Bronfenbrenner), as well as a reply by Banaji and Crowder added additional fuel to the conflict between basic and applied researchers. Alternatively, Klatsky (1991) and Baddeley (1981, 1993) argued that it was time to set the controversy aside and proposed that basic and applied cognitive researchers progress most effectively if they work collaboratively (Baddeley, 1981, 1993; Zacks & Hasher, 1992). When the third Practical Aspects of Memory Conference was held in 1994, harmony between basic and applied researchers prevailed.

While the Practical Aspects of Memory Conferences were occurring, applied cognitive psychology was developing in other ways. Other researchers sought to establish journals that might regularly report applied cognitive research. The journal Applied Cognitive Psychology was first published in 1987. In the same year, Berger et al. (1987) published the first book on applied cognitive psychology, consisting of a collection of research articles from this new field. In 1992 a special issue of the journal *Memory & Cognition* was devoted to memory and cognition applied.

In 1994, *Society for Applied Research on Memory and Cognition* was formed. Since its founding, this society has met every year or two. In 1996, a second journal, *Cognitive Technology*, was founded by the society to provide an outlet for applied research that leads to technologies that aid cognition (e.g., Nickerson, 1997).

THE GROWTH OF APPLIED COGNITIVE PSYCHOLOGY

As the history above reveals, applied cognitive psychology has developed rapidly as basic cognitive psychology has grown. Over the past three decades many researchers have successfully applied basic cognitive theories to understanding everyday problems (Barber, 1988; Berger et al., 1987; Benjafield, 1997; Galotti, 2003; Gruneberg & Morris, 1992; Gruneberg, Morris, & Sykes, 1978, 1988; Herrmann, McEvoy, Hertzog, Hertel, & Johnson, 1996a, 1996b; Izawa, 1993; Payne & Conrad, 1997). Many applications have been developed through this period (Hoffman & Deffenbacher, 1992, 1993) as have many new products and services (Clegg, 1994). Thus, applied cognitive psychology has succeeded in developing its own unique view of cognition, a view that has a somewhat different focus from other fields that address cognition, including basic cognitive psychology (Ellis & Jones, 1994); Guenther, 1998; Haberlandt, 1997) and cognitive science (Gardiner, 1985; Gardner, Kornhaber, & Wake, 1996; Mandler, 1985; Simon, 1980).

The range of real-world problems tackled and solved by applied cognitive psychologists is impressive (Payne et al., 1999; Walker & Herrmann, 2004). Products and services have been devised to remedy situations in which people have difficulties in perceiving, comprehending, learning, remembering, reasoning, and problem solving. For example, principles of cognitive psychology have been successfully applied to improving surveys, identifying flaws in computer screens in commercial software, and developing treatments for cognitive problems due to neuropsychological impairments, and as well as numerous other products and services intended for the home, business, industry, and government worldwide.

Moreover, considerable research raised serious questions about legal and judicial practices. For example, applied cognitive findings highlight concerns about the use of eyewitnesses in court. Such findings also were used to evaluate new procedures proposed by the Food and Drug Administration to regulate advertisements of over-the-counter drugs. Because of the way humans process information, it is easy to present advertisements that will be distorted and misremembered so that people incorrectly make certain assumptions about what products do.

For example, strategically deleting portions of text in an ad can make the ad more effective, as can omitting a stated conclusion (Sawyer & Howard, 1991). When we draw our own inferences and conclusions, we are less likely to question the message we have inferred.

Memory applications became very common. Products and procedures focused on memory include assessment measures (Poon et al., 1986), external aids to memory (Intons-Peterson & Newsome, 1992; Yoder & Herrmann, 2003), memory improvement strategies (Herrmann, Weingartner, Searleman, & McEvoy, 1992; McEvoy, 1992; Poon, 1980), and cognitive rehabilitation (Bergman, 1998; Bracey, 1996; Herrmann & Parente', 1994; Parente', 1998; Parente' & Anderson-Parente', 1991; Schacter & Gilsky, 1986; Solberg & Mateer, 1989; Wilson, 1987). The promise of applied cognitive psychology lies especially in the products and services it fosters as solutions to everyday problems.

WHAT APPLIED PSYCHOLOGY IS NOT

Applied cognitive psychology may originate in ecologically valid research or applicable research, but these kinds of research are not sufficient to develop applications. In principle, applied cognitive psychology is derived from basic psychological theory, but it is also motivated to produce a strategy, technique, or product that is generalizable from situation to situation (Chapanis, 1967; Chapanis & Morgan, 1949; Herrmann & Raybeck, 1997; Intons-Peterson, 1997).

It is important to point out that certain sub fields of psychology have arisen that specialize in providing particular kinds of applied cognitive applications. Cognitive engineering, cognitive rehabilitation, and cognitive therapy have all devised applications appropriate to the main focus of these fields. Survey methodology, an interdisciplinary field, has developed its own cognitive methods for designing and administering surveys (Jabine, Straf, Tanur, & Tourangeau, 1984; Loftus et al., 1985; Sirken et al., 1999). Historians have applied their understanding of cognition to improving methods of historical research. Table 1.1 presents the names of several different fields that are related to applied cognitive (Sanders & McCormack, 1993).

WHAT APPLIED COGNITIVE PSYCHOLOGY MAY BECOME

In addition to the many problems already solved by applied cognitive psychology, this new applied field holds the promise of solving a wide variety of problems that confront individuals, organizations, and institutions. Applied cognitive psychology also has the potential to reveal those aspects of current cognitive theory that are

TABLE 1.1

Terms Pertaining to the Application
of Cognitive Psychology in Related Fields

Cognitive Psychology - basic cognitive research investigates the fundamental cognitive processes through controlled experimentation and observation

Cognitive science - multidisciplinary investigation of the origins, development, components, and deployment of knowledge in human and nonhuman systems

Ecologically valid cognitive research - investigation of basic cognitive processes in natural real-world settings

Applicable cognitive research - investigation of potential applications of basic or ecologically valid cognitive research (sometimes called mission oriented)

Cognitive applications - use of basic cognitive psychology to solve a practical problem

Cognitive technology - applications that may be generalized across situations and people, applied repeatedly to common cognitive tasks

Engineering
Human factors engineering - engineering applied to the design and use of machines

Cognitive engineering - engineering that takes account of cognitive processes

Cognitive ergonomics - equipment design that optimizes cognition

Communication
Instructional technology – knowledge of how instruction is maximally effective

Information-processing theory - the theory of how information is represented and transmitted;

the most powerful and most productive in terms of creating new technologies and services (Herrmann, Yoder, Parente, & Schooler, 1997; Walker & Herrmann, 2004). How we think and process information is a product of many cognitive and noncognitive factors.

Along with human factors, cognitive ergonomics, and cognitive engineering (Harris, 2001), applied cognitive psychology assumes that the traditional cognitive psychology approach does not adequately embrace all of the complexities of human information processing. Instead of a responsive, optimally functioning cognitive unit (e.g., a university undergraduate), which is often assumed in cognitive psychology, applied cognitive psychology suggests employing a cybernetic model of human responding. This type of model takes account of how a person acts and interacts with the environment. Interactions are recognized as outcomes of different kinds of processes. The cybernetic model specifically relies on the concept of feedback. A person presumably receives feedback that originates from all pertinent social, physical, and motivational factors that affect how we know. By recognizing the role of different kinds of feedback in shaping outcomes, and the interaction of the person and the environment, the model can provide a comprehensive account of responding.

WHAT YOU WILL LEARN FROM THIS BOOK

An applied approach to cognitive psychology calls attention to a wider array of issues than are normally covered in a standard cognitive psychology text. Here are the topics that you will learn especially well from this book.

The nature of applied research
The nature of the relationship between basic and applied research
The fundamentals of basic cognitive research
The fundamentals of applied cognitive research
Examples of application research for different cognitive processes
How to generate creative ideas
How to transform a creative idea into a legitimate application
The nature of the career of applied cognitive psychologists

SUMMARY

In this chapter, we considered what applied cognitive psychology is, what it is not, and what it might become. Simply put, it is the application of scientific knowledge to investigate and design products and services that may be used in one or more situations. Applied cognitive psychology has roots in the ideas of Francis Bascon who, nearly four centuries ago, wrote about the relationship of basic science and its application. Applied cognitive psychology has a strong allegiance to basic cognitive theory. However, its focus overlaps with cognitive ergonomics, cognitive, engineering, and human factors (Payne & Blackwell, 1997). The goal of applied cognitive psychology is to apply knowledge of cognitive psychology to make valuable contributions to the common good of society.

2

Similarities and Differences Between Basic and Applied Cognitive Research

Science discerns the laws of nature. Industry applies them to the needs of man.

- Author unknown

It is likely other parts of your education have already given you a good sense of the differences between basic and applied research. Nevertheless, there are some subtle but important distinctions you may not know. Even some professionals are not totally aware of certain differences between these two parts of science.

For a variety of reasons, basic researchers and applied researchers conduct their investigations in different ways. Basic researchers identify the effect of a variable while controlling as many other variables as possible and ignoring the rest. Applied researchers identify the effect of one or more variables that are key to an application, often while not controlling other variables. Instead of ignoring the remaining variables, an applied researcher measures how these variables may influence an application's effectiveness.

Suppose that the Federal Aviation Administration (FAA) wants to find a way for air traffic controllers to communicate faster with pilots. Basic researchers would test how accurately a group of pilots comprehend messages that vary in complexity as well as the speed of transmission. The pilots would have comparable amounts of training and experience, they would be tested after having approximately the same sleep, and they would be tested at the same time of day.

Applied researchers would test the comprehension of a group of pilots in the same ways as basic researchers when possible, but the testing may be abbreviated and expedited. Applied researchers often have pressures on them to come up with answers faster than basic research. For example, determining the optimal message speed, that can be used by controllers for good comprehension by pilots, may be needed because an accident has just occurred and the FAA needs to make changes for safety reasons. When circumstances require a fast answer from research, the applied researcher may not insist that all pilots have the same background. They also may test the pilots when they are available, rather than scheduling them all to be tested at the same time of day. In addition, the applied researcher may get access to recorded radio messages in which the messages could be measured for their speed of presentation and the pilots' reactions could be assessed for degree of comprehension. Basic researchers would normally not be called on to listen to radio messages to identify the need for changes.

This chapter explains the important ways basic and applied research differ in their operations. Basic research attempts to explain why things happen. On the basis of these explanations, applied research develops applications and technologies to meet society's needs (Herrmann, 1995, 1997a; Payne, Conrad, & Hager, 1997). Basic researchers focus on questions concerned with the structure of cognition (Anderson, 1983; Gillian & Schvaneveldt, 1999; Squire, Knowlton, & Musen, 1993) or the process of cognition (e.g., Jacoby, Lindsay, & Toth, 1992), whereas applied researchers take a decidedly more pragmatic and functional approach to cognitive problems. You will find that an appreciation of the reasons for operational differences between basic and applied researchers will increase your grasp of what these two groups offer to science and society. Whether or not you continue your study of psychological science, this knowledge will serve you well in the future when reading about science.

TRAINING AND SPECIALIZATION

You might be surprised to learn that applied researchers and basic researchers are trained at the same schools and at the same time. That is, they take the same classes and sometimes even conduct the same types of research as students.

In centuries past, it was possible and even expected that all scientists be experts in both kinds of research. Indeed, generalists in basic and applied science were common in all sciences as late as the beginning of the 20th century. Today, because of the vast increase in both information and methods, and because of the physical and institutional separation of basic and applied research, cognitive scientists of all stripes are pressured to choose between being either a basic researcher or an applied researcher. This choice is made either in graduate school or when leaving graduate school for employment.

Once employed, basic and applied researchers specialize differently. In recent decades the explosion of basic research in various fields has made it necessary for basic cognitive researchers to read and to commit to memory a large number of studies, and also to become familiar with the literature in only a few narrow research areas.

In contrast, the applied researcher rarely can specialize. Because the applied researcher is assigned to work on one application after another, the applied researcher is constantly shifted from one research topic to another. Given these different demands, applied researchers tend to be generalists, equipped to develop a broad range of cognitive applications and technologies.

ORIENTATION TO PRACTICALITIES

More than many kinds of scientists, applied cognitive researchers have a vision of what cognitive psychology can do for the world. They have a firm grasp of a wide range of empirical research and related theory, as well as practical, real-world problems. Once applied cognitive psychologists have studied an application problem, they are better prepared to develop creative and useful solutions to problems involving human cognitive processes than other types of specialists (Gillan and Schvaneveldt, 1999).

CONCERNS OF BASIC AND APPLIED RESEARCHERS

Scientists begin by identifying variables. They identify variables that are held to produce a phenomenon. These variables are sometimes called independent variables. Scientists also identify variables that characterize the phenomenon. These outcome or performance variables are sometimes called dependent variables because they presumably depend on the independent variables.

Specifying the precise form of the functional relationship between variables is perhaps the major objective of science. The relationships identified by basic research are said to be basic because they supposedly apply to a wide set of situations and natural occurrences. Basic research is regarded as pure (Chapanis & Morgan, 1949; Wright, 1978) in that, in principle, research should generalize across situations. Indeed, basic researchers are described as being concerned with developing explanatory accounts of phenomena of interest (Payne et al., 1997). It is assumed that applications apply directly or with a small amount of adjustment for situational influence (Pedhazur & Schmelkin, 1991).

Applied researchers investigate the applicability of fundamental principles to resolve specific problems and to design and implement applications (Chapanis & Morgan, 1949). Through investigation, an attempt is made to extend basic principles to applicable research and eventually application (Hawkes, 1973; Herrmann, 1995; Herrmann & Gruneberg, 1993; Lens, 1987; Wright, 1978). If the principles appear to fail to apply to a problem even when appropriate changes are made then in theory the applied researcher could submit this problem to the basic researcher for further study and revision. After learning about a possible flaw in a basic principle, the basic researcher could then seek to discover the factor that was missing in the original formulation of the fundamental principle.

THE BASIC-APPLIED ACCOUNT IN PSYCHOLOGY

The tendency to separate basic from applied research in psychology was acknowledged early in the history of psychology. Ebbinghaus (1885/1913) established a tradition of investigating memory from a basic research tradition. The tradition he established lasted for almost 100 years before researchers felt sufficiently comfortable to investigate memory from an applied perspective (Barber, 1988; Berger et al., 1987; Hoffman, 1997; Hoffman & Deffenbacher, 1993).

Currently, the standard account of the relationship of basic and applied research is based on a division of scientific labor. Basic research identifies the principles that are fundamental to phenomena. Applied research determines how these principles may best be applied to particular situations. This division of labor has been successful in psychology (Herrmann, Raybeck, & Gruneberg, 1998; Intons-Peterson, 1997; Wright, 1978) and in many other sciences for several decades (Schultz, 1979, see Table 2.1). An example of the division within the sciences generally and within the field of psychology is provided in Table 2.2.

TABLE 2.1
The Division of Labor in Basic and Applied Sciences

Basic Science	Applied Science
Physics	Engineering
Chemistry	Chemical Engineering
Biology	Medicine
Psychology	Applied Psychology

TABLE 2.2
The Division of Labor in Basic and Applied Sciences

Basic psychology	Applied psychology
Abnormal psychology	Clinical psychology
Social psychology	Industrial/Organizational psychology
Psychology of mental abilities and Personality	Psychometrics Psychological assessment
Neuropsychology	Cognitive rehabilitation
Health psychology	Behavioral medicine
Psychology of motivation	Consumer psychology
Cognitive psychology	Applied cognitive psychology

Interdisciplinary Approaches

Applied research has traditionally been more interdisciplinary than basic research (Schonflug, 1993a). Because application projects occur in the real world, applied research often requires input from several disciplines to isolate the variables responsible for what is being investigated (Johnson & Field, 1981). Because basic research seeks to isolate fundamental principles, such research limits the number of independent variables, and that type of approach is usually easier to achieve within one or two disciplines. Even when basic research is interdisciplinary, fewer disciplines are involved than in applied research.

Communication Differences

Basic scientists tend to present research at conferences and in peer-reviewed publications, whereas applied researchers communicate using prototypes, standards or specifications, and reports that are not distributed widely because of industry competition and security. One outcome of these differing philosophies and communication styles is that each group tends to regard the other with considerable suspicion. Basic researchers see applied researchers as using inadequate experimental procedures and not fully incorporating all of the research knowledge available. Applied researchers see basic researchers as out of touch with real-life concerns and much too slow to get anything of consequence accomplished.

Moreover, basic and applied researchers are not very effective at working together. Basic researchers need to be able to communicate with each other so that their ideas will be used. Similarly, applied cognitive psychologists have to be able to communicate with each other but they also must sell their ideas to supervisors, executives, and consumers.

If applied researchers are disinclined to consider communicating about their contributions to products and services, their earning power will be restricted and, in addition, the creation of new products and services will be retarded. The public will not necessarily understand new cognitive products and services just by being told about them. That is, it may be necessary to find powerful ways to demonstrate the cognitive-saving or time-saving properties of new products.

AN EXAMPLE OF APPLIED COGNITIVE RESEARCH

Lineup procedures are commonly used by police to identify a suspect in a group of similar-looking others. In this hypothetical illustration the fictitious Downsberry Police Department has received media criticism for using lineup procedures that supposedly had framed some suspects and set free some very likely felons (Herrmann & Gruneberg, 1993). To confront this criticism, the police department contracted with a research psychologist to develop ways to improve its procedures. The psychologist then obtained data on past lineups conducted at the Downsberry Police Department. The psychologist proceeded to analyze data as a function of various aspects of these lineups (e.g., physical characteristics of those in the line, the backgrounds of the officers conducting the lineups, the intervals between the crime and the lineup). In addition, research was conducted comparing different lineup approaches used by the police. Based on the data analysis, the psychologist developed specific recommendations to improve the Downsberry Police's lineup procedures; however, these recommendations apply primarily to the Downsberry police (Gruneberg & Morris, 1992a; Gruneberg & Sykes, 1993; Wells, Seelau, Rydell, & Luus, 1994; see also Egeth, 1993; Loftus, 1979).

The psychologist's recommendations in a study such as this one concerning the Downsberry Police usually will be limited in generalizability. This is because, like most applied research, certain conditions of the study are unusual or at least not typical of lineup procedures of police departments everywhere. Obviously, the Downsberry Police Lineup Study cannot be generalized directly to all other police departments because other departments are somewhat different from the Downsberry department. Nevertheless, these results can still contribute to conclusions about lineups in general when its findings are considered along with other findings from similar studies. For example, if the results of two or more lineup studies, conducted in different police departments, conform to a pattern, then this pattern may suggest fundamental mechanisms at work.

In short, this example illustrates that, unless there are many investigations that report the same findings, applied research may make no claims about generalizability to other different settings. In contrast, well-established basic research assumes that its findings do generalize across other situations (although this assumption is inaccurate in some cases; Herrmann et al., 1998).

The Use of Basic and Applied Research for Society

Basic cognitive researchers try to determine the fundamental processes that underlie all cognitive phenomena. Basic researchers generally believe that their research ultimately is of the greatest value to society (Farley & Null, 1987). To many basic researchers, applied research is only valuable to the extent that it is based on basic principles. Alternatively, applied researchers generally believe that their research is of greatest value to society. To many applied researchers, basic research is only valuable because applied research makes it possible to realize the use and value inherent in basic principles.

It might be assumed that basic researchers need to know little or nothing about applied research. Applied researchers obviously must know basic research to apply it, but the reverse is not necessary. Nevertheless, there are good reasons for basic and ecological researchers to become familiar with applied research.

First, as noted earlier, knowledge of applied research can suggest effects of fundamental variables that otherwise would have to be rediscovered by basic research (Herrmann & Chaffin, 1988). Second, applied research forces the development of a sophisticated understanding of phenomena. Applying basic theory is usually much more difficult than envisioned by basic researchers (Chapanis, 1967).

Laboratory or ecologically valid findings are commonly designed to focus on the effect of a few variables, making the findings appear easier to apply to complex problems in the real world than they actually are. For example, actual lineups (as conducted in police stations) generally involve crimes that are far more serious and complex than those staged by researchers. In addition, real crimes are often committed by individuals who come from different economic, ethnic, and social classes than the police.

In contrast, in ecological research, the confederate criminal and the researcher usually originate from the same strata of society. In addition, real crimes are frequently embedded in a larger social phenomenon, such as poverty or drug addiction, whereas staged crimes are not a genuine manifestation of social phenomena. It is clear now that many variables can affect the likelihood that a witness will identify a criminal in a lineup (Deffenbacher, 1996; Lindsay, 1999; Loftus, 1979, 1993; Yuille, 1993; Yuille & Cutshall, 1986).

Mutual Dependence

Whether recognized or not, the success of applied research is critically important to the support given to basic research. The public tends not to finance basic research that does not lead to worthwhile applications. On the other hand, basic research provides applied researchers with a foundation on which to begin their thinking. Applied researchers almost never are so fortunate as to be able to isolate the effects they endeavor to understand, predict, or alter. Most problems in the real world cannot be cast into a fully controlled experiment because practical considerations and ethical concerns preclude doing so. While there are often considerable differences in approach, both groups work toward better understandings of how people function.

A TIME OF CHANGE

Prior to the 1970s, few everyday phenomena involving basic cognitive processes had been investigated outside of the education (Neisser, 1978) and applications of cognitive psychology (Gruneberg, Morris, & Sykes, 1978). Today applied cognitive psychology can take considerable satisfaction that many cognitive applications have been developed (Walker & Herrmann, 2004). However, applied cognitive psychology cannot afford to be indifferent to the progress in other competitive scientific groups.

Different real-world cognitive problems vary in how much they have been investigated. Based on a count of the literature conducted for this text; the most frequently investigated topic since 1970 was eyewitness testimony. The least investigated topic was the role of cognition in motor movements (Adams, 1987) although this is changing with more available neuroimaging methodologies. As shown in Table 2.3, the frequency of applied cognitive research articles in each of the areas listed fall into four bands that represent the degree to which topic has been addressed by published research articles.

TABLE 2.3
Amount of Applied Research as a Function of Research Topic

Amount	Topic for Applied Research
Very High	Eyewitness research, educational research on instruction, learning, sports
High	Cognition in legal and court issues, health, mnemonics, social cognition, business
Medium	Individual differences in cognition, assessment of cognitive performance, higher level cognitive functions (reasoning, problem solving, decision making), external cognitive aids, driving, emotions, autobiographical memory, surveys, sensory processes
Low	The arts, computers, motor movements, safety

SUMMARY

This chapter showed how different backgrounds and environmental demands lead basic researchers and applied researchers to conduct their investigations in different ways. Basic researchers identify the effect of a variable while controlling as many other variables as possible and ignoring the rest. Applied researchers identify the effect of one or more variables that are key to an application, often while not controlling other variables. Instead of ignoring the remaining variables, an applied researcher measures how these variables may influence an application's effectiveness.

3

Methodology
of Cognitive Research

If your methods are improper, the results
cannot make sense.
                                   - Author unknown

It is important to acknowledge that cognitive phenomena are not directly observed (e.g., no one has ever seen a mental image or a thought). Rather, these phenomena are indirectly measured through behaviors that indicate mental representation and processing. This chapter explains how cognitive phenomena are investigated in psychology.

We begin by examining the nature of cognitive phenomena. Investigating cognitive phenomena requires that different kinds of tasks be used to assess different types of thought processes (Fleishman, Quaintance, & Broedling, 1984). Different kinds of tasks require different types of cognitive skills with appropriate measurements. As with any science, proper use of methodology requires that certain knowledge sources be consulted to be sure that the tasks are properly implemented and that cognitive performance is fairly scored. Also, cognitive methods today are sometimes paired with brain imaging technologies to see how the brain responds to different stimuli and tasks. Finally, we discuss several ways to interpret observations of cognitive phenomena and then finish the chapter by reviewing how such observations are tested, evaluated, and used to refine cognitive theory and create cognitive products.

We wish to point out that you may already have read or be reading a cognitive psychology textbook that provides more detail on the methodology of cognitive research, such as textbooks authored by Anderson (2000), Galotti (2003, Jahnke & Nowaczyk (1998), Leahey & Harris (1997), Matlin (2005), Medin, Ross, & Markman (2004), Norman (1998), Payne & Wenger (1998), Pinker (1997), Reisberg (1997), Solso (2001) among others. It may also be helpful to consult individual articles to develop a more comprehensive understanding of particular methods.

MEASURING COGNITIVE PERFORMANCE

Cognitive performance does not necessarily equate with actual competence or ability to perform cognitive tasks. How we perform is also based on whether or not we understand what is expected, how motivated we are, whether we are able to focus our attention, as well as many other factors. Well-designed research should consider how these possible variables may influence performance.

Cognitive performance may be described in many ways. Usually, it is necessary to talk precisely about what aspect of cognitive performance is of interest. For example, we may be interested in the accuracy of memory performance, the speed of response or more subjective aspects of performance. In most studies, different measures of performance are collected.

The critical issue in cognitive research is to identify the characteristics of the cognitive situation on which the performance (or the phenomenon) depends (Goschke & Kuhl, 1994). Researchers first formulate certain statements or hypotheses of what is likely to occur. These hypotheses are then converted or operationalized into specific definitions of terms and procedures that can be tested in consistent and systematic ways. Conventionally, the characteristics of the cognitive situation on which performance depends are called independent variables. The goal of research is to identify which independent variables affect performance and then to develop explanations for why such effects occur. Since performance measures depend on the influence of independent variables, these outcome measures are called dependent variables.

The Nature of Independent Variables in Cognitive Tasks

Over the centuries, different kinds of characteristics have been identified as affecting cognitive phenomena. As might be expected, different cognitive phenomena depend critically on some independent variables than on others. For example, how well we remember information we just read in our textbook depends on how attentive we are, what we already know, how well we connect this new information with that knowledge, and how relevant that information is to us. In other remembering situations, such as seeing two cars hit each other from a car length away, ability to recall what happened is also dependent not only on whether or not we were attending but also on what happened immediately before and after the event and on how we are asked to recall the event. The literature on research design points to certain independent variables essential to understanding psychological phenomena. These variables may include a permanent characteristic of the subject, antecedent events that recently happened to the subject, ways that a task was explained to the subject, ways that stimuli are presented to the subject, the particular stimuli presented to the subject, and the kinds of situations in which a person must perform a cognitive task. These variables are listed in Table 3.1.

TABLE 3.1

Classes of Variables That Affect Registering, Retaining, or Remembering Information

Organismic variable (O) – a permanent characteristic or trait of an individual, such as gender, ethnicity, or personality characteristic, that influences how a particular cognitive task is performed

Antecedent variable (A) – something that recently happened to a person that temporarily affects how a cognitive task is performed

Task variables
> Instructional (I) – how instructions or procedures regarding how to accomplish a task are explained when presenting a cognitive task
>
> Presentational (P) – aspects of the way stimuli are presented to the person performing a cognitive task
>
> Stimulus (S) – the kinds of information or material presented to the person performing a cognitive task
>
> Context (C) – the kinds of situations in which a person must perform a cognitive task
>
> Retention (R) – the length of the interval, the presentation rate, the interference, the information that precedes or follows a memory task, and recall opportunities
>
> Task/Test (T) -- cognitive procedure to be implemented (recall, recognition, relearning, problem solving, decision making, reasoning)

Creating good research, and recognizing poor research, hinges on an awareness of the status of the variables in Table 3.1. Organismic variables (O) dispose a person to perform well or poorly. These variables pertain to a person's general capability for cognitive tasks, such as whether a person is a slow or fast learner or whether the person is a conservative or foolish guesser. Organismic variables may include any trait or characteristic, such as personal motivation, that a participant brings to a cognitive task that affects performance. Antecedent variables (A) may temporarily affect a person's typical level of performance. Such variables can range from degree of the previous night's sleep to the amount of other cognitive work required just before task performance. Without knowledge of antecedent variables, a researcher may be fooled by the results of a study.

There are any number of task variables that can influence how well we perform a task. Instructional variables (I) can prepare participants to perform a cognitive task intentionally by telling them what to expect and what to do. Presentation variables (P) affect the appearance of stimuli. The stimulus variables (S) refer to the kinds of materials to be learned or that may be used to aid remembering. Context variables (C) can range widely from the laboratory to the classroom or the workplace or the shopping mall (Block & Morwitz, 1999; Davies & Thompson, 1989). Retention variables (R) affect a participant's capability to remember what someone said or what a person looked like. Task/test variables (T) affect how a person is led to structure his or her responses (such as how one organizes a response to an unexpected request for information).

The different types of independent variables in Table 3.2 can combine in some fashion, although the relative contribution of these independent variables differs depending on particular tasks. One way to provide a general description of the scientific process is to determine how the different independent variables combine to affect cognitive performance. The simplest description of how the independent variables combine (following Woodworth, 1938) is expressed symbolically in this equation, where performance (P) may be a function (f) of the separate and joint effects of all the independent variables:

$$P = f \ [O, A, I, T, S, R, C]$$

Effects of Independent on Dependent Variables

Cognitive phenomena are assumed to be mediated by the components and processes of the nervous system. Mediating variables influence dependent variables, but they often work by having different effects on different levels of an independent variable. These mediating components or processes are labeled as hypothetical because they are inferred and cannot be directly measured. Instead we attempt to measure them with various paper-and-pencil tests or physiological or observational measures in ways that we believe validly get at the components or processes of interest.

When someone performs a cognitive task, we cannot see the inside of his or her brain and observe the part of the brain where cognition occurs. Instead, we see the test stimuli, and we hear or see the person's response to the task. Even with the new scanning methods that present images of areas of the brain that are active when a person performs a task, these images do not reflect all aspects of the brain process. With or without images of brain activity, researchers have to carefully monitor the changes in participant's responses as stimuli change.

Ultimately, research seeks to identify the processes that mediate the changes in performance (Druckman & Bjork, 1994; Roediger, Nairne, Neath, & Surprenant, 2001). Trying to understand the nature of mediating variables is often one of the key challenges for basic and applied researchers. There are two kinds of mediating variables.

Architectural mediating variables refer to the ways the nervous system is wired and how that affects cognitive performance. Architectural variables include the supposed physical relationship of short-term memory and long-term memory. For example, many researchers are persuaded that there are different physiological mechanisms for how memories are stored for short-term memory and long-term memory (Atkinson & Shiffrin, 1968; Cowan, 2001). Other researchers do not believe that short- and long-term memory involve different mechanisms but, instead, hold that short-term memory is an activation of part of the contents of long-term memory.

Process mediating variables refer to those aspects of how information that has been learned or gained from experience is processed (Anderson, 1983). Process variables refer to how the cognitive system functions based on previous learning and experience. For example, depending on their early experiences with education, children are more or less likely to learn in a classroom. Many factors are involved, but some important ones are their parents' attitudes about education, how much reading and exposure to information the children have received, and the kinds of teachers the children have.

OBSERVING COGNITIVE PHENOMENA

Primary Measures

Variables that are of key interest to the researcher's hypotheses constitute primary measures. Typically, these are the dependent variables that are believed to be associated with the independent variables and also, perhaps, influenced by powerful mediating variables. Although there are an almost infinite number of ways to measure what a person knows about a past event or some other designated information in memory research, we typically rely on some version of recall or recognition to measure this knowledge. Recall involves asking participants to remember what they can about the item of interest. In contrast, recognition typically involves asking participants to select from a group of choices which item they had previously seen or experienced.

Typically recognition tasks are easier than recall tasks in part because it is easier to retrieve information with cues or even to guess than to retrieve with no cues at all. If a question on a recognition test presents three wrong answers for every right answer, it is clear that, on average, a guess will be right 1 in 4 times. A common procedure is for a recognition test to consist of a series of items, presented earlier during learning, and to have participants classify each item as having, or not having, been presented earlier. With this procedure, there are two ways to be right. You may score a hit by identifying an old item as having been presented previously. Or you may score a correct rejection by identifying any new items as not having been presented during learning. Similarly, there are two ways to make a recognition error. You can overlook old items that had been presented before, scoring a miss; or you can identify new items as having been previously learned, scoring a false alarm. The overall patterns of these four types of responses can provide useful insights into how people are performing a recognition task.

Recall tasks permit several kinds of responses. You can correctly recall an item from a previously learned set of items. You can be wrong by failing to recall all or part of the information, or by recalling an item that does not belong to the previously learned set. The recall of an incorrect item is called an intrusion. Although accuracy of recall or type of intrusion is often important, sometimes how quickly people respond is the key variable of interest. For example, in some concept formation and matching tasks, it is assumed that everyone can do the task, so speed is the primary factor that discriminates individual performances.

In problem solving and decision-making, the quality of the response is typically evaluated. In some studies, primary measures might also include ratings of feelings of what one knows about a topic and ratings of confidence in cognitive responses. In other tasks, a primary measure may involve generating a response based on ability to consider and combine information provided or already known.

Secondary Measures

Secondary measures are typically not as central to the researcher's hypotheses as are primary measures. Nevertheless, researchers use secondary measures when a variable may influence outcomes and could provide interesting information that better explains outcomes. Secondary measures are sometimes variables that are recognized as being possible mediators of the independent-dependent variable relationship. In general they are important because they help us better understand correct or incorrect responses.

Secondary measures may provide information about physiological or psychological activity. For example, the response of the brain evoked by a cognitive stimulus, as measured by PET scans and CAT scans can give an index of cognitive processes. Secondary measures may assess participants' ratings of their subjective feelings and attitudes present during a cognitive task. However, whether a variable is a primary or a secondary measure is best understood in the context of a particular study. That is, what constitutes a primary and secondary measure depends on the central hypotheses of interest.

DETAILS OF METHODS

Stimulus Materials

Basic as well as more applied cognitive research examines cognitive performance for materials presented in the laboratory and in everyday life. These materials involve verbal items, such as words, numbers, lists, sentences, paragraphs, and conversations. Depending on the purpose of the study and the researcher's orientation, these verbal stimuli might be words selected that are unrelated, newspaper articles, or lunchroom discussions. But symbols, diagrams, maps, and pictures are used as well. These may take the form of geometric patterns, ambiguous drawings, or pictures of people, objects, and scenes.

Tasks

For decades, basic psychologists felt that cognition might best be understood by studying the mechanisms of how people perform a few elementary tasks. Sometimes the findings about performance on elementary tasks indicate how to create an application. For example, presenting paired associates, where two items are presented together initially, is a common method used to study associations created when forming memories. When we learn new terminology or when we learn a new language, similar techniques might be employed where we first learn to discriminate stimuli and possible responses and generate appropriate associations. Other times, research analyzes what is required in an application task and then may explore basic research for more information that may be helpful. Therefore, cognitive research must carefully select the task used to study a phenomenon.

Group versus Individual Analyses

Most cognitive research is conducted comparing groups of individuals. Because people bring so many individual characteristics to a task that can affect performance, most research designs plan to balance out this uncontrolled variation (e.g., error) through random assignment to experimental groups. Usually, an investigation involves measuring the performance of a group of people, but sometimes there are reasons to conduct case studies. For example, many of the effects of brain damage are examined in one person at a time because usually a person's damage is unique (Shallice, 1979). Alternatively, sometimes individuals have such particular expertise that it is not possible to conduct group studies. For example, chess masters have been studied for their particular reasoning skills, and mnemonists' memory abilities have been studied for their uncommon encoding, storage, and retrieval skills.

RESEARCH PROCEDURES AND STANDARDS OF SCIENTIFIC EVIDENCE

No particular cognitive study involves testing the entire population of human beings. Only a small proportion of people are ever tested. The group of people tested is called a sample. With the help of inferential statistics, we can estimate how likely it is that the behavior of the people in the sample is representative of people in general (Ayres & Wood, 1999).

Many research findings today are based on the likelihood of occurrence or probability. Typically we start with a hypothesis-testing procedure where we state our experimental hypothesis as well as what is called a null hypothesis. Typically we are interested in finding support for the experimental hypothesis. Our experimental hypothesis, such as "Procedure A will produce better memory for names than typical strategies people use to remember names." is what we are interested in finding. The null hypothesis simply states that you expect no difference between your comparisons. In this case, our null hypothesis might be "Procedure A will produce no better memory performance when compared to typical strategies people use to remember names."

Because it is not possible to ever test every possible sample, the standard hypothesis testing procedure is to show that the null hypothesis of no difference is not likely to be true. It comes down to comparing your distribution of scores to a distribution of scores that would occur by chance alone. For example, the chance distribution might be the memory performance people will get when not using Procedure A. If the difference between your sample and a sample of scores due to chance is great enough, you can conclude that your sample is really different from differences that would be expected simply because of random variation that naturally occurs among people.

Whether a difference is large enough to conclude that Procedure A was more effective than people's usual strategy of remembering names is determined by the probability, or alpha level, which is set before you begin your study. Most of the time, this probability level is conventionally set at .05. If the difference between your comparison groups reaches a level of .05, then the difference is large enough that, if the null hypotheses were in fact correct, it could only have happened by chance in 5 of 100 studies. Generally, when a probability of .05 is reached, it can be concluded fairly safely (95 times out of 100) that the null hypothesis can be rejected. When this happens, you have found support for your experimental hypothesis.

Why is probability routinely set at .05 in much scientific research? One of the key reasons is researchers do not want to report that a procedure is effective when it is not. When we conduct a study, we can be correct in determining that the null hypothesis should be rejected and the alternative hypothesis should be accepted. However, we can make an error in rejecting the null hypothesis, when it is really true. That is, if there is really no difference when we think there is, this is called a Type I error. The likelihood of a Type I error is the same as our probability level. That is, there is a 5% chance that we have made such a mistake.

In other cases, our comparison might not reach the required probability level. In such cases, we may have correctly learned that our procedure A was really no more effective than people's typical memory strategies. However, our conclusion may have been in error, in that our procedure may have had an effect, but this effect may not have been large enough for us to detect. Concluding that no effect occurred, when it actually did but was too small to detect, is called a Type II error. Table 3.2 summarizes the logic of drawing conclusions about research findings using inferential statistics.

TABLE 3.2

The Occurrence of Correct Decisions and Errors as a Function of the Kind of Conclusion About the State of the World and the Actual State of the World

Conclusion About the State of the World	Actual State of the World	
	No Difference	Difference
No Difference	Correct	Type II Error
Difference	Type I Error	Correct

When all is considered, it is crucial that our measures and procedures be reliable. For findings to be credible, there has to be a fair amount of stability in how people respond over a period of time. In addition, findings are reliable if they happen repeatedly under predictable circumstances. Conducting a series of studies that replicate the key findings is considered good scientific practice. Reliability and statistical significance alone do not mean that a finding is important.

If an occurrence is statistically significant, its importance can be assessed in other ways. A significant finding can vary from being relatively small to large. Generally a practice effect that lessened response time about a half a second would not be as impressive as a reduction in response time of several seconds. Larger effects will usually be regarded as more important. Observations or outcomes that support or refute a theory will usually be judged as important.

Obviously, in investigating any phenomena, it is essential that selected measures reveal the aspect of cognitive functioning the researcher had in mind. If a task measures what it is believed to measure, the measures are said to be valid. For example, a researcher may be interested in understanding how people comprehend a textbook. To have a valid measure of comprehension, it is obviously important to choose materials from the text that are not already known to your reader but not too difficult based on your reader's expertise.

Argument and Counter-Argument

The overall approach to discovering valid conclusions about cognitive phenomena, applied and basic, involves examination and reexamination of observations and conclusions about observations. An important part of this process of examination and reexamination is the adversarial method, in which different investigators take opposite sides regarding the validity of a theory. As in court where the prosecutor and defense counsels oppose each other, different theorists advance different theoretical explanations of a particular phenomenon. Studies are designed to assess theories. The better explanation of a phenomenon emerges, as in court, through the airing of different points of view and a series of studies that support and refute these hypotheses.

Although resolution of which theory is best will rely on the available data, sometimes the resolution is also affected by attitudes of researchers. The classic conception of science is that it involves forming hypotheses, deducing observations that follow from the hypotheses, and then checking to see if those observations actually occur in the way predicted by the hypotheses. This is called the hypothetico-deductive method.

However, researchers are human beings who sometimes apply other criteria beyond the consistency of observations with hypotheses, such as the plausibility or the importance of the phenomena and explanations. In addition, there are increasing numbers of scientists who prefer an abductive approach to science in which findings accumulate and theories are constantly revised to accommodate new information. Instead of viewing a theory as right or wrong, this approach suggests that theories are valued to the extent that they account for and consolidate current findings (Rozeboom, 1997).

Tasks for the Application of Cognitive Psychology

Everyday cognitive tasks, small or big, can become the target of application efforts. The need for application is in the eyes of the client or customer. Although the number of tasks that could be studied seems endless, the desire to improve performance at a task is limited by the needs of people today. Table 3.3 presents examples of everyday cognitive tasks that may be enhanced by future applications of cognitive psychology.

TABLE 3.3
Everyday Cognitive Tasks

Reasoning and problem solving
Remembering what is in the news
Reasoning what may happen next given current events
Finding a file
Giving someone directions to your home
Deciding which candidate to vote for in an election
Providing an answer to a question
Navigating a route in a new city
Organizing information stored on your computer
Selecting a car or cable company
Using a map of a shopping mall to find a specific store
Using a calendar or electronic device to maintain your schedule
Using the Internet to search for information
Learning and remembering special numbers (Social Security,
        license, address)
Learning someone's name during an introduction
Learning and remembering phone numbers
Recognizing a business acquaintance in a crowded room
Remembering whether you did something
Remembering what someone said to you at a previous occasion
Remembering when some event occurred
Remembering how to operate machinery
Remembering how to solve a problem
Remembering your or someone else's point of view on an issue
Remembering your schedule and to make appointments
Remembering when to complete tasks on time
Remembering when to start something at a certain time
Remembering that you must take a certain item to work or a
        meeting
Remembering how to perform an action you have done before
Remembering where you are in an action that has several steps

SUMMARY

Three decades ago, few everyday cognitive phenomena had been investigated. Today research is focused on improving our understanding of general cognitive phenomena as well as everyday cognitive events. Independent variables, dependent variables, and mediating variables of cognitive phenomena are now routinely investigated in the laboratory and in real-world applications. Regardless of where research is conducted, many psychologists seek to better understand human cognition. Observations are critically evaluated against statistical standards and with respect to the reliability and validity of hypotheses about cognition and applied cognition. In the next chapter, you will see that, although basic and applied researchers are grounded in the same scientific method, they sometimes approach research with different procedures and sometimes interpret findings differently. Also, differences in their communication customs may foster discrimination and prejudice between basic and applied researchers. Learning about the differences in their approach to research and communication customs will enable you, if you want, to speak the language of either group.

4

Approaches and Methods of Applied Research

Learning is often hard … but unlearning
is harder. It is best to get it right the first
time.

Author unknown.

Differences in the assumptions and practices of basic and applied researchers need to be addressed if science overall is going to advance as it should. Such differences may lead basic researchers to misunderstand applied research outcomes. Similarly, these differences may lead applied researchers to misapply basic research. However, if there is greater awareness of the differing assumptions between applied and basic research, the contributions of applied research are more likely to be recognized. Moreover, a greater awareness of the differing assumptions will enable basic researchers to prepare applied researchers to make the most of their basic principles and findings.

APPLIED APPROACHES TO SCIENCE

Although both basic and applied researchers understand the scientific method in the manner defined by Bacon (1620/1905), their implementations of this method are often different. Despite basic and applied researchers usually having been trained in the same graduate programs, several years' experience in either the basic research world or the applied world create differences in the way science is conducted. Table 4.1 summarizes the assumptions on which basic and applied researchers are likely to differ when carrying out scientific investigations. In the following paragraphs, we discuss these assumptions. An awareness of the differences listed in Table 4.1 enables basic researchers to communicate more effectively with applied researchers and for applied researchers to communicate more effectively with basic researchers. An awareness of these differences also prepares anyone to read about science more intelligently and interact with scientists in the most productive manner.

TABLE 4.1
Assumptions About How Science Is Conducted

Philosophy of science

    The discoverability of truth
    The generalizability of basic principles
    Inferential processes

Research approach to experimental and Observational designs

    Control of variables
    Orientation to what is scientifically important
        Usefulness of basic research
        Usefulness of applied research
    Research experience
        Pace of research
        Continuity of research
    Statistical Practices
        Methods
        Imputation of data
        Regard for the null hypothesis
        Type I versus Type II error
        Number of variables
        Replication in basic and applied research

DIFFERENCES IN THE PHILOSOPHY OF SCIENCE

As discussed earlier in this book, although basic and applied researchers both accept the basic tenets of science, they often appear to accept some fundamentally different assumptions about the philosophy of science (Herrmann et al., 1998; Levy-Leyboyer, 1993). Apart from philosophical assumptions, there are also differences in approaches to designing experiments and observational investigations, as well as how to interpret the results of research.

Discoverability of Truth

Applied researchers know that if their results turn out to be unreliable, misleading, or not relevant, they may lose a raise, promotion, or even a job. Consequently, applied researchers sometimes distrust basic findings or theories until there is considerable evidence that these findings are correct and the theories sound. Alternatively, because basic cognitive researchers seek truth, they are dubious about applied claims that are not clearly linked to basic theories and findings. A basic researcher who wrongly advances a finding as reliable or a theory as valid, will almost never lose his or her job after receiving tenure, although their credibility will be damaged sometimes beyond repair.

The Generalizability of Basic Principles

The standard understanding of basic principles is that they generalize across all situations. This understanding is valid in the abstract. However, all principles are only approximately generalizable at best. For example, when people attempt to recall an event from their past, basic research says that such recall is based on episodic memory. However, a person's recall of the past is influenced by his or her general knowledge about similar such events. In addition, people may sometimes recall what they think others want them to recall. An adequate account of recall in everyday life cannot be done solely with basic assumptions about episodic memory if they do not take account of other knowledge and social influences (Jobe & Herrmann, 1996; Payne, 2000a, 2000b).

It is important that applied cognitive researchers recognize why basic theories are not fully generalizable across situations. Without an awareness of the limits to the generalizability of basic research, an applied researcher will not be sufficiently sensitive to those situations in which the theory best applies. There are several reasons why basic findings and theories are not fully generalizable.

First, all research is necessarily incomplete (Campbell & Stanley, 1966). The purpose of research is to push into the unknown. Hence, any principle discovered today can be expected to require revision in the light of findings from tomorrow's research.

A second reason basic research may fail to generalize is because the research is formulated without concern for application. As a result, the journal article reporting the research or theory often fails to specify the rules of correspondence that would permit extending the theory to the conditions and constructs of everyday life (Payne et al., 1997). Theories that lack bridging principles make it difficult to connect the theory with observable events and may be difficult to apply (Hempel, 1966).

A third reason given for a lack of generalizability is that basic research is often based on unrepresentative samples of participants. Basic research in psychology typically uses what applied statisticians call a convenience sample. In other words, such a sample consists of whatever people the basic researcher can find to participate. Many basic principles are established without clarifying how they may apply to people with different backgrounds and characteristics. For example, the common use of college students as participants in social psychology has limited some of that field's conclusions to students only (Schooler, 1989a, 1989b; Sears, 1985, 1987). Obviously, conclusions based on intelligent, verbal, and well-educated participants at the peak of their intellectual powers may not generalize well to other groups.

Fourth, the generalizability of basic findings and theories is also restricted by differences in the laboratory context and the contexts of real life where the findings and theories might be applied (Payne & Conrad, 1997). However, basic research usually does not specify which outside variables are likely to moderate results. Without guidance on how contexts affect results, applied researchers cannot anticipate how the theory or findings may be used most effectively.

A fifth factor limiting the generalizability of basic research is that findings are rarely described in terms of the size of an effect produced by variables. Effect sizes assess the degree of relationship between variables of interest, often the proportion of variance in the dependent variable that is associated with levels of the independent variable. Without knowing the size of a basic effect, it difficult to apply basic research pertaining to effects that are smaller than expected. For example, in the past three decades cognitive researchers have come to recognize that cultural differences affect cognitive processes (Cole & Gay, 1972; Cole & Means, 1981; Cole & Scribner, 1974; Lave, 1988), However, little basic research on cognition has addressed how important these differences are to how culturally diverse people approach tasks.

Applied cognitive psychologists need to be aware that they should not take literally the tenet of basic research that fundamental principles have generalizability (Chapanis, 1967, 1986, 1988). For example, laboratory research has shown that effort is important in recall, but survey research has shown that effort alone is not sufficient to account for recall on surveys (Jobe & Herrmann, 1996). In addition, the effect of effort varies with the syntax of a question (Miller & Herrmann, 1998) and the pace of an interview (Jobe, Tourangeau, & Smith, 1993). If an applied cognitive psychologist uncritically accepts the generalizability of a basic finding, he or she may not be listened to in the future (Baddeley, 1993b; Conway, 1993; Gruneberg, Morris, & Sykes, 1991; Payne & Conrad, 1997; Schonflug, 1993a, 1993b; also see Banaji & Crowder, 1989; Crowder, 1994). On the other hand, others have argued that the processes by which respondents answer surveys conform to a stage model similar to that found in basic research (Tourangeau, 1984).

Although basic research usually provides a useful starting point, applied cognitive researchers are wise to replicate a basic finding in their applied domain to determine how the basic principle should be adjusted. Sometimes basic theory turns out to be irrelevant to the particular mission of the applied researcher (Boneau, 1994; Bryan, 1972). If there are not sufficient basic findings to assess a situation, the applied researcher must attempt to estimate how people would respond on the basis of expert knowledge of the domain (Hoffman & Deffenbacher, 1993).

Inferential Processes

Applied research and basic research isolate critical effects by eliminating confounding influences of other variables. Confounds occur whenever other variables not of interest are contaminating the relationship between the factors of interest. For example, we believe a certain method of language learning results in better learning. Although we find that groups exposed to this training technique learn better, we later learn that this is because they are more motivated to learn because the method is more interesting and engaging. Level of motivation or interest is confounding the relationship between training and learning. Not surprisingly, real world situations frequently confront the applied researcher with many more variables than are, or could be, addressed in basic research.

To properly recognize the complexity of a problem under investigation, applied research often includes as many relevant variables as possible. For example, different forms of instructions to a survey may be field tested with a sample essentially identical to the final survey sample, permitting an analysis of numerous variables (Wright & Hull,1999) . To better understand how participants might respond, a researcher may analyze responding as a function of individual characteristics of the respondent, such as age, gender, or particular opinion of interest or the interviewer. A researcher may also measure the amount of time that respondents use to answer questions. The basic researcher generally uses tight logical reasoning: if x is the case, then y should follow. The applied researcher uses this reasoning whenever possible. However, the applied researcher is often forced to reason more like a judge or a clinician, relying on expert knowledge to interpret effects that are due to the influence of several possible variables (Popper, 1959).

Clearly, basic and applied scientific methods are not mutually exclusive, but they do reflect differences in approach and in investigatory priorities. The basic researcher gives primacy to laboratory data, whereas the applied researcher attaches more importance to environmental observations. Furthermore, if a manipulation is effective, the applied researcher is often not concerned with which aspect of a manipulation may be effective but rather with the overall result. A typical example of this is the study of the effectiveness of job environments, where a variety of variables are simultaneously considered as a group.

DIFFERENCE IN RESEARCH APPROACH: EXPERIMENTAL AND OBSERVATIONAL RESEARCH DESIGNS

Control of Variables

More than basic research, applied research often employs observational, quasi-experimental, or experimental methods (Campbell & Stanley, 1959). Basic researchers seek to control all extraneous variables in an experiment (Sidman, 1960) by ensuring that a variable has the same value in all conditions. For example, a researcher may want to compare two advertisements for their impact on consumers. Various characteristics of the advertisements (e.g., degree of action, amount of language, duration of exposure) would need to be held constant. If these variables were not controlled in this manner, any difference in the impact of the advertisements could be attributed not to their message but to any uncontrolled characteristics of the experiment.

Another way to deal with extraneous variables is to let them occur randomly and make the assumption that, on average, the value of the variable will be approximately the same in all experimental conditions. However, random variation sometimes allows one condition to actually have unequal values of the variable across conditions. For example, if the brightness of the advertisements was allowed to vary randomly and the advertisements turned out to differ in brightness, the results of the experiment could not be interpreted if brightness is a critical influence on advertising effectiveness.

Applied researchers seek to control as many extraneous variables as possible, but they usually control fewer variables than do basic researchers because naturalistic settings invariably preclude complete control (Gruneberg & Morris, 1992a, 1992b; Gruneberg, Morris, Sykes, & Herrmann, 1996; Hedrick, Bickman, & Rog, 1993; Herrmann & Gruneberg, 1993; Wright, 1997). Whereas a basic researcher can narrow down the number of variables that affect a phenomenon by placing certain restrictions on the environment, the task, or the respondents, it may not be possible or even desirable for the applied researcher to narrow the set of variables in this manner. Also, applied research has a practical goal of trying to identify any or all variables that might seriously affect the effectiveness of a product and a service. The applied researcher cannot afford to miss detecting unanticipated variables that may also be at work.

Other factors sometimes make it difficult for applied research to have the control achieved by basic research. Sometimes applied research is precluded from having a control group (DiTomasso & McDermott, 1981). For example, it is typically seen as unethical to withhold a new medicine or other treatment from control subjects because doing so may lead the participants in the control group to become more ill or even die. At other times, there are constraints on the investigation that require the use of a quasi-experimental design in which participants are not randomly assigned to conditions (Campbell & Stanley, 1966). For example, noise is known to have a significant effect on the comprehension of speech, but research into such effects in industrial settings usually has to be observed with the naturally occurring amount of noise, rather than at levels predetermined experimentally. Single case designs, or case studies, are used mostly by applied researchers (Kearns, 1986; Yin, 1994), although basic research will sometimes use a case study (Shallice, 1979) to document an unusual cognitive performance.

Orientation to What Is Scientifically Important

Differential reliance on experimental and observational research design may be seen to grow out of differences in a researcher's orientation to what is scientifically important. The principles that basic cognitive researchers select for investigation are those receiving considerable interest in the empirical and theoretical research field, sometimes referred to as the Zeitgeist, and by funding agencies that determine the topics eligible for research funds. For example, many basic cognitive researchers are currently devoting investigative effort to false memories and eyewitness testimony. Almost no researchers studied the phenomenon of false memories until it became topical. Whereas eyewitness memory has been studied for nearly one hundred years, the current Zeitgeist has also energized research on this topic over the last two decades.

Applied researchers, for the most part, focus their investigations on topics dictated by their employers or their clients. These clients and interested parties, having a stake in the outcome, are often able to insist on changes in procedure and repeated attempts to get a certain effect that has been hard to observe. The applied researcher's choice of research questions is not guided by the Zeitgeist. Instead, the perspective that inspires research topics in the applied world is motivated by factors such as profit, safety, public policy, and public relations (Fischoff, 1990; Johnson, 1996).

Research Experience

Basic and applied researchers experience a somewhat different pace of research. Applied researchers are faced with many deadlines. The fiscal and programmatic requirements of the application world necessitate making decisions by certain times, which in turn force the applied researcher to complete work on a project by the deadline. Applied research is primarily driven extrinsically, by the needs of employers. Hence, applied research often is driven by more time pressure than basic research. In contrast, basic researchers often establish their own deadlines by choosing to apply for grants that award funds on set dates. However, there are constraints as well on basic researchers; for example, they must meet the deadlines set by a granting agency and funding, and sometimes job reappointments may depend on steady completion of projects. The pace of basic research is primarily driven intrinsically, out of the scientists' interest in a project and sense of competition. New findings often change the pace and direction of inquiry.

Basic and applied researchers experience projects that vary in continuity. Applied researchers are often forced to work on several applied projects at a time. Consequently, they often have to switch from one project to another. Projects are often unrelated to the previous research assignment. The requirement that applied researchers shift research topics based on employers' needs can make it difficult to complete research.

In contrast, most basic researchers pursue one line of research or rotate projects which researchers work on indefinitely. However, most basic researchers teach in colleges or universities, responsibilities that applied researchers in industry and the government do not have to contend with.

Statistical Practices

Although statistical training is essentially the same for basic and applied researchers, each requires somewhat different statistical practices that are not apparent when reading basic or applied research journals. We briefly discuss these differences according to methods of analysis, imputation of data, regard for the null hypothesis, Type I versus Type II errors, number of variables investigated, and the use of replication in research.

Applied research makes use of more methods of statistical analysis than basic cognitive research. More methods are used by applied researchers because their research usually employs less control than basic research. Whereas basic research tends to focus on one level, with a few carefully selected variables, applied research is often multilevel (Hedrick et al., 1993), encompassing a broader range of variables and requiring more complex analyses than single-level research. For example, in the analyses of advertisements, it is necessary to evaluate at least two levels, such as visual appeal and content. In addition, an applied researcher correlates a variety of additional variables that a basic researcher would ignore because the basic researcher assumes these variables vary randomly or controls some of these variables within the study.

Basic researchers are taught to avoid fishing expeditions in which they continue to test the effects of variables until they identify a variable that has a big effect. Such explorations unfortunately may lead to finding an effect due to chance. Applied researchers are also taught that non-theory-driven statistical testing can yield false knowledge. Nevertheless, they are encouraged to explore their data because overlooking a potent variable can end up costing a lot of money.

Basic and applied researchers sometimes impute data for statistical purposes. Imputing refers to estimating missing data. In some cases, missing data requires that an entire set of results be thrown out. However, if one can impute data that resembles the missed data, then an analysis can be completed and the data set need not be thrown out.

Consider how imputation may actually be done. Suppose that one participant failed to show up for part of an experiment. To make use of the participant and avoid throwing out data for the part of the procedures that were completed, imputation might be used. This procedure requires that it be assumed that, had this person been tested, he or she would have gotten the similar scores in the missed parts of the test as in the part that was completed. For example, the mean, median, or mode for a given variable may be substituted. The imputed data are regarded as hypothetically representative of scores of a person who was fully tested.

Basic researchers generally avoid imputing data for missing data, and many reviewers may reject manuscripts for publication because of imputation. Because research in the real world cannot tightly control conditions in the same way that lab research can, missing data is not unusual and imputation is common. From the applied viewpoint, it is best to have estimates that provide some description of the data so that application is based on the best information.

Basic and applied researchers differ in their regard for the null hypothesis. Applied researchers usually report all findings, null or otherwise. They do so for two reasons. First, upper level managers typically require that they be told which treatments are ineffective, as well as effective. To best guide their projects, managers need to know what does and does not work. Second, nearly all applied research is done on a budget that requires a strict accounting of funds. If findings are not reported, it appears that allocated funds have either not been spent or not spent as intended. Organizations operate on budgets and must know where the money has been used. In contrast, basic cognitive researchers strive to reject the null hypothesis and accept the experimental hypothesis. As a result, basic cognitive researchers typically do not report findings that support the null hypothesis. If a basic researcher obtains a null finding, he or she will often discard the results and try again. Rarely will a null result be accepted and reported by basic researchers (Smart, 1964). Null findings are generally regarded as occurring as a result of artifacts, inappropriate experimental designs, poor measurement or sloppy logic.

These two approaches to null findings contribute to prejudice between the two kinds of researchers. Basic cognitive researchers look at applied cognitive reports and sometimes conclude that the applied researchers are inept for reporting null findings. Applied researchers, who are aware of how common null findings are, look at basic reports and believe that the findings are as easy to apply as the basic research indicates (Herrmann & Gruneberg, 1993). The many variations and efforts to achieve the effect are rarely described.

Applied researchers worry more about a Type II error (failing to detect an effect that actually did occur) because they want to avoid spending money on an investigation that could have discovered a procedure of use to their employer. Basic researchers often are very concerned about a Type I error (concluding an effect was observed in an investigation when in fact it did not occur) because an invalid finding may lead other researchers astray. To counteract this possibility, repeating experiments and observations is a necessary part of research.

As discussed earlier, applied research necessarily must pay attention to more independent and dependent variables. Consequently, the number of variables addressed in applied research reports is typically greater than the number of variables addressed in basic research reports. Applied research does so, fully aware of the complications that added independent variables pose for interpretation. Nevertheless, institutional pressures require the applied researcher to make as complete a report as possible.

Both basic and applied researchers recognize the importance of replication of prior results, but the conditions requiring replication are somewhat different between basic and applied research. Replication means that an experiment is repeated with all or most of the conditions identical to procedures followed earlier. If the same results are obtained, it is said that the second experiment replicated the findings of the first experiment, whose findings have implication for an application. A successful replication is required by management before substantial sums are invested in developing an application based on these findings.

Although basic research journals increasingly require a replication of the critical effect, replications or near replications may be regarded as less necessary to basic research unless a finding seems inconsistent with previous findings. Basic research findings are assumed to be replicable when they are published.

Because of their different perspectives on the use of replication, as well as the customs for reporting replications, basic and applied researchers sometimes misinterpret each others' research. Basic cognitive researchers sometimes feel that applied researchers fail to understand the rationale when they read an applied report that mentions a number of null findings. Alternatively, applied researchers read basic articles and are suspicious when null findings are never discussed because they know that null findings are not unusual.

SUMMARY

The differences in approaches to science are sufficiently great that scientific translators can make a good living telling the other side how communications from the other camp should be interpreted. The difficulties in communication between the basic and applied researchers are similar to the communication problems experienced by Americans and the British when they talk to each other. It is not uncommon for basic and applied researchers to view each other as unskilled or incompetent because each is ignorant of the other's scientific approach. These differences originate in what their group assumes about control of variables, what is scientifically important, the way in which research experience differs between the groups, and the statistical practices that each group respects.

5

Phases of The Basic-Applied Cycle: The Yin and Yang of Science

To truly understand a debate, you must first appreciate both sides of the argument.
Fortune Cookie

Explicit in Bacon's (1620/1905) account of research is a cycle of discovery and application, called here the basic-applied cycle. This cycle describes the standard way that basic and applied scientists cooperate to advance science (Bickman, 1981; Garner, 1972; Hedrick et al., 1993; Salomon, 1987; Schultz, 1979). As discussed earlier, basic researchers presumably discover the principles that are fundamental; applied researchers and practitioners apply these principles (Adams, 1987), until inadequacies in an application are revealed. On discovery of these inadequacies, applied researchers communicate perceived deficiencies in the principles; basic researchers then investigate the conditions of the deficiency until they can discover an improved description of the original principle (see Fig. 5.1).

Some have judged the standard account of the basic-applied relationship as overly simplistic. If basic research generalized to variables in the real world as the basic applied cycle anticipates, applied research would be very easy. However, several factors make it difficult to apply basic research. As basic research advances, it gets more complex with greater awareness of variables' influence on performance. As a result, basic theory requires understanding of many caveats relative to what was known a few decades ago. Because of the increased complexity, some researchers have questioned whether the basic-applied cycle should be revised and elaborated (deWolff, 1993; Hoffman & Deffenbacher, 1992; Prohansky, 1981; Reagan, 1967; Schonflug, 1993a, 1993b; Vicente, 1994). In the first chapter, distinctions were briefly described that divide basic research and applied research into subtypes. Here we elaborate further on these subtypes.

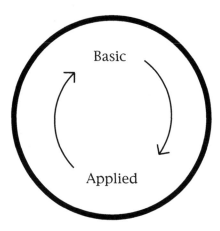

FIG. 5.1. The Basic/Applied Cycle

BASIC RESEARCH

Ecologically Valid Research

Some researchers have assessed the degree to which fundamental principles inferred from basic research are observed in everyday contexts (Barker, 1968; Bronfenbrenner, 1977; Brunswick, 1956; Neisser, 1976; Wright, 1997). The supposition underlying much ecological or naturalistic research has been that those discovered principles will be potentially useful when applications are attempted (Bruce, 1985). Ecologically valid research attempts to eliminate the artificiality of the laboratory that sometimes makes it difficult to generalize findings to the real world.

Mission-Oriented/Applicability Research

Some researchers have assessed the degree to which fundamental principles inferred from basic research have the potential to be applied to a stated mission of a business, industry, or any other organization, such as a government agency. Hence, this research may be referred to as mission-oriented (Featherman, 1991). This research attempts to discover how to optimize a planned application of a fundamental principle to a particular real-world problem. Such mission-oriented research seeks to carefully capture whether a functional relationship described by a fundamental principle can be shown to systematically differ from what is expected (Branscomb, 1995). For example, research on the influence of post event information on the memory of eyewitnesses to staged events is potentially applicable to memories of witnesses to actual crimes or accidents (Loftus, 1979; Yuille & Cutshall, 1992; see also Chapman & Underwood, 2000).

The reason for conducting mission-oriented research has been that the results should require less modification to achieve a successful application than a principle that has been shown only to be ecologically valid (Dubin, 1976; Herrmann & Gruneberg, 1993; Nogami, 1982). Although ecologically valid research is naturalistic, it may or may not be conducted in a way that is consistent with a certain practical application. For example, slides have been presented to subjects that depict an auto accident as it unfolds step by step, but however closely slides might mimic an actual auto accident, slide presentation probably does not affect participants in the same way as experiencing an actual auto accident. Consequently, although slide or video presentation may be useful for certain research questions, these methods are probably less effective for assessing what people remember from an actual auto accident.

Alternatively, when a principle fails the applicability test, it is shown to lack potential for application and as a consequence is unlikely to represent a fundamental cognitive process. For example, a great deal of cognitive literature indicates that people use strategies that enable them to reconstruct past events and information. On the basis of this literature, researchers in the survey industry have made heroic attempts to facilitate the answering of survey questions by encouraging respondents to use strategies to recall information (Jobe & Mingay, 1991). The technique was not particularly effective with survey responding. The survey researchers' findings do not invalidate the conclusion that strategies are useful in recall, but their experience does cast doubt on the generality of strategy use and reveals that we need to learn more about the conditions that give rise to using strategies to recall information.

APPLIED RESEARCH

Application Research

Some researchers have tried to assess the degree to which fundamental principles can be applied successfully in the real world (Spurgeon, Davies, & Chapman, 1994). Clients often insist on such an assessment before investing in full fledged product development. An evaluation of the actual application of fundamental principles, therefore, assesses application validity for these principles.

In the views of many basic and applied researchers, application validity provides the strongest support for the fundamental nature of a principle (Chapanis, 1967). When a principle fails the application validity test, the principle's status as representing a fundamental process is undermined (Cronbach & Meehl, 1955). However, application research requires that one or more prototypes of the final application be developed. Thus, although application or evaluation research is very powerful, it requires a stage of development that is typically not completed by either ecologically valid research or applicability research.

Technology Research

An application refers to solving a particular problem. Once research has developed effective lineup procedures at the Downsberry Police Department, only that department has benefited. If the lineup procedure is adapted to suit a range of different police departments, the application becomes a technology. This is not to suggest that all applications can become technologies. The procedures developed for the Downsberry Police Department may not work elsewhere because these procedures have been created to capitalize on strengths of their staff.

CONDUCTING RESEARCH IN STAGES

The existence of different subtypes of basic and applied research opens the door to combining the subtypes in a series of investigative stages. The two-stage approach of basic and applied research is becoming a thing of the past (Sirken et al., 1999). Each stage of research leads to revision and subsequent research and an eventual application (Landy, 1993). Figure 5.2 illustrates some of the relationships that may occur among these new research camps. The figure presents five multistage combinations to the standard two stages of the basic-applied cycle (Herrmann, Raybeck, & Gruneberg, 1999),

Three Stages	Three Stages	Three Stages	Four Stages	Five Stages
Basic Research	Basic Research	Basic Research	Basic Research	Basic Research
|	|	|	|	|
Ecologically Valid Research	Applicability Research	Application Research	Ecologically Valid Research	Ecologically Valid Research
|	|	|	|	|
Application	Application	Application	Applicability Research	Applicability Research
			|	|
			Application	Application

FIG. 5.2. Multistage alternatives to the standard two stages of the basic applied cycle. These alternatives are suggested by the beliefs of different research camps in the need for ecologically valid, applicability, and application research.

& Gruneberg, 1998). The findings of the final stage for every alternative in the figure are expected to lead back to basic research and complete the cycle. Each alternative is presented in a sequence from beginning to end. These alternatives may be elaborated further by assuming feedback loops from the later stages back to earlier stages. For example, in the three-stage model, findings from ecologically valid research influence the application stage and success of the application stage thereby influence basic research.

An Example of Multi-stage Basic-Applied Research

Basic cognitive researchers discovered early on that retention decreases over time in an exponential fashion (e.g., Ebbinghaus, 1885/1913; Luh, 1922). Several generations of were taught that forgetting is initially rapid and then levels off. However, researchers with applied interests discovered more recently that the retention function varies according to the kind of information held in memory. The retention function was found to be linear for autobiographical memory, to maintain with very little decay over decades for recognition of pictures in yearbooks, and to decrease, plateau, and decrease again for knowledge of a foreign language (Searleman & Herrmann, 1994). Similarly, Linton (1975, 1982) did a diary study where she wrote short descriptions of daily events in her life over a 6 year period. She found that everyday memories were remembered well. In fact, those events that she was unable to recall did not have distinctive cues to help her remember them or were similar to other events so that those events did not elicit any particular memory (see also Wagenaar, 1986; White, 1982. 1989).

These kinds of studies indicate that the shape of the retention function varies with the content of information remembered. This realization that memory processes are more complex than originally suggested by laboratory research has lead basic researchers to identify the variables associated with these and other performance differences. Another example of multi-stage research may be found in the face recognition literature, see Figure 5.3 from Herrmann, Raybeck, & Gruneberg, 1998.

Kind of Research	Stimuli
Basic	Patterns
Ecologically-valid	Faces
Applicability	Faces in a staged crime
Application	Faces from an actual crime or potential crime

FIG. 5.3. Kinds of stimuli in investigations relevant to face recognition as a function of kind of research.

THE LACK OF COLLABORATION BETWEEN BASIC AND APPLIED RESEARCHERS

Sometimes it has been argued that the information exchange between basic and applied research in psychology is not effective (Schonflug, 1993a) because there is little communication between these two groups of researchers (Brewer, 1985; Schonflug, 1993a, 1993b). However, although communication between basic and applied researchers is limited, each new generation is taught primarily by basic researchers who impart basic research skills common to graduate training at the time. Additionally, there are a growing number of newly trained scientists who opt to go into the applied world. As a consequence, as the number of applied cognitive researchers grows, there are more scientists who have friends in the other camp. With more cross-group communication (Smith, Randell, Lewandowsky, Kirsner, & Dunn, 1996), it seems likely that many of the distinctions between basic and applied researchers will be better understood. Greater understanding will result in better collaborations. Better theoretical models, more comprehensive empirical investigation, and better artifacts are likely to be primary outcomes.

INVENTING COGNITIVE PRODUCTS AND SERVICES

Sometimes an executive knows the kind of application that needs to be developed, giving the applied researcher the responsibility of creating and perfecting the application idea. In other cases, the applied researcher is asked to conceive of the application needed in a situation. Thus, the applied researcher either invents the final form of an application or the application in its entirety.

There are a number of ways to think up new applications. First, an aspiring application developer (an inventor) may study the basic research literature with the goal of identifying findings and theories that have yet to be transformed into an application. Once such findings and theories are identified, the aspiring inventor freely associates situations that seem related to these findings and theories. Once a potential situation is found, the aspiring inventor seeks processes and behaviors that are critical to the situation. Finally, the inventor attempts to imagine a device or a service that might take over the processes for a person or might assist somehow in executing the behavior. Other aspects of the process of invention (Petroski, 1994) are discussed later in the chapter on problem solving. For example, a great deal of research and common sense indicate that a person's physiological states affect cognition. One situation in which these states affect cognition is at work. A device that might be useful could measure physiological states before going to work. If these states were suboptimal, various activities aimed at improving physical well-being could be used to improve physical state, which in turn would improve cognitive functioning.

A second way to conceive of a possible application is to study cognition in everyday life to identify hypothetical applications that could be developed to improve outcomes. Once a potential application has been identified, the aspiring inventor studies the situations to which the application seems to apply. Once relevant situations are identified, the next step involves specifying the processes and behaviors that the application will address. Finally, the inventor attempts to imagine the way in which the application (device or service) might somehow assist or actually execute the targeted behavior. For example, many people have recognized for years that it is difficult to remember appointments. Planners were developed and used effectively by many people. However, the planner reminds a person only if he or she is looking at the planner near the time that something has to be done. In the past decade many inventors recognized that some kind of palm-top computing device could signal upcoming events. Accordingly, several companies developed palm-top reminders (sometimes called personal data assistants), which provide cues that improve likelihood of remembering (Herrmann, Brubaker, Yoder, Sheets, & Tio, 1999.

Conceiving new products and services requires creativity. One might ask, how can we become more creative? One answer to this question is the philosopher's stone, a mythical object that if held in one's hand enables a person to know everything. Obviously, such a stone is fantasy. Everyone has the potential to be creative.

Different people are often creative in different situations but one key to creativity is knowledge. For someone to think of a situation, process, or behavior that could benefit from assistance and application, you must have the necessary expertise or information. Some of the knowledge may come from a book, but other aspects of knowledge have to do with understanding and being able to identify the salient issues in that particular situation. One way to discover a new application is to seek out an unusual problem or an unusual solution to an old problem. However, unusualness for its own sake will not be enough.

New ideas regarding potential applications ultimately have to be useful. If you are familiar with, or make yourself familiar with, particular tasks at work or in your personal life, you may be able to discern when something interferes with success. Alternatively, a critical element may be missing that thwarts completion. Remaining mindful and attentive to what is involved in successful performances enhances the likelihood of identifying creative opportunities.

Another way to conceive of a potential application is to study an old application in light of new information. For example, coming out of the behaviorist tradition common in the first half of the 20th century, many teaching machines were developed and sold to guide learning. One could argue that some of today's interactive learning programs reflect this old tradition but with a new updated look.

We invite you to think of possible applications as you read this book. Record your ideas in your course notebook or in a separate ideas notebook. However, because good ideas can be valuable, if you come up with an idea that strikes you as brilliant or at least profitable, take the following actions to protect your idea.

Procedure for Protection of Ideas Short of Copyright or Patent

Do not discuss your idea with anyone whom you do not trust. Not everyone is honest. Write a detailed description of the application you envision. If you can draw a sketch of the application, do so, although it is not necessary to do so. If the idea requires electronics or chemistry that you do not yet understand, do not worry. Write as good a description as you can. Then put the description in an envelope addressed to you. Go to the post office and send the envelope to yourself as certified mail.

When the envelope arrives in the mail, sign the form provided to you but do not open this envelope. Store the envelope in a safe place. By doing so you will have evidence that you conceived of the idea for the product or service on or before the date on the envelope.

This process protects your idea from being stolen. For example, suppose some dishonest person overhears you talking about your brilliant idea and then sells it to a big corporation for several hundred thousand dollars. You would be able to sue the person because you could prove that you had the idea before the thief claimed to think of it. You prove it was your idea by taking your envelope to court, where the judge can see that the envelope was sent on a certain date, never opened prior to the trial, and contained the brilliant idea. The details of a registered letter on the envelope shows that the U.S. Post Office officially recorded the date that the brilliant idea was sent in the mail, proving that you thought of the idea on or before that date.

The students in several classes of ours have generated potential applications. Every student has been able to conceive of a creative idea with potential application. Some of the ideas would not make a lot of money because the idea applied to a small group of people or even to just one person. Other ideas have had clear money-making potential, so the students involved did take the steps to protect their idea in the manner we described. If our students can be creative in this manner, so can you.

SUMMARY

However conceived, the relationship of basic and applied research needs to be better understood. For scientific endeavors to be the most effective, collaboration between basic and applied research groups should be an organizing principle.

Both camps can better meet their individual goals while achieving more comprehensive theoretical understandings and practical applications to advance science.

This chapter described different models for cooperation between basic and applied researchers. Knowledge was presented that may help basic and applied researchers collaborate more productively. Finally, the process of inventing was described in detail. It was seen that anyone can invent new products, services, and technologies with sufficient preparation.

6

Basic Cognitive Psychology: Framework for Application

Always begin with the fundamentals.
- Author unknown

THE CHALLENGE TO APPLIED COGNITIVE RESEARCH

Tasks that confront us in everyday life vary in the demands on our cognitive processes (including perception, learning, remembering, reasoning, problem solving, decision making, and communicating). Many of the tasks could benefit from cognitive applications that pertain to activities of daily living. Whether we are paying bills, organizing records, remembering necessary chores, or executing learned skills at home, we depend on a range of coordinated processes to comprehend and execute designated tasks. Alternatively, different occupations rely on cognitive processes differently. Nevertheless, tasks at work also depend on basic cognitive processes. Thus, an applied cognitive psychologist must be able to improve cognitive performance at home and work.

To develop ways to assist cognition in everyday life, it is necessary to understand and influence general cognitive processes and the specific process used to address a certain task. As we have all experienced, each cognitive process is vulnerable to failure (Baars, 1992: Broadbent, Cooper, Fitzgerald, & Parks, 1982; Norman, 1981, 1988; Reason, 1990; Reason & MyCielska, 1982; Sellen, 1994; Senders, & Moray, 1991). Table 6.1 lists some common ways we routinely experience cognitive failures.

TABLE 6.1
Cognitive Failures With Corresponding Everyday Examples

Perception involves interpreting sensory information. Failures occur when we misperceive, fail to discern stimuli, fail to discriminate, or misinterpret sensory stimuli.

Attention involves focusing on certain stimuli. Failures occur when we fail to attend, do not concentrate, are withdrawn or preoccupied, are unaware.

Comprehension typically involves understanding oral or written communication. Failures occur when we misunderstand, misclassify, misinterpret, overgeneralize, or create inappropriate associations or when our personal interests influence our ability to process information accurately. Comprehension is also affected by the clarity of the material and its complexity relative to our expertise (Kintsch, 1974).

Learning is a relatively permanent change in performance. Failures occur when we do not organize material effectively, when we do not associate new information with what is already known, and when we do not understand the meaning (Conway, 1993).

Retention involves the storage and retrieval of encoded memories. Failures occur when we fail to attend, do not try to remember, fail to create distinctive cues or when noncognitive modes, such as physical states (e.g., tired, too many parties), interfere with remembering. Many times, failing to remember information reflects never having learned it in the first place.

Reasoning is inferring conclusions from premises or initial information. Failures occur when we misjudge or misconstrue information, when we fail to critically evaluate key elements, when we are overinclusive, or when we fail to see the bigger picture. Prejudice and bias can contribute to problems.

Problem-solving is essential for living effectively. Failures occur when we fail to understand the problem appropriately; when we persist in doing things as we've done before, even when the situation is different; and when we fail to break problems down into manageable steps.

Communication failures occur because we are misinformed, have misspoken, or provide too much or too little information. Although we generally assume that people are being truthful, many communications are deceptive, cryptic, or involve distortion intended to misrepresent the communication.

Planning failures occur when we are shortsighted, rash, careless, negligent, impulsive, compulsive, perseverative, inaccurate, or inconsistent (Das, Kar, & Parrila, 1996).

A FRAMEWORK FOR APPLYING
COGNITIVE PSYCHOLOGY

Applications of applied cognitive psychology have grown steadily over the past three decades. To get a sense of common areas of application are, we classified articles in Applied Cognitive Psychology, Cognitive Technology, Journal of Experimental Psychology: Applied and the Handbook of Applied Cognition (Durso et al., 1999) according to the applied topic addressed by each article. Table 6.2 lists these areas.

TABLE 6.2
Areas of Applied Cognitive Applications

Arts - performing: music, dance; visual: painting, sculpture
Business - advertising, management, sales
Culinary arts
Communication industries - news media, survey field
Education - instruction, learning, assessment
Engineering - operation of computers, design of
    machines and environments
Industry - manufacturing and production
Law - police activity, lineups, and interrogation;
    eyewitness testimony; use of the courts
Health - medical treatment
 Physical illness - diagnosis, treatment
 Mental functioning- diagnosis, treatment, reading comprehension
    Assessment of cognition in everyday life
    Assessment of autobiographical memory in everyday life
    Treatment of memory problems
Military
Recreation
Sports
Transportation - automobile driving, aviation, safety

How we create and adapt our mental representations depends on a variety of cognitive functions, including perception, learning, and reasoning. However, simply understanding the elements that comprise our cognitive system is insufficient to fully understanding how cognition works. Research clearly indicates that cognitive processing is not only due to these and related cognitive functions but that such processing is also affected by other psychological systems that are extrinsic to the cognitive system (Baddeley, 1993a, 1993b; Barnard & Teasdale, 1991; Herrmann, Plude, Yoder, & Mullin, 1999). Thus, a person's physical state, attitude, social interactions, expertise, and culture influence what is learned, retained, remembered, and analyzed (Rabin, 2003). Considering the impact of these multifaceted performance contributors can greatly facilitate understanding how people think and remember.

Therefore, applications can aid cognition by improving not only cognitive factors but also noncognitive factors (such as health, emotion). To develop applications that may facilitate cognitive performance, this chapter explains the multimodal approach to cognition. Systematically considering the elements in the multimodal approach should suggest a broad range of applications for particular situations.

COGNITIVE ABILITIES

Psychological research shows that cognitive abilities are not uniformly good or bad across all situations. Instead of one general ability, each person has many cognitive abilities, each suited to different kinds of cognitive tasks (Gardner, 1993; Sternberg, 1986). Of course, there are some independent as well as many related cognitive abilities, but performance across tasks may be quite variable (Guilford, 1967). Some of these processes are sometimes labeled as lower level and some as higher level. Lower level cognitive processes are those that bring information into the cognitive system (sensation, perception) and hold that information (learning, retention, remembering) for additional processing. Higher level cognitive functions (reasoning, problem solving, decision making) derive new knowledge or potential new knowledge on the basis of information available in storage.

Each of these abilities is discussed from a cognitive perspective in the following chapters. The purpose of this chapter is to show how these cognitive processes fit within the entire psychological system.

MODES OF THE HUMAN COGNITIVE SYSTEM

Our cognitive system enables us to see, learn, remember, reason, solve problems, and communicate with others. The functioning of these systems obviously depends on how much knowledge and experience we have. Cognition is a function of a variety of mental processes (perceiving, comprehending, encoding, learning, retaining, remembering, reasoning, solving problems, making decisions). Moreover, there has been increased recognition of how the functioning of our cognitive system is affected by several noncognitive modes, such as the physical, emotional, and attitudinal state of the learner; motivation to perform; social interaction; and use of external aids (Herrmann & Searleman, 1990; Newell, 1990). Changes in noncognitive modes can positively or negatively affect cognition. Sometimes the non-cognitive modes may interact with each other in influencing cognitive processing. Fig. 6.1 below illustrates how cognition is dependent on these different modes.

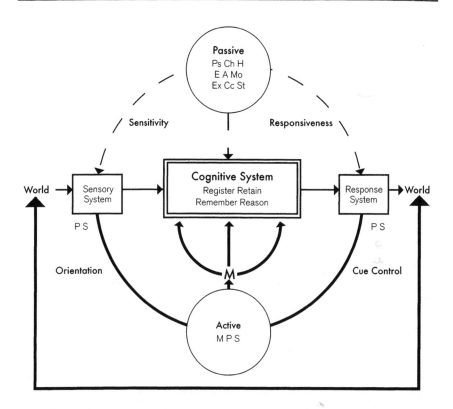

FIG.. 6.1 The multimodal model I. Note: Strength modes: Ps-physiological state; Ch-chemical state; H-health state. Emotional modes: E-emotive state; A-attitudinal state; Mo-motivational state. Individual modes: Ex- expertise; Ce-cognitive competence; St-cognitive style. Information modes: M-mental manipulations of cognition; P-manipulations of the physical environment; S-manipulations of the social environment (Herrmann & Searleman, 1992).

Noncognitive modes are particularly important to those who do applied cognitive work because careful scrutiny of these factors can suggest possible applications. By checking how a possible application affects a user's modes, it is possible to decide whether manipulating a particular mode will yield the most effective application. Considering how noncognitive modes affect cognition results in optimizing what is taught in this book. The procedures presented here provide a template for you to develop sound applications of cognitive psychology.

The multimodal model assumes that the human psychological system is made up of four categories of modes: mental activity modes, physiological modes, emotive modes, and response readiness modes. The mental activity mode includes the processes that are involved in cognitive processing per se, in reacting to the social environment and in making use of the physical environment. The remaining modes are fundamentally noncognitive, but, because of the way our nervous system is organized, these modes may affect cognition. The nature of how this occurs is the focus of the rest of this chapter.

To optimize cognitive performance, it may be helpful to prevent the physiological, emotive, and response readiness modes from not functioning well (Mullin, Herrmann, & Searleman, 1999; Rabins, 2003). Even the best cognitive products and services in the world may be of limited use if the user is fatigued or under great stress. In the following sections, we discuss some general principles about how modes affect cognitive performance.

MENTAL MANIPULATIONS

Cognitive Processes

Cognitive processing begin with sensation and perception. These processes often occur automatically. At night, we recognize patterns and movements of light as other vehicles, buildings, or animals. We may consciously use strategies or logic to facilitate cognition. For example, to remember certain facts for a test, we sometimes depend on first-letter mnemonics. Another commonly used strategy for novices wishing to read music is learning the line notes on the treble clef with the mnemonic *Every Good Boy Does Fine*, or *FACE* for space notes. Distributing versus massing practice is still pertinent to what someone learns from studying (Seabrook, Brown, & Solity, 2005). Also we need to manage the amount of information we are processing in that an overload impedes processing and makes it more vulnerable to error (Schvaneveldt, Reid, Gomez, & Rice, 1998).

Environmental Control

In addition to perceiving the world around us, people are able to study and manipulate the environment (Norman & Shallice, 1986). Environmental features can foster encoding or help cue retrieval. The idea here is to determine the salient elements in an environment that cause people to learn, think, or remember in certain ways. The goals of environmental study and manipulation are to improve accuracy and acuity of our evaluation or performance. Cues may not only be concrete but abstract as well (Mace, 2004). Usually, studying and manipulating the environment depend on acquired knowledge and skills in addition to fundamental cognitive functions. Thus, although the mental activity involved in controlling the environment is not a cognitive strategy per se, it is how people manage their environment.

Other times concrete aspects of the environment influence cognitive processes. Room temperature can affect cognitive performance (Wyon, Anderson, & Lundqvist, 1979). For example, slightly cool temperatures lead to the best cognitive functioning. Also, use of an optimum level of sensory stimulation for cognitive performance can be important. Would you believe that noise can actually improve some college students' cognitive performance (Daee & Wilding, 1977). Other factors that are important include reinstating cues present during learning when attempting remembering (Geiselman & Fisher, 1998) or arranging alarms to serve as reminders for tasks we need to accomplish (Herrmann, Brubaker, Yoder, Sheets, & Tio, 1999).

Social Interaction

People are often more likely to fail cognitively when they are with others than when they are alone. Being in a social environment requires more cognitive processing than being alone (Best, 1992). To interact socially, people study and manipulate social situations to improve cognitive processes, such as communication and memory (Wyer & Srull, 1986). As with the physical environment, managing the social environment also depends on acquired knowledge and skills in addition to the use of the fundamental cognitive functions.

The social environment can be used to improve cognition. For example, we can arrange to perform a cognitive task in the presence of patient and tolerant others who will provide cues and necessary information. We can avoid cognitive failures by conversational ploys, such as redirecting a topic, slowing the pace of discussion, and remembering what is important to others. Others in the environment may help us monitor comprehension and recall of events. Companions may validate our recollections, challenge our interpretations, or present new information that we had not considered (Stephenson, Kniveton, & Wagner, 1991). However, research in naturalistic settings indicates that collaboration with others may not improve prospective and retrospective memory (Johansson, Andersson, & Ronnberg, 2000). In particular, older adult married couples and arranged pairs performed more poorly than individual controls on a range of tasks.

STRENGTH MODES

Physiological Condition

Cognitive performance may be affected by factors that alter the physical state of a person's body. For example, one way in which physical condition may affect cognitive performance is through its influence on arousal or alertness. Another way is through the influence that arousal has on selective attention (Eysenck, 1982; Hockey, 1983, 1984; Jennings, 1986a, 1986b; Parasuraman & Davies, 1984; Posner, 1984).

Some influences on physical condition facilitate cognitive performance. Not too long ago it was reported that ingesting glucose enhances learning (Gold & Greenough, 2001; Gonder-Frederich et al., 1987; see also Benton, 1993 and

Foster, Lidder, & Sunram, 1998). Imbibing glucose shortly after learning results in enhanced recall (Manning, Stone, Korol, & Gold, 1998). The level of glucose naturally occurring in the blood has also been shown to be related to memory performance (Donoho & Benton, 1999). Exercise enhances cognitive performance during and after exercise occurs (Kramer et al., 1999; Powell, 1974; Stamford, Hambacher, & Fallica, 1974). Whereas physical fitness generally facilitates memory, food consumption often adversely affects cognition (Smith, 1988). Excessive as well as insufficient eating negatively influences thinking and memory.

Circadian rhythms also can affect cognitive performance (Folkard, 1979; Folkard & Monk, 1980). Memory performance is optimal shortly after waking (Tilley & Statham, 1989), with the best performance occurring in the mid morning, although the optimal time differs across tasks (Folkard & Monk, 1980). Disruptions of the sleep cycle can impair memory, although there are some situations in which some sleep loss may be facilitative (Blagrove & Akehurst, 2000; Idzikowski, 1984). The level of performance of some memory tasks may also vary across the days of the week (Koriat & Fischhoff, 1974) and months of the year (Pillemer, 2001; Pillemer & Goldsmith, 1988). And for premenopausal adult females, memory performance varies with a woman's menstrual cycle (Hartley, Lyons, & Dunne, 1987).

Health State

It is well known that certain diseases or conditions, such as Alzheimer's disease, Korsakoff's disease, and low blood pressure, can have a conspicuous effect on cognition (Khan, 1986). However, it is almost not discussed in the cognitive literature, except for cognitive aging research, that a variety of other health conditions impair cognition. Physicians are well aware that cognitive symptoms are apparent in a wide range of illnesses, from irreversible serious and progressive disorders (brain tumors, heart failure, syphilis, some forms of epilepsy) to serious conditions more amenable to medical attention (toxemia of pregnancy, anemia, pellagra) to more routine disruptions of health, such as the common cold (Miller, 1956; cf. Willis, Yeo, Thomas, & Garry, 1988) or diminished sensory capacities (Cutler & Grams, 1988). A person is best prepared to perform cognitive tasks when free of physical or emotional disease or other debilitating conditions.

Chemical State

Various substances may also impair cognition. Alcohol, tobacco, and various psychotropic substances, such as marijuana, impair memory (Block & Wittenborn, 1984; Schwartz, 1991). Under certain conditions, coffee can impair memory processing (Humphreys & Revelle, 1984; Petros, Beckwith, Erickson, Arnold, & Sternhagen, 1987; Revelle, Humphreys, Simon, & Gilliland, 1980), although it may enhance performance in other cases. Interestingly, it seems to interact with the personality trait of extroversion (Corr, Pickering, & Gray, 1995; Stelmack,

1990). Many medicines (antidepressants, antibiotics, antihistamines, tranquilizers) interfere with cognition (Bowen & Larson, 1993). Excessive exposure to various environmental agents (such as paint fumes, electric shock) can lessen cognitive functioning permanently (Singh, Dwiedi, & Saxena, 1987; Stollery, 1988). Obviously, proper chemical balances are associated with optimal cognitive performance, although stimulants may improve cognitive performance but only when one's chemical balance is abnormal.

EMOTION MODES

Emotive State

Regardless of how we feel, sometimes we must execute certain cognitive tasks. Emotional states have physical and chemical concomitants (Wolkowitz & Wein-gartner, 1988). It has long been known that verbal materials with different kinds of content elicit different kinds and amounts of affect with different effects on memory (Kleinsmith & Kaplan, 1964). Additionally, it is well established that people, whether alone or with others, tend to remember pleasant experiences better than unpleasant ones (Matlin, 2005), although it is a function of our current emotional state (Bohanek, Fivush, & Walker, 2005; Bower, 1981; Hertel, 1996). Investigations have found a link between mood and memory (Singer & Salovey, 1988), especially in depression (Johnson & Magaro, 1987; Williams & Dritschel, 1992; Williams & Scott, 1988), where negatively valenced material is remembered better.

Stress, a major factor in moods, is known to impair cognition as well (Hammand, 2000; Reason & MyCielska, 1983). For example, nurses who work on highly stressful wards experience more cognitive failures than nurses who work on less stressful wards (Broadbent et al., 1982; Reason, 1990). Stress has also been implicated in cognitive problems identified in women undergoing mastec-tomy (Reason, 1988) and in people convicted of shoplifting after they forgot that they had a product in hand when leaving a store (Reason & Lucas, 1984).

Attitudinal State

A person is likely to perform well when there is an interest or inclination to perform a task, when sufficient effort is dedicated to performing the task (Herrmann, 1984, 1989; Klatsky, 1984; Morris, 1984), and when positive incentives affect arousal level (Fowles, 1988). These attitudes may originate out of dynamic processes that protect one's self-concept (Greenwald, 1980, 1981) or as a result of experience. For example, two groups matched on prior performance at learning nonsense syllables differed in a subsequent attempt at such recall simply because they were falsely told they were superior or inferior at learning nonsense syllables (Sullivan, 1927).

We are inclined to better register information that is consistent with, rather than inconsistent with, our metacognitive beliefs (Greenwald, 1981; Levine & Murphy, 1943; Metcalfe, 2002; Perfect & Schwartz, 2002); however, it depends on how much we reflect on the material (Eagly, Kulesa, Chen, & Chaiken, 2001). Moreover, we are disinclined to perform cognitive tasks when the social stereotypes that apply to us indicate that we cannot perform well, such as the stereotypes associated with age (Best, Hamlett, & Davis, 1992) or gender (Crawford, Herrmann, Randal, Holdsworth, & Robbins, 1989; Halpern, 2002; Herrmann, Crawford, & Holdsworth, 1992; Loftus, Banaji, Schooler, & Foster, 1987).

Changing our attitudes can facilitate cognitive performance. Improving the desire to attempt a certain task leads to better cognitive performance of that task. In addition, adopting a realistic appreciation about what one can and cannot do will also enhance cognitive performance (Herrmann & Searleman, 1990).

Motivational State

We may be motivated to strategically and intentionally employ cognitive processes such as attention, reasoning, and memory to achieve goals. Rewards motivate us to perform certain responses, whereas punishments may suppress a response. Improving one's motivation is especially useful when one needs to perform cognitive tasks in distracting circumstances. However, a person can be motivated so much (Yerkes & Dodson, 1908) that it interferes with optimal performance.

INDIVIDUAL MODES THAT INFLUENCE APPROACH

Expertise

People differ in their readiness to perform cognitive tasks as a function of intelligence, personality, experience and expertise Brunas-Wagssraff, 1998). Experts represent problems in-depth and spend more time considering the nature of the problem relative to less experienced people. As a result, the cognitive performance of an expert is more efficient, and their memory for cognitive tasks is more complete (Chi, Feltovich & Glaser, 1981; Ericsson, 2005; Hoffman, 1996). Vocational and avocational experiences may equip us with specific skills toward certain cognitive tasks. For example, after extended work with numbers, a person may develop a high level of skill in recalling numbers. Some servers in restaurants become unusually skilled at remembering orders, and some programmers become increasingly able to minimize the number of steps needed to execute an action. Of course, experience with hobbies also create additional opportunities to perform cognitive tasks.

Individuals need to identify the cognitive tasks for which they are most competent in order to know how we can maximize our cognitive abilities. Cognitive assessment may help people identify strengths, although most of us rely on our own evelution of how effective our cognitive performances may be. It has been proposed that, while self reports on memory performance are sometimes valid, the processes undelying memory performance are beyond introspection (Nisbett & Wilson, 1977). Subsequent research has indicated that under some conditions people do have insights into cognitive processes (Cohen & Schooler, 1997). For example, people may be able to know what processes that led short-term memory to be successful or unsuccessful but not know what processes underlie a long term memoruy failure. Other research has indicated that people can recognize some of the causes of a memory failure (such as a distraction) while remaining unaware of the processes that are trigger by a cause (such as the attention processes that are disrupted by a distraction ; Herrmann, Gruneberg, Fiore, Torres, & Schooler, in press).

Cognitive Competence

People vary in their ability to perform cognitive tasks. People also differ in their willingness to attempt cognitive tasks because of beliefs about abilities. With increasing age, there may be decreasing confidence in cognitive functioning that interferes with willingness to even attempt cognitive tasks. Increases in confidence leads to the best possible performance of cognitive tasks if the confidence is realistic.

Cognitive Style

Everyone is both similar and different in how they approach cognitive tasks. Some people are error prone . Other people are very careful not to make errors; such people may avoid cognitive tasks unless they are sure they will succeed. Some people have a need for information, which leads them to learn information in detail (Cacioppo & Petty, 1982).

MONITORING READINESS TO PERFORM COGNITIVE TASKS

A person should monitor the modes discussed earlier at least several days before performing an important task, such as a job interview. If appropriate, the person can then take steps to maximize cognition. When you monitor yourself, decide whether or not each of the modes is average, below average, or above average. Assign each mode a score of -1, 0, or +1 for each mode. Total your score. If your score is below or near 0, try to avoid situations where your cognition is tested. Alternatively, if you are in the positive range, feel free to get tested. Fig. 6.2 presents another visual presentation of the multimodal model. In comparison to the figure of the model shown earlier in the chapter, this figure stresses the interdependency of the four categories of modes.

Research based on the multimodal approach has demonstrated that cognitive failure can be due to noncognitive variables, a fact not frequently investigated by most basic cognitive research. Thus, the multimodal model, which originated out of applied research, demonstrates that applied research sometimes leads to observations that are useful for basic, as well as applied, research.

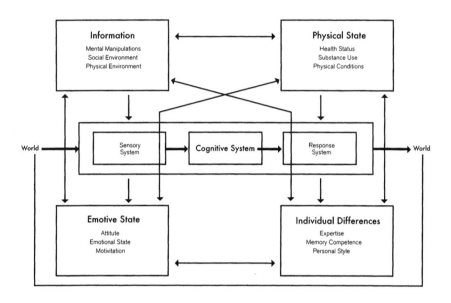

FIG. 6.2 A second depiction of the multimodal model that illustrates the role of the different modes on cognition (Herrmann, Plude, Yoder, & Mullin, 1999).

The multimodal model provides a guide to design cognitive applications, such as in education (Herrmann et al., 1998), by taking account of a person's biological, psychological, and social nature. General and specific procedures of an application may have different goals and outcomes depending on the physical, emotional, and mental state of the user. When you want to design an effective application, assess modes that may affect particular cognitive processes and manipulate modes that will be influenced by the application.

APPLICATION

The multimodal approach has guided recent efforts to refine methods of memory improvement and memory rehabilitation. This approach has been taught in classes, in books, and on the Web and training has been provided on CD-ROMs (Herrmann & Searleman, 1990, 1992; Herrmann et al., 1992) to improve memory (Zacks & Hasher, 1992). Searleman and Herrmann (1994) published a textbook that summarizes basic research findings within a multimodal context. The multimodal approach has also been shown to be useful for rehabilitating the memory and cognition of individuals who have suffered brain damage from head injury (Harrell, Parente', Bellingrath, & Lisicia, 1992; Kreutzer & Wehman, 1991; Luria, 1973a, 1973b; McEvoy, 1992; Parente' & Herrmann, 2003; West, 1985) as well as other neurological impairments, such as brain damage due to toxic solvent exposure (Bendiksen & Bendiksen, 1992, 1996).

SUMMARY

The multimodal model assumes that the human psychological system is made up of four categories of modes: mental activity modes, physiological modes, emotive modes, and response readiness modes. The mental activity modes include the different cognitive processes that are the focus of the next group of chapters. The mental activity category also includes the cognitive processes that are involved in reacting to the social environment and in making use of the physical environment. The remaining modes are fundamentally noncognitive, but they still regulate how we learn and remember. To optimize cognitive performance, it may be helpful to control the physiological, emotive, and response readiness modes. Even the products and services in the world may be of limited use if the user is fatigued, poorly motivated, or believes that the task-at-hand is beyond his or her capabilities.

II

Application

7

Attention, Perception, and Imagery

Seldom seen, soon forgotten. Often seen, not forgotten. Imagined, remembered well.

— Author unknown

ATTENTION

Focusing attention depends on our ability to be sufficiently aroused to attend to certain stimuli while blocking out other stimuli (LaBerge, 1995; Norman, 1968; Pashler, 1998). The number of items that can be attended to at one time is referred to as the span of attention. If we are overaroused or are too tired to make ourselves alert, we have difficulty focusing. Attention is important for almost all cognitive processes that are required in real-world tasks. If we want to remember information, often called explicit memory, attention is required. Some perceptual information that we learn automatically and without effort may not require attention, but conceptual information, even learned incidentally, probably requires attention (Jacoby et al., 1992).

The likelihood that information in working memory will be encoded and will be available for retrieval from stored memory depends on how carefully we attend to the information in working memory. Attention is critical to successful reasoning, problem solving, and decision making.

Attention sometimes occurs automatically, whereas at other times deliberate effort is required. Because the world confronts us with an amazing amount of information, attentional mechanisms must filter and limit the information that reaches higher levels of thought (Holyoak & Thagard, 1994). Paying attention consumes mental capacity. When we are paying close attention to something, it is difficult to get our attention. A limited amount of attention is available to us (Broadbent, 1958), and attending to one event takes away from the capacity to attend to something else. Thus, by increasing the level of attention we give to a task, we may be able to enhance the quality of cognitive performance (Craik & Lockhart, 1972).

SENSATION

Our sensations begin with our sensory systems representing stimulus energy as chemical and electrical changes which result in neural firing and end with our recognizing the stimulus. Sensation is primarily associated with structure, physiology, and general sense receptor activity. The beginning of a complex chain of interdependent events is caused by the activation of sensory receptors by energy changes in the physical environment where certain sense-related information is extracted. As with any chain, the strength of the entire sequence of steps is determined by the weakest link. If any of the sensory/perceptual processes fail, our perception will fail or will be inaccurate. Our sensations are considered the representations of uninterpreted energy. Sometimes we hear a sound, sniff a smell, or see something and are not sure what it is. At this stage, we experience sensation but only that. If, as time goes on, we figure out what the stimulus is, we are said to perceive the stimulus.

PERCEPTION

Whereas sensation involves registering events in the outside world, perception involves interpreting how the energy conforms to a structure (Garner, 1962). Perception is the study of how we attach meaning to what our senses detect. Sometimes we should be skeptical of what we think we see, hear, feel, smell, and touch. Believing in one's perception does not mean our interpretation is accurate. For example, if someone is color deficient and has never been informed of this deficiency, this person will not sense colors as others do, resulting in incorrect color perception. Even if a person is informed of a deficiency, he or she still may not be able to form accurate perceptions because the output of the deficient sense does not provide enough information to accurately adjust response to a stimulus.

Misperception may also result because because receptor impulses are not conveyed fully to the afferent nerves that project to the appropriate cortical area, or because the cortical detectors are not sufficiently aroused by the afferent impulses. Sensory information may be imprecise or missing. A person may not have enough experience with a stimulus to recognize it easily. Alternatively, because we expect certain events, we may misconstrue stimuli, thinking the stimulus represents what we expected and not what is actually available. Noncognitive modes, such as emotional or physiological states, may also affect perceptual acuity.

IMAGERY

The fundamental cognitive function that enables people to envision what is not presently directly perceived is imagery, or our ability to create mental pictures (Pylyshyn, 1973, 2003; Richardson, 1999). This function allows a person to move into the future and invent, to return to the past and appreciate what life must have been like, or to transform the present with new possibilities. Imagery allows us visualize encounters with important others to review past occurrences, influence future encounters, and even maintain conflicts (Honeycutt & Cantrill, 2000). Imaging gives us the capability to solve problems that we might not be able to solve without having the problem in front of us. We can also create mental models of objects that might be useful in certain situations. Imaging a properly executed performance does result in athletes performing their sports more effectively at a later time (Martin, Moritz, & Hall, 1999).

Amazing as it may seem, our imagery follows some of the same rules as actual perception (Kosslyn, 1995). People can mentally rotate images, zoom in to see more closely, and search an image in their mind's eye. Nevertheless, images of objects are not as accurate as direct perception of those objects and are more susceptible to our understanding of what we imagine. However, in spite of a few differences, creating and using visual images activates many of the same general areas of the brain that are important for visual perception.

APPLICATIONS OF ATTENTION RESEARCH

The Effects of Practice on Attention

Increased practice at attending leads to better attention skills. Additional practice may eventually result in less attention and more automatic performances. When dividing attention between two tasks or stimuli, we do not pay attention to either as well as we can to each alone. However, with extensive practice over time, we can approach the accuracy of focused attention for both events together. How long it takes the dual-task skill to develop also depends on the difficulty of the task (Payne, 1991; Shiffrin & Schneider, 1977). Spelke, Hirst, and Neisser (1976) demonstrated that motivated students could take dictation while also reading and comprehending short stories.

The Effects of Continuing to Pay Attention

Real-world tasks sometimes require sustained attention. Some people's jobs require them to monitor displays for specific, infrequently occurring events over long time intervals. Sustained attention or vigilance is important in processing and quality control in manufacturing, baggage inspection, and national and corporate security. Detecting ambiguous targets in the midst of background noise depends on both cognitive and noncognitive factors.

Although practice at paying attention is generally regarded as critical to effective cognition, there are situations where less is more. Prolonged effort at certain tasks can lead people to become bored or fatigued, regardless of their general level of skill. Similarly, if a person has to perform the same task repeatedly, well beyond the time in which their skills increased, they become more inclined to make absentminded errors (Reason, 1988). For example, senior test pilots become more accident prone with extended trials requiring attention, despite the fact that they are probably among the most skilled pilots in the world.

Deficiencies in Ability to Pay Attention

Absentmindedness refers to a lessened ability to keep track of what one is doing. When we are absentminded, we have more difficulty than usual paying attention (Reason, 1988; Reason & MyCielska, 1982). People differ in their powers of attentiveness. Clearly, some occupations (such as air traffic controllers) require an above average ability to sustain attention (Vortac et al., 1996).

Situations that fatigue or upset a person can adversely affect one's ability to focus. Although problems with attention are symptomatic of other medical conditions (e.g., depression) and can be a side effect of many medications and drugs, problems with attention rarely require medical intervention. There are, however, some conditions of impaired attention that can benefit from medical care. Two common examples are attention deficit disorder (ADD) and attention deficit disorder with hyperactivity (ADDH). Both of these involve difficulty in sustaining attention, with the latter being coupled with overactivity and restlessness. Inability to focus results in poorer learning and knowledge acquisition over time.

Attention Training

Changing how we approach a task can remedy deficiencies that normally lower attention. Attention can be improved when we actively implement successful strategies. You would not be alone if you wished to permanently and effortlessly increase your ability to attend (Plude, 1992) and a number of training protocols have been shown to improve attention.

First, attention training can be as simple as practice listening for faint, unpredictable sounds or looking for dim, unpredictable lights (Neisser, 1992). For example, you may practice increasing attention by searching for predator birds in trees along the highway or monitoring squad cars with radar. A second kind of attention training attempts to increase your ability to divide attention. As we noted, practice can improve your ability to pay attention to two things simultaneously (Neisser &

Becklin, 1975). A third kind of attention training attempts to increase your ability to notice details. Research shows that practice at picking out a detail in a scene or a sound in a mix of sounds results in improved performance at selective attention (Biederman, 1987). A fourth kind of attention training attempts to increase your ability to resist distraction. Research has found that practice can improve one's ability to pay attention to something despite distractions.

If you want to improve your attention, target the necessary skills and practice the desired task. For attention training to be effective you must practice extensively, perhaps over several months, depending on the complexity of the task. Attention training is no simple proposition. In addition, optimizing other factors within you and in the environment (as discussed in chapter 6) is also important.

Where Attention Matters

Attention is crucial for successful performance in a number of domains. Here are a few examples of applied use of attention research.

Sports.   The findings and theories of attention may be applied to a variety of life's events, such as improving the effectiveness of sport performances, such as tennis (Williams, Ward, Knowles, & Smeeton, 2002).

Military Sentry.   Serving as a guard requires a person to conduct detection tasks including maintaining a vigilant awareness of the environment and detecting the enemy or accidental intruders (Rogers, Rousseau, & Fisk, 1999).

Education.   Research has shown that personal data assistants (PDAs) can help students get more out of college (Walker & Andrews, 2001, 2004). For example, use of PDAs by students improved their memory for events in their weekly schedules, a key factor in time management. PDA use was also associated with increased memory for telephone numbers, also a time saver. It appears that teachers can produce better performance in class by encouraging PDA use in general.

Technologies can facilitate learning in other ways. If children do not attend to information, they have little chance of learning. In the case of children and adults with ADD or ADHD, they have difficulty staying on task. Carefully structuring activities can improve focus. Understanding the cognitive problems that plague such people has benefited from a cognitive theory of attention (Barclay, 1992). People with ADHD often forget what they were doing and start doing something else. Recently, a device, called a MotivAider, has been developed that is similar to a pager to remind a person to stay on task. The device can be set to vibrate at certain intervals. The person carrying the vibrator is asked to consider what he or she should be doing when the vibrator is activated. Initial reports indicate that this is helpful for some individuals.

Applications of Attention and Perception

Pursuit Driving by Police.   Car chases are extemely dangerous, involving complex coordination of perceptual and attentional skills. Crundall, Chapman, France, Geoffrey, and Phelps (2005) recorded eye movements of police drivers with simulated driving tasks. They found that police are better than other drivers at directly attending to possible hazards, such as pedestrians.

Perceiving Traffic Signals. Although most of us have little trouble understanding the information provided by traffic signals, roughly 8% of men and 0.5% of women have difficulties discriminating red and green. Having a reduced ability to detect color may affect reaction times and accuracy in responding to traffic signals. Work by Atchison, Pedersen, Pain, and Wood (2003) explored color vision problems with different kinds of signals. They identified a particular shade of green signal that people with several different types of color deficiencies could correctly identify.

Avoiding Read-End and Parking Collisions. Accidents have been clearly linked to cognitive problems (Wagenaar, Hudson, & Reason, 1990). In the 1980s many rear-end collisions occurred because a driver did not notice the brake lights of another vehicle until it was too late. As a result, another brake light was added to the rear window. Improving perception by installing the center-mounted brake light has been credited with preventing thousands of accidents (Theeuwes & Alferdinck, 1995; Voevodsky, 1974). Another product was developed to alert people to avoid fender benders in their garage or in parking lots. This product provides feedback on potential obstacles. It has three lights (red, yellow, and green) aligned vertically and can emit an infrared signal that causes the lights to change depending on proximity to obstacles. If the car is not close to other objects, the green light is on. When the car gets within a foot or so of an object, the yellow light goes on. When the car is within inches of an obstacle, or actually collides with something, the red light goes on. Why did the inventor of this product come up with this idea? Because depth perception is difficult for many people with normal vision and more problematic if a person wears glasses. Without an aid such as that described, our perceptual and attention systems may not be up to the job.

Relearning to Drive. An innovative use of basic understanding about visual sensory memory has made it possible to rehabilitate the driving skills of people with head injury. Such injuries sometimes interfere with memory. It is not unusual for head-injured people to report difficulties remembering what traffic signs mean. People are shown a series of slides, each for about a half a second in length, reproducing the fleeting images when driving. This training of the very short-term memory of traffic signs has been shown to help head-injured people regain their ability to recognize these signs, a skill that is essential if the person is to return to driving (Hamid, Garner, & Parente', 1996).

Phonics. Phonemic processes in children's listening and reading have been clarified by considerable research. The production of sounds has been mapped onto the reading process. Teachers and therapists are more able today to use phonemics to improve performance (Crain-Thoreson, 1996). In particular, research has demonstrated that training in phoneme recognition transfers to instruction in sound-symbol correspondence (Gelzheiser, 1991).

Cognitive Problems of the Deaf.

In part because it relies on kinesthetic cues in a person's fingers, sign language is different from spoken language. Sign language consists of visual cues, augmented by kinesthetic cues and lipreading cues (Vitkovitch & Barber, 1996). Signs can be combined according to subject, verb, direct object, and indirect object but normally communication by sign is not done this way. In practice, many signs are equivalent to a phrase or sentence. Thus, a message often consists of paralinguistic gestures, such as making facial grimaces that correspond to asking a question or making a point firmly. For example, instead of producing signs for each term in the question "do you want to go eat," a person may simply make the sign "to eat" accompanied by a questioning facial expression.

Because sign communication often relies on global signs, the encoding of the visual and kinesthetic cues is often slower or less precise than the encoding of speech. Research has shown that short-term memory may be of less help to deaf individuals than hearing individuals because of the differences in what is encoded (Logan, Maybery, & Fletcher, 1996).

Perceptual Problems Introduced by Poor Design of Man-made Objects.

Some objects, natural or manufactured, are harder to use than other objects. Generally, many of the products we use in everyday life have not been designed with cognition in mind. Norman (1988) showed that many products are designed in ways that make them hard to use and hard to remember how to use in the future. For example, the first generation of VCRs was notorious for being difficult to understand.

The clock on the VCR was particularly hard to use; most owners ended up leaving the clock flashing 12:00 because of the myriad steps involved in setting the timer. Another example noted by Norman is the placement of small and large burners on an electric stove. The placement varies from one manufacturer to another and in ways that may not be indicated by the controls. Norman makes clear that the designer's concept of a product and the concept of the product held by a consumer are not necessarily the same thing.

Design of Visual Displays. People differ from each other in which stimulus situations foster awareness (Durso & Gronlund, 1999). A stimulus may not be perceived and responded to appropriately because the nature of the display is inconsistent with the demands of the task (Payne, Lang, & Blackwell, 1995). Also, people are vulnerable to perceptual illusions. Because there are so many ways for us to misperceive, it is important not to take for granted the accuracy of perception in various situations. In addition to the various vulnerabilities of the human perceptual system, difficulties in perception of manufactured objects may be introduced by poor product design as in some automobile instrument panels. Just because you believe something happened does not mean it actually did. An awareness of the fallibility of the perceptual process is important to carefully in-corporate in the design and testing of any new products and services.

Designing effective visual displays often involves multidiscplinary ef-forts. Combining research from vision, object recognition, and psychophysics, Witus and Ellis (2003) created a computer model that predicts the presence of military targets in daylight that are likely to be spotted by humans. The VDM2000 program was based on data from human responses to photographs of military ve-hicles and simulates the visual receptors' adjustment to light. Witus and Ellis report that field testing provided good validity for the program.

Statistical Graphics. A statistical map is one kind of graphic that has been investigated extensively by applied cognitive researchers. The maps present statistical information by shading geographic regions according

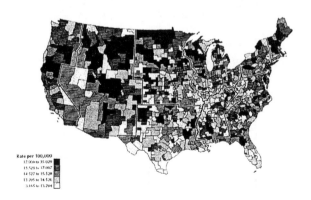

FIG. 7.1. A statistical map. Such maps illustrate the geographic distribution of a statistic, such as the rate of mortality due to a certain disease (Herrmann & Pickle, 1996).

to each region's value on a factor (see Fig. 7.1). They are used in a variety of fields to analyze the geographic influence of some variable of interest. For example, statistical maps are used to present the mortality rate of particular diseases in different regions of the United States. However, the perceptual characteristics of many maps sometimes exceed the human ability to interpret these characteristics. Nevertheless, Lewandowsky and Behrens (1999) cite an example of a statistical map reported by Pickle, Mason, Howard, Hoover, and Fraumeni (1987). The map clustering of cervical cancer in West Virginia resulted in funding to detect and treat this disease; the increased attention ultimately resulted in a decline in mortality rates (Maher, 1995)

In the first half of the 1990s, the National Center for Health Statistics made a coordinated effort to develop a theoretical framework to account for how people read statistical maps and develop guidelines for designing maps that report the national mortality rates of various diseases. Moreover, methods were developed to assess the phenomenon of clustering, in which map readers see certain regions on a map as exhibiting similar statistical values (Lewandowsky, 1999; Lewandowsky, Behrens, Li, Pickle, & Jobe, 1993). Additionally, after careful study of the literature, it was evident that many studies concerning statistical maps were consistent with the assumptions of cognitive stage theory advanced over a century ago by Donders (1868/1969). This theory assumes that a series of information-processing stages intervene between a stimulus and a response. In recent years, stage theory was expanded to include the selective influence of individual stages of information processing (Sternberg, 1975).

Stage theory has been enormously successful in explaining how people read statistical maps (Hastie, Hammerle, Kerwin, Croner, & Herrmann, 1996; Herrmann & Pickle, 1996; Pickle & Herrmann, 1995). For example, Sternberg (1969, 1975) concluded through an analysis of the latency of recognition responses indicated that memory search includes an encoding stage, inference involving a memory search, mapping, application, and a response stage where each stage involves qualitatively different processes. In similar fashion, time data for reading statistical maps were consistent with five separate stages of statistical map reading: orienting to the map, reading the legend, integrating the map and the legend, and extracting the relevant data from the map before the final response. Accuracy data also indicated the influence of different variables on these stages. The evidence from different measures and from different experiments suggested that these five stages were often executed sequentially.

Without the perspective of stage theory, developed by basic research in cognitive psychology, it is unlikely that researchers would have recognized that statistical map reading unfolds in stages. Two decades of research on statistical maps had failed to recognize that map reading involves specific stages of information processing, probably in large measure due to the lack of input from a cognitive psychology perspective.

Separate from the statistical map research area, other aspects of map use have been investigated by applied cognitive psychologists (. Eley (1993) demonstrated that there were differences in topographical map interpretation as a function of training. For example, even with a map, people with less training are more likely to get lost than people with more training. Research has been done on new ways to design cartographic symbols to optimize utility (Phillips et al., 1990).

Graph Reading. Graphs and tables are important ways to present information. Ever since Huff's (1954) powerful little book, *How to Lie with Statistics*, a number of applied cognitive psychologists have explored how information is extracted from tables and graphs and how this may be done more accurately (Carswell, Bates, Pregliasco, Lonon, & Urban, 1998; Kosslyn, 1989; Meyer, Shamo, & Gopher, 1999; Spence & Lewandowsky, 1991). For example, Kosslyn (1989) suggested a global information-processing approach that likens comprehending graphs to using short-term memory and analyzing perceptual, meaningfulness, and pragmatic (congruence between graph and viewer goals) elements. Although graphs support efficient processing of information, one concern has been how to maximize display designs to create a plausible, comprehensible graphic summary. Another issue has been judging proportions with graphs (Hollands & Spence, 1998). Another concern has centered on task and user goals. A variety of theoretical and empirical research has been reviewed by Lewandowsky (1999) and Friendly (1999) on how people make sense of information intended to be conveyed by graphs.

Human Computer Interface. Anyone who can recall the interfaces available on computers a decade ago can attest to the improved quality of this exchange in recent years. Applied cognitive psychologists were among those who have helped improve interface characteristics, often referred to as human-computer interaction (Baguley & Landsdale, 2000; Murphy, 2000; Newlands, Anderson, & Mullin, 2003; Norman, 1997; Pirolli, 1999). One method that has been especially helpful in improving use has been the usability test. The interface is developed first by the concept person who conceived of a particular program, such as a program that does arithmetic. Next, a computer programmer develops the arithmetic program. Finally, a computer graphics specialist adds programming to make the screens of the program appealing and helpful. A couple of decades ago, this was the end of the development process after which program was given or sold to whomever was supposed to use it. Then the usability test was developed to catch flaws in the design process.

The usability test is introduced after the design process was seemingly complete but before a product was released. Such a test involves having a group of potential users attempt to use the program while voicing their questions and difficulties. The results of the usability test are then provided to the design teams who corrects problems identified by potential users (Payne, Wenger, & Cohen,

1993; Schneiderman, 1987). Virtually anyone who has used, observed, or participated in a usability test can attest to its power to catch glitches in design that would not have been recognized until the consumer had the product in hand.

Another problem that was quickly apparent was that some people appeared to be technophobic. In essence, they were hesitant to operate new technologies (Weil & Rosen, 1994). Unfortunately, these users discovered that the screens presented to them, and the logic behind the programs were incomprehensible. Many users could not get a program to execute simple operations, and they blamed themselves rather than a flawed design for their difficulties. The usability test helped to decrease the number of problems and, in turn, the number of technophobic people. In addition, instructional procedures permitted more exploratory learning, increased consumer comfort with technology, and resulted in more consumers.

The Arts. Applied cognitive psychologists have not been preoccupied with the application of cognition to the arts, but they have made some contributions. For example, research has been done on aspects of music (Biel & Carswell, 1993; Chaffin & Imreh, 1997), paintings (McLaughlin, Dunckle, & Brown, 1999; Schmidt, McLaughlin, & Leighten, 1989) and film (Glass & Waterman, 1988). Also psychologists have devoted efforts to maximize teaching opportunities in museums (Loftus, Levidow, & Duensing, 1992). For example, displays attract more attention if the lettering is sufficiently large. Many museums have prepared displays that use a font legible from about a foot away but illegible from a typical viewing distance of 2 to 3 feet.

Applications of Imagery Research

Simulations and Training. A dramatic application of imagery has been used in training programs. As you know, computer simulations can recreate stimulus situations that help us learn complex tasks. Flight simulators have been useful in training people to pilot planes, and many people benefit from car simulators in driver education classes. Simulators can even let you practice your softball hits.

Even without a physical image, people can envision activities and actions in their mind that assist task performance. For example, basketball players who imagine practice can demonstrate improvement in the game better than those who do not engage in such practice and sometimes as well as those who actually practice the game. Musicians commonly practice playing their instruments without touching them.

Imagery and Learning. Imagery is the key to many kind of mnemonics, as discussed in the chapter on learning. One dramatic example of the power of imagery is in the learning of foreign language vocabulary and syntax. Here, in the key word method, the learner creates images that connect the foreign language with one's well known native language. Raugh and Atkinson (1975) demonstrated that students learned Russian vocabulary almost twice as fast with the keyword technique than without this mnemonic. Since then, Gruneberg (1985, 1987) has applied the key word technique to the development of courses pertaining to several languages: French, German, Spanish, Italian, Greek, Russian, Dutch, Portuguese, Hebrew, and Welsh. The keyword method has been somewhat controversial (Ellis & Beaton, 1993), partly because some foreign language instructors fear the method does not emphasize the meaning of terms learned. Nevertheless, considerable research demonstrates that the keyword method is more effective than other methods of vocabulary training.

SUMMARY

Many applications in cognitive psychology depend on appropriate attention and perception. To use such applications, it is necessary to focus on certain stimuli, while blocking out other stimuli. Sensory processes must represent stimulus energy properly and relay this representation up to perceptual centers where the sensory representation is interpreted. Applications that cannot capture the necessary attention, sensory representation, and perception will fail.

When perceptual representations are incomplete or unavailable, imagery may provide supplementary information. The effectiveness of attention depends in part on practice. Increased practice at a task fosters better attention skills. However, continuous use of an application may lead people to become less attentive and absentminded. Abilities to register sensations, form perceptions, and create imagery are also well known to be critical in many applied areas, such as in the military, education, manufacturing industry, computer graphics, human computer interactions, statistical graphics, and more. In some situations, training that facilitates these processes is key to a successful application.

8

Comprehension and Learning

Many complain of a bad memory when their real problem is a lack of understanding.

– Author unknown

Meaning occurs at different linguistic levels. Phonemes are the smallest units of sound that are combined to make language. For example, *ta* and *da* are phonemes. Phonemes are combined into words. Morphemes are the smallest sound-letter combinations that convey meaning. For example, morphemes include some root words, prefixes, suffixes, and even tense markers.

Meanings occur also in combinations of words (Klix, 1980) and syntax structure. Phrases and clauses are combined into sentences, which compose conversation, speeches, stories, and reports. In addition, meaning at any level may be regarding as denotative or connotative. Denotation refers to the particular or explicit meaning of a word or concept. The denotation of car refers to four-wheel machines people drive around town. Connotation refers to the feelings or associations that we have about a particular word or concept. Most people feel that cars are useful, so their connotative meaning is useful or positive, unless their car is always breaking down.

AMBIGUITY IN COMMUNICATION

Messages may be clear when we have a context and sufficient time to understand. However, oftentimes people are compelled to devote only a limited amount of time to comprehending a message. In such cases, comprehension is affected by the content and the structure of that content. At other times, content is made intentionally ambiguous. "THE STUDENTS ARE REVOLTING."

At first glance this short sentence appears to convey one thought. Actually, it can be interpreted in at least two ways, although we usually apply one meaning but not the other. Gernsbaker (1993) found that when good readers try to read ambiguous words that have multiple meanings, they suppress the inappropriate meaning based on the context and apply the appropriate meaning of the word more effectively than poorer readers.

LEARNING

Learning is a relatively permanent change in behavior, produced by different encoding processes and different transfer processes (Hintzman, 1990). The amount learned varies according to the strategy used in learning. Methods of encoding that involve elaboration, organization and understanding are more effective in promoting long-term learning. Learning results in different kinds of mental representations depending on the nature of the content. Remembering is discussed in the next two chapters as depending on the mental representation produced by learning. This chapter presents the major principles of learning processes as judged by the authors to be most useful in applied research and in application.

Some memories are ephemeral, whereas others may last indefinitely. Representations vary according to how completely they are encoded and how long they last in our memory. Very short-term memory registers our initial sensations. The sensory representation of this kind of memory lasts about only a .5 sec. Information is transferred from very short-term memory or working memory. Information will remain in working memory for up to 20 to 30 sec. if the information is not rehearsed. Generally, the amount of information held in short-term storage is relatively small, but it depends on our existing knowledge about that information. Alternatively, when we engage in rehearsal (intentionally or unintentionally), information is transferred to long-term memory which allows us to remember the information for use in the future. A traditional schematic of the memory system is shown in Fig. 8.1 but nowadays most conceptualizations of memory include a more specialized working memory that actively focuses on the task at hand.

Regardless of which memory metaphor is used, we have limits on how much information we can process at one time. Baddeley (1981, 1990, 1995) describes working memory as an active workspace, which can direct how we manage and monitor information. Working memory consists of a central executive, which controls information, and two systems to keep acoustic and visually coded information available. The phonological loop is an auditory mechanism that allows us to maintain information through subvocal rehearsal, whereas the visuospatial sketch pad maintains a visual icon to aid retrieval. When first exposed to information, we may convert the information into an auditory code. We then use our phonological loop to briefly hold information in its buffer before we subvocally rehearse what we want to learn or remember.

Rehearsal is limited to a fixed amount of time, approximately 1.5 to 2 sec., and when we need to retain more information, rehearsal must be faster. Alternatively, we may translate information into imagery using the sketch pad. What we actively think about is handled by the central executive, which coordinates getting and holding information through directing attention. Working memory thus involves an active effort to learn or retrieve information from longer term memory and keep it available for use. To ensure memory is available over time, information needs to be elaborately processed in ways so that it is meaningful to us.

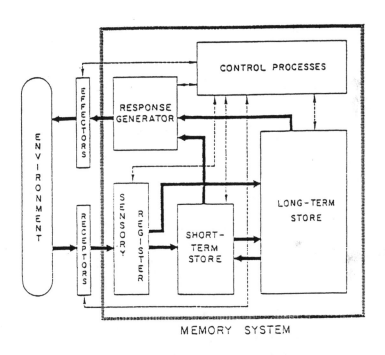

FIG. 8.1 A multi-stage model of memory processes from Atkinson, Herrmann, & Wescourt (1974), based on models advanced by Atkinson & Shiffrin (1968) and Atkinson & Juola (1974).

Cognitive psychology assumes that our experiences are represented physiologically as well as mentally. Biologically, we experience learning through the development of networks of neurons that are activated by a particular pattern of energy. We experience memory as changes in chemistry that allow the neurons to later fire when similar patterns of stimulus energy occur. Though not the focus of most cognitive research, the field of cognitive psychology assumes that cognition must be analyzed at the level of representation (Gardner, 1985). That is, the primary focus is on how information is transformed and processed between input, when we first get information, and output, when we respond. Rather than analyzing how nerve cells work in the brain, the main task is to understand how an experience is perceived and understood when we attend. A cognitive representation of experience includes sensory images, percepts, and concepts, as discussed in the previous chapters.

Whether transfer occurs intentionally or incidentally, the amount of detail represented in memory depends on other factors besides intentionality. Knowledge is specific, as are the skills for using knowledge. For example, Thorndike and Woodworth (1901) failed to find that students who had learned Greek or math were necessarily any better than students who had not studied these disciplines. Prior to that work, the general assumption was that training in Greek and math enhanced general processing abilities of the learner.

APPLICATION OF RESEARCH ON COMPREHENSION

Visual Graphics

Pictures are worth a thousand words. They specifically teach us by presenting considerable information efficiently. Whether reading musical notes or icons, pictures are increasingly common ways to elicit comprehension in a range of human-machine interactions. To improve comprehension, Norman (1997) emphasized the need for consistency in the design of graphical-user interfaces so that users can work out appropriate responses even when working with new machines or programs.

Measurement of the Meaning of Occupational Terms

Meaning is represented in the brain in an organized fashion. When people indicate the relatedness between words, their responses are very consistent. For example, people typically see the concepts of nurse and doctor as more similar to each other than doctor and lawyer (Smith, Shoben, & Rips, 1974). Such consistencies in meaning may be revealed by spatial mapping; e.g., a map of the meanings for nurse, doctor, and lawyer with greater proximity between nurse and doctor while lawyer and doctor are more distant because of weaker association. Ratings of the relationships among words are so sensitive to differences in meaning that the map of people for one culture differs with the map of people from another culture. Even within heterogeneous cultures, agreeing on terminology is critical for effective communication (Harris, 2004; Schwartz, 1996). For example, the Bureau of Labor Statistics employed multidimensional scaling of occupational terms to guide their surveys of salaries of different occupations (Conrad, 1997).

Problematic Comprehension in Surveys

One factor that impairs comprehending surveys is sentence length and complexity. Complex sentences take longer to comprehend than simple sentences and are more likely to be misunderstood (Miller & Herrmann, 1998). One difficulty is that complex sentences require more memory than simple sentences. Generally, sentences under 15 to 20 words are understood more easily than longer sentences (Miller & Herrmann, 1998). Complex sentences may also engender different responses to different elements of the statement. As a result of such studies, survey designers strive to employ simple sentences. Applied cognitive psychologists have solved a variety of practical problems concerning quality of respondent comprehension and legitimacy of survey response.

Legal Implications of Comprehension.

Advertising provides many example of how applied cognitive psychology has been helpful in dealing with legal issues. For example, companies sometimes get into legal wrangles over which company has the right to use a certain name for a product - that is, a case of trademark infringement. Several years ago, Proctor and Gamble challenged Johnson & Johnson for the use of the word sure in a new feminine hygiene product called sure and natural. Proctor and Gamble felt that it had laid claim to the word *sure* years before as the name for a deodorant. An applied cognitive psychologist testified in court that *sure* was the 300th most common word in the English language, based on word counts. The judge ruled that the word *sure* was so common that any company is free to use it.

In another trial, Frank Sinatra's lawyer attempted to sue the *Wall Street Journal* for libel. The Journal had noted that Frank Sinatra, his lawyer, and a friend had just bought a legitimate mining stock. Because Sinatra and friends normally invested only in Las Vegas hotels associated with organized crime, the Journal assumed they must have gotten a tip that the stock was a good one and that everyone better follow their lead. Sinatra's lawyer complained to the Journal that Sinatra and all his friends only invested in good businesses. The Journal published the lawyer's letter of complaint with the headline: "Sinatra's Mouthpiece Replies." The lawyer chose to sue because he had been called a mouthpiece.

In court, an applied cognitive psychologist presented survey results that showed people regarded a mouthpiece as less valued than a lawyer or an attorney but more valued than a shyster (Herrmann & Rubenfeld, 1985). Also, a substantial number of people reported not knowing that the term mouthpiece might denote a lawyer for a mob. The lawyer argued that Sinatra's reputation might wrongly suffer if people believed that he worked for the mob. When people were asked about the prestige of mouthpieces who might work for someone famous, Sinatra's mouthpiece was rated clearly higher than Charlie Manson's mouthpiece, about the same as Richard Nixon's mouthpiece (a president who had almost been impeached), but lower than Pope John Paul's mouthpiece. The court ruled in favor of the Journal, noting that the psychological evidence rendered mouthpiece not too derogatory.

Reading

Many applied psychologists have implemented principles of cognitive psychology to reading. A recent focus has been on applying working memory theory to the analysis of reading. Reading problems have been traced to difficulties in auditory rehearsal (McIntire & Miller, 2000), the size of the phonological loop, and the coordination of executive components in reading (Larigauderie, Gaomac'h, & Lacroix, 1998). The size of a person's phonological loop has also been implicated in vocabulary development (Gathercole, Service, Hitch, Adams, & Martin, 1999) and language learning (Baddeley, 1992). For example Baddeley (1992) reported that word length, phonological similarity, and suppression all affected the functioning of the phonological loop when people learned Russian. Interestingly, the phonological loop's function was not affected when people memorized familiar word pairs.

College Aptitude Assessment

Another application of basic research to comprehension has been in the testing field. Comprehension tasks are routinely included on intelligence tests. Similarly, college and graduate school admission exams probe comprehension skills in ways that take account of differences in the background of different applicants (McIntire & Miller, 2000; Sternberg, 1986). If background is not considered, some individual applicants may not be given fair consideration.

APPLICATION OF LEARNING RESEARCH

Effective use of Mnemonics

Mnemonics are tools or strategies we apply when we want to remember information. When we need to remember a list of items, a commonly used mnemonic we use is creating a word from the first letter of each of the items to be remembered. By now, most of us have learned that mnemonics can boost test performance. Although Loisett (1896) championed the cause of verbal mnemonics over imagery mnemonics (McLaughlin Cook, 1989), at least in the past century imagery mnemonics have been more dominant in memory training. For example, the method of loci mnemonic requires a person to imagine locations in a well-known building, such as their home, and then mentally visit these chosen locations in the same sequence. After locations are well rehearsed, the person can mentally place items to be memorized in these different locations, preferably where the item visually interacts with the space. Another way to use this method is to imagine a path that you routinely take when out walking and then mentally place the items along the path. This mnemonic is generally very effective (Bellezza, 1982; Bower, 1970; Higbee, 1988a, b).

Comparing the effectiveness of imagery to verbal mnemonics may be a bit like comparing apples to oranges. You might like both, but they are distinctly different. Applied cognitive psychologists have found support for both approaches. Research has demonstrated that appropriately designed imagery mnemonics successfully improve memory performance (Higbee, 1999), such as the method of loci (Cornoldi & de Beni, 1991) and the key word technique for learning vocabulary and languages (Desrochers, Wieland, & Cote', 1991; Gruneberg, 1998; Kasper & Glass, 1988; Wang & Thomas, 1999). Alternatively, a variety of verbal mnemonics also facilitate learning (McLaughlin Cook, 1989). In at least one case, verbal mnemonics can interfere with registration of images. When people try to remember faces, encoding the features of faces verbally interferes with subsequent visual memory for the faces (Schooler & Engstler-Schooler, 1990; also see Brown & Lloyd-Jones, 2003). That is, describing what you saw may impair your ability to imagine.

One mnemonic that uses language but not imagery is the phonetic mnemonic. The person learns a set of pairings between consonants and the numbers from 0 to 9. After learning the pairings, the person can readily encode letters with numbers and vice versa. Past and recent research has shown that the phonetic system can aid people in learning (Higbee, 1998a, 1988b, 1999; Patton, D'Agaro, & Gaudette, 1991). However, considerable research indicates that people who have been trained in the classical imagery techniques usually stop using these techniques because they require so much personal effort (Park, Cavenaugh, & Smith, 1990; Searleman & Herrmann, 1994; also see chapter 12).

New Mnemonics

Although most mnemonics originated centuries ago (Yates, 1966), applied cognitive researchers have shown that it is still possible to identify or create other mnemonics. For example, people can improve memory by applying the learning strategies of professional actors (Noice & Noice, 2002, 2004; Noice, Noice, Perrig-Chiello, & Perrig, 1999). Noice et al. (1999) used the social interaction of acting to increase memory ability in a 5-week theatrical training program. Practice remembering lines in an intentional way, based on actively experiencing their character's motives and goals in the context of their character's exchanges with others, resulted in better recall and recognition. Also, we remember better if we can create cues rather than simply learning cues others have generated (Grosofsky, Payne, & Campbell, 1994; Payne, Neely, & Burns, 1986). When self-generation is not practical or reasonable, experts in various lines of work can use their expertise to guide learning in novices (Bellezza & Buck, 1988). Additionally, computers can deliver mnemonics that facilitate performance of a variety of everyday memory tasks (Davies & Logie, 1993; Leirer, Tanke, Morrow, & Kahn, 1997).

Task Specific Mnemonics

Besides extending traditional mnemonics and developing new mnemonics, some researchers have studied particular everyday memory tasks to develop schemes for improving memory performance at everyday memory tasks. For example, researchers have discovered that rehearsal is especially effective when increasing the time between successive rehearsals of the to-be-learned information (Landauer & Ross, 1977; see also Carpenter & Delosh, 2005). Metacognition, or how one thinks about one's cognitive abilities, can help a person remember a shopping list (Block & Morwitz, 1999; Mazzoni, Conoldi, Tomat, & Vecchi, 1997; Reason & Lucas, 1984). If we enjoy cooking, committing a short list of grocery items to memory may be easier than if we feel less informed about cooking. Also, being knowledgeable about food will likely result in some ideas about how to best register and organize a list in memory.

A great deal of research has been done in the past two decades on remembering intentions. This kind of memory was called prospective by Meacham (Meacham & Kushner, 1980; Meacham & Leiman, 1982; Meacham & Singer, 1977; see also Harris. & Wilkins, 1982) who demonstrated that people were more likely to remember tasks they are supposed to complete if they were calm, rewarded in some fashion, and had to remind them . Several reviews of prospective memory research are available (Brandimonte, Einstein, & McDaniel, 1996; Einstein & McDaniel, 1990; Ellis, 1988, 1996; Kvavilashvili, 1998; Mantyla, 1994; Maylor, 1990; McDaniel & Einstein, 2000; Morris, 1992).

Much of the research on memory for intentions has investigated how the timing of tasks influences our ability to remember to do them (Ceci, Baker, & Bronfenbrenner, 1988; Wilkins & Baddeley, 1978). Other research has been concerned with how remembering prospective events is guided by cues present in a situation (Herrmann, 1996). For example, a person may have to remember to have a car serviced once a year in a certain month. Alternatively, people remember to put gas in their car when the gas gauge shows that the tank is empty. In addition, research has verified that people remember important prospective tasks better than less important ones (Andrzejewski, Moore, Corvette, & Herrmann, 1991).

Key factors that influence prospective memory are our motivation, attention, type of competing tasks, and timing. Altering these factors or teaching people how to compensate can improve performance (Druckman & Swets, 1988; Wichman & Oyasato, 1983). Some research has also shown that prospective memory can be improved in neurologically impaired people (Cockburn, 1996; Parente' & Herrmann, 2003) and victims of Alzheimer's disease (Camp & Foss, 1997; Camp, Foss, Stevens, & O'Hanlon, 1996; Terry, Katzman, Bick, & Sisodia, 1999).

Different mnemonics have been shown to be more useful in learning in certain domains than others. Table 8.1 shows the rated usefulness of several mnemonics by faculty who teach in some disciplines (Herrmann, 1990). These mnemonics include flash cards, outlines, reading aloud, note taking, examination of different sources, categorizing of information, visualizing of information, first letter mnemonics, diagnosis and explanation of information, and studying of key terms and facts.

TABLE 8.1
Mean Ratings of Study Skill Usage Recommended
For Introductory College Courses in Different Disciplines

Discipline	Mnemonic Technique										
	Flash Cards	Out-line	Aloud	Notes	Sour	Categ	Vis	Mn	Diag	Terms	Facts
Physical Sciences	1.4	4.6	2.0	5.6	3.9	5.2	6.4	2.5	3.8	6.5	4.2
Social Sciences	1.1	4.2	2.7	4.2	3.2	6.3	3.6	2.2	2.7	5.8	3.9
Humanities	1.0	4.5	5.5	5.2	4.8	4.9	6.3	4.0	3.1	5.8	5.0
Behavioral Sciences	1.7	6.0	2.4	5.7	2.6	5.6	4.7	3.6	2.9	5.9	3.6
Language	5.2	3.6	4.7	3.7	2.6	5.9	4.3	5.0	3.0	5.9	3.0

A rating of 1 = "never" and 7 = "always." This table was abbreviated from Herrmann (1990).

Note. Mnemonic Technique abbreviations: sour-source; categ -categorization; vis-visualization; mn-mnemonics; diag-diagnosis

Physical sciences included faculty from biology, physics, geology; social sciences included government, history, art history, linguistics, and philosophy; humanities included English, speech, and theater; behavioral sciences included psychology, sociology, anthropology, and economics; languages included German, French, and classical languages.

Education
Comprehension and learning are obviously central to education. Some classrooms use language and analogy carefully to increase understanding of societal problems. For example, Wortham (2001) described a classroom discussion of Sparta's practice of infanticide to highlight social processes in the United States' welfare system.

Using analogy, questions, and careful commentary with meticulously selected language, teachers were able to guide critical thinking in a classroom discussion of values and contemporary social relations. Students' performance indicated that comprehension and learning were advanced through this approach.

Applied cognitive psychologists have played an important role in developing new methods of instruction (Bruning, Norby, Ronning, & Schraw, 2003; Dennis & Sternberg, 1999; Donovan, Bransford, & Pelligrino, 1999; Embretson, 1999; Mayer, 1999a, 1999b). For example, mind maps have come into vogue (Dansereau & Newbern, 1997; Gruneberg & Mathieson, 1997).). A mind map is created by physically organizing related concepts on a piece of paper where the distance between concepts increases as the concepts become less related. Also, close associations are placed near the concepts they describe to reveal salient qualities of a particular concept. In other words, mind maps strength association through organizing facts or ideas. Research shows that mind maps can facilitate learning (Gruneberg & Mathieson, 1997) partly by creating a series of mental locations, as in the method of loci.

A great deal of work has been done to identify different learning styles in high school and college (Naveh-Benjamin, McKeachie, Lin, & Lavi, 1997; Speth & Brown, 1990). However, style alone is not sufficient to account for what is learned. It is also necessary to examine interrelationships among study activities, the learner's concept of academic ability, knowledge of content, test anxiety, and other educational variables (Safer, 1998; Sweller, 1989; Thomas et al., 1993; Wilding & Valentine, 1992, 1997).

Students need note-taking skills to provides an external record of information and to facilititate encoding and storing information (Kiewra, 1989; Piolat, Olive, & Kellog, 2005; Smyth, Collins, Morris, & Levy, 1994). Taking notes over key points is generally more effective than verbatim conventional note-taking (Kiewra et al., 1991), with research showing that the best students do not necessarily take the most notes (King, 1991; Lambiotte, Skaggs, & Dansereau, 1993; Morgan, Lilley, & Boreham, 1988; Wilding & Hayes, 1992). Rather than copying nearly every word your professors say, you will learn faster by writing down key ideas. Although taking notes may be something you think you will give up once you earn your degree, note-taking skills are related to adult-world success as well. Research has shown that note-taking affects interviewer memory and even the appropriateness of civil jury decision making. Juries, who take notes, make better decisions (Horowitz & Borden, 2002).

Reading

As your behavior at this moment indicates, people in modern societies obviously need to read. Consequently, successful teaching of reading is essential for modern as well as developing societies. Research continues to develop ways to teach reading by using phonics (Crain-Thoreson, 1996; Gelzheiser, 1991), although other methods (e.g., whole language) are sometimes popular. From the perspective of phonics, it is not surprising that research has shown that the size of a child's phonological loop is related to the ease of learning to read (Gathercole et al., 1999; Larigauderie et al., 1998). Creating an awareness of what is implied or can be inferred from material may also be helpful in improving comprehension (Yuille & Oakhill, 1988). Given the increasing rates of learning and reading disabilities in today's youth, other work has focused on assisting dyslexics in college with their reading (Watson & Brown, 1992).

Spelling

Applied cognitive psychologists have demonstrated that the acquisition of spelling skills is affected by the beliefs children possess. For example, research has assessed the beliefs of children about how letters should be combined and found children's attitudes were related to their spelling performance (Kernaghan & Woloshyn, 1995; Rankin, Bruning, & Timme, 1994). Kernaghan and Woloshyn provided students with multiple spelling strategies and found that spelling performance improved.

Advertising

From an advertiser's point of view, the ideal advertisement should be shown once, whereupon the consumer sees it and is duly influenced. Of course, this rarely happens. Some people may intentionally focus on an advertisement, whereas others may observe an advertisement without intending to remember it (Krishnan & Shapiro, 1996). Interestingly, memory for advertising is influenced by the programming in which the advertisement is embedded. When people watched programming with violent or sexually explicit content, they were less likely to recall or recognize advertisements as compared to recalling ads embedded in neutral programming (Bushman & Bonacci, 2002). How well we remember ads depends on placement.

One question about advertising that has readily lent itself to cognitive analysis is the degree to which advertisements are remembered as a function of the number of exposures. Research has shown that news programs often require considerable repetition for people to encode them (Gunter, 1987). The same may be expected of advertising. Advertisements may be remembered but not elicited by a particular context, so the ad does not influence our behavior. This problem appears to be partly the effect of context in the advertisement and the context in which a person might think of the advertisement (Braun & Loftus, 1998; Furnham, Gunter, & Walsh, 1998; Norris & Colman, 1996). Even distinctive corporate symbol may not be readily remembered (Green & Loveluck, 1994).

Learning to Use Computers

An important part of the computer revolution has been the various ways that have been developed to teach people to use computers. As some of us may concede, learning how to use a computer can be cognitively challenging. Research has shown that multimedia instruction splits attention (Kalyuga, Chandler, & Sweller, 1999) and requires a person to learn new skills to use a computer (Chandler & Sweller, 1996). Computers were once thought to be an interest of the young but recent research indicates that older adults increasingly make use of computers (Morrell, Mayhorn, & Bennett (2000), The innovations of computer systems have advanced the development of cognitive models, which in turn have led to the use of connectionist models in practical applications (Anderson, 1990). However, it has been argued that computers require as much work to learn and use as the time they are supposed to save (Landauer, 1996).

Using Computers to Facilitate Learning

Teaching machines were popular in the 1940s to aid children in learning various topics taught in school (Benjamin, 1988). The machines presented information guided by reinforcement and shaping principles. The popularity of these machines faded, partly because they were not fun to use and partly because enthusiasm faded as behaviorism gave way to cognitive psychology.

In the past two decades, teaching machines have had a comeback in the form of computers. Programs, called intelligent tutors, increase a student's learning through hierarchical presentation of data and testing that capitalize on a student's habits of learning (Anderson, Conrad, & Corbett, 1989; Anderson, Corbett, Koedinger, & Pelletier, 1995). These programs make use of psychologically-based techniques that research has shown to improve learning (MacLachlan, 1986). Fortunately these programs are much more effective in helping people learn than their behaviorist predecessors (Wenger, 1987).

Improving Memory Abilities of Phone Operators

Computers have eliminated the need for phone operators when making local calls. However, information requests, person-to-person calls, and some long-distance calls require a phone operator as do the older PBX phone systems. One problem for phone operators has been to remember the phone number that was requested between the time when the operator first obtained the number and when the operator provides it to the person who requested it. Although this is a short time, phone operators search out so many numbers daily that proactive interference makes it easy to forget a number even during a short interval. Nevertheless, the operator of today is still under pressure to seek out and briefly retain information. To help operators remember the phone numbers, the patterns of operators' number rehearsals were studied by psychologists under the employ of Ma Bell. Similar to education-based research, they found that continuous rehearsal was much less effective than spaced rehearsal. Spaced rehearsal involves saying the number to oneself, waiting a few seconds, saying it again, waiting longer and so on (Landauer & Ross, 1977). Expanding the time between attempts at retrieval resulted in a stronger memory for a number. By expanding the retrieval interval, a phone number was more likely to be learned in new and varied ways, which is more resistant to forgetting.

Improving the Reading of Head Injured Individuals

Not only does spaced rehearsal work effectively for people such as phone operators and students who have too much to remember, but cognitive rehabilitation therapists have also found that neurologically impaired patients benefit from using this technique when trying to learn new information (Wilson & Moffat, 1984, 1992). Presenting head injured individuals with repeated exposures of verbal material has been found to enable head injured individuals to relearn reading and comprehension abilities (Hamid et al., 1996).

SUMMARY

Comprehension of written or spoken language is essential to many applications, either in developing an appropriate understanding of a product or service from a manual or in the actual use of the product or service. The speed and accuracy of comprehension is affected by the content of a message and the means of expression. In addition, comprehension also depends on the characteristics of the speaker, the characteristics of the receiver, the nature of the message, and pragmatic understandings of the social rules of communication.

Research on comprehension has been applied to numerous products and services, such as in using computer graphics, understanding occupational terms, using surveys, understanding the law, educating people, and especially learning. Applied research on learning has developed effective use of mnemonics in educational and other settings. For example, students can develop improved study skills by bettering encoding practices, creating outlines, taking class notes, visualizing information, and using appropriate mnemonics. In addition, comprehension and learning processes are central to a variety of applications, in advertising, computer use, and communication systems, and in helping neurologically impaired individuals cope with cognitive tasks.

9

Retention and Remembering

Don't learn and remember too much unless you are willing to be called on to do
a great deal.

— Author unknown

Part of the focus of the last chapter was on learning, relatively permanent changes
in cognition or behavior. In this chapter we move on to memory, sometimes
described as retaining or recalling information that has been learned. Although
these areas are highly related and often difficult to separate, a primary distinction between them is the methods used to study them. Anderson (2000a, 2000b)
suggests that a key difference is that learning experiments typically include
an induction phase where the learner must determine what is important. By contrast, memory research often involves explicit instructions about what should be
remembered.

Retention

As we all have experienced, memories are more difficult to retrieve as time passes.
Over time, some events or information may be remembered only vaguely; other
events are not remembered at all. Although some information is remembered
throughout our life, our focus in this chapter is with memory that becomes harder
to remember with time, despite our desire to remember whenever we want.

Given that information has been stored, remembering is not as simple
as whether we can or cannot remember. Many factors make it more or less likely
that we will remember when we want. Some of these factors include the means

by which remembering is expressed (e.g., recognition versus recall), whether the memory was intentionally created, the orientation of remembering (to information or events from the past or the future), our awareness of our potential to remember given sufficient time (we often quit trying to remember much too soon), and the level of encoding and organization of the memory, and the degree of learning (Rohrer, Taylor, et al., 2005).

Remembering procedural knowledge depends on expertise (Zeitz & Spoehr, K.T. (1989).. For example, elementary and high school gymnasts, with little or considerable experience, studied cards featuring gymnastic actions. Tenenbaum, Tehan, Stewart, and Christensen (1999) found that expert gymnasts rapidly encoded the meaningful information in ways that could be retrieved immediately and after a one -week delay. Ericsson (2005) suggested that experts can use long-term memory to extend working memory even with interruptions and interference (see also Charness & Schuletus, 1999; Goldman, Petrosino, & the Cognition and Technology Group at Vanderbilt, 1999; and Rikers & Pass, 2005).

What we appear to know depends in part on how we try to remember. If you know that you are going to be tested by a certain means (e.g., multiple choice versus essay), you can organize your preparation in different ways. We retain memories more effectively if we sleep or rest after exposure to the event, review memories periodically, and if we avoid trying to remember information that is similar and therefore easily confused with what we want to remember.

Also, it is beneficial if we anticipate remembering situations - that is, prepare ourselves mentally to retrieve information. Some information is readily recalled, although poorly understood material will rarely be remembered. Memory retrieval failures occur for many reasons (Anderson & Schooler, 2002). However, people forget different types of information at different rates. Theorists have conceptualized that different kinds of information are retained in different types of long-term memory systems which are briefly described in Table 9.1.

Remembering

How much a person remembers depends partly on how well that information is initially learned. Recent research has also shown that retention over time is also based on how one expresses what has been retained (Searleman & Herrmann, 1994). What is expressed depends on our success at retrieving what we are trying to remember (Roediger & Guynn, 1996). Our ability to communicate what we know at any given time can affect our ability to remember that same information at a later time.

Cognitive research has demonstrated that the amount remembered varies with how remembering is attempted: recall, cued recall, recognition, as well as the number of cues available that were also present during learning. The nature of a remembering experience can be described in several ways. Implicit remembering refers to when people remember spontaneously whereas explicit remembering occurs when we deliberately recall a certain event or item of information.

TABLE 9.1
Long-Term Memory Systems

Retrospective memory

The declarative memory system includes information that we can actively state that we understand; knowledge is organized into semantic and episodic systems (Tulving, 1972) as well procedural memory.

Semantic memory involves culturally based knowledge that is typically acquired in school or through informal training (e.g., 33.8 ounces equals 1 liter).

Episodic memory has to do with remembering information that is autobiographical in nature. It involves the episodes and moments in our lives that are personal and meaningful (e.g., remembering senior prom).

Procedural memory retains information about sequences of decisions and behavior and coordinates movement (e.g., remembering how to cook lasagna or play an instrument).

Prospective Memory.

The prospective memory system retains our intentions that are future oriented. These memories may be time-based (e.g., scheduled appointments) because they are to be executed at a certain time or event-based because they are to be executed when a certain event occurs (e.g., taking out the garbage when the can is overflowing).

Retrospective memory refers to remembering the past, whereas prospective memory refers to remembering future events. Sometimes serious memory loss occurs. Retrograde amnesia refers to when a person cannot remember events that occurred prior to a neurological damage. Anterograde amnesia refers to memory loss that occurred after a neurological impairment so that new information cannot be learned.

People base their answers to questions about something they supposedly remember on retrieval (direct, indirect) and guessing (educated, wild). Using retrieval heuristics involves a search of specific content in the memory system and improves the chance of retrieving information (Reder, 1987, 1988). However, sometimes we fail to remember because of mismanagement of physiological, emotional, and motivational states, which compromise optimal cognitive performance. That is, we may be indifferent or unmotivated to reconstruct a valid response.

APPLICATIONS OF COGNITIVE RESEARCH ON RETENTION

The Shape of the Forgetting Curve for Material Learned in School and in Other Training

Ebbinghaus (1885/1913) established the shape of the forgetting curve on the basis of his own forgetting of nonsense syllables. Nonsense syllables were chosen to minimize other associations that might improve or impair memory. For almost a century psychology taught that the shape of the forgetting curve for recall involves a rapid decline, as in a ski slope, followed by a plateau near zero recall. The curve for recognition had a similar shape but at a higher level, showing that more was retained than was indicated by the recall forgetting function. This retention function was believed to characterize all kinds of memory, including that learned in school.

Then, after almost a century, psychologists began to investigate memory for other kinds of material. Linton (1975, 1986, 2000) recorded daily events of her life over a period of six years. At different times she tested her memory for the events that occurred after various retention intervals, ranging from 1 month to 6 years. She found that, contrary to Ebbinghaus, her memory for her daily experiences decreased with a constant rate with time, i.e., in a linear manner.

A series of investigations by Bahrick and colleagues (Bahrick, Bahrick, & Wittlinger, 1975) discovered other shapes for the forgetting function. Young and old adults were tested for their memory of classmates as depicted in their pictures in high school yearbooks . The percentage of accurate recognition of classmates decreased very little initially. Subsequently, recognition remained at a high level of accuracy for about 50 years, after which the decline in retention was rapid. Thus, the forgetting function for yearbook pictures was very different from that of everyday memory or of nonsense syllables. Similarly, military training research has found that motor memory for putting on a gas mask and disassembling equipment (e.g., weapons) or visual memory for discriminating different types of aircraft is retained well for long periods; obviously, if this kind of information is not retained, the consequences can be dire (Hagman & Rose, 1983).

In other investigations, Bahrick and colleagues assessed the retention of courses that are central to high school or college curriculum, such as a language Spanish (Bahrick, 1984; Bahrick & Phelps, 1987) and algebra (Bahrick & Hall, 1991). This research found that memory for material learned in school conformed to another retention function. For example, the amount of Spanish retained by students over a 40-year period decreased considerably in the 10 years after first studying Spanish, whereupon the retention of Spanish leveled off for the remaining 30 years (Bahrick, 1984).

The research findings concerning retention functions teaches an important lesson. If the forgetting curve for a particular kind of material has not been assessed, it cannot be assumed. When it is not possible to measure forgetting, we should be careful in making assumptions about how forgetting occurs. Now it is recognized that the steep slope occurs mainly after learning difficult and meaningless material. Specifically, our forgetting of nonsensical material declines rapidly, whereas our memory for everyday events declines much more gradually. Material learned in school appears to decrease and then plateau. Some memories, such as for yearbook pictures, apparently involve almost no forgetting until very old age when the forgetting is very rapid, followed by a leveling off. Thus, the rate of forgetting over time varies with the nature of the task and conditions of remembering (Healy & Bourne, 1995; Marsh & Tversky, 2004).

APPLICATIONS OF COGNITIVE RESEARCH ON REMEMBERING

Use of Remembering Heuristics on Surveys

A number of recall heuristics, or strategies, have been developed to assist in reconstructing a probable answer to a question. However, it should be noted that sometimes a strategy elicits a probable answer that helps us gain access to the actual information in memory. Here are some well-known remembering heuristics that can reconstruct a probable answer or precipitate a successful retrieval.

The anchor and adjustment strategy refers to when people are more effective answering when they are provided with a baseline answer (or anchor) that they can adjust to derive an appropriate response (Lessler, Tourangeau, & Salter, 1989; Means, Habana, Swan, & Jack, 1992; Means, Nigram, Zarrow, Loftus, & Donaldson, 1989). That is, sometimes 'putting words in people's mouths' can get them to activate the associations necessary to actually retrieve a memory. On the other hand, it can unnecessarily limit how we think about a problem.

We recall events, outcomes, or information more easily when we first recall (reinstate) the context of, or the reasons behind, the events or behavior (Belli, 1998; Lessler et al., 1989; Means et al., 1992; Parker & Gellattly, 1997).

With cue utilization, we often benefit from having certain reminders or cues provided when we are asked to retrieve information. Some students prefer multiple choice questions, which provide many cues, to essay questions, which typically provide less information as to the appropriate response. In many cases, these cues help us retrieve more complete memory when provided with the question (Lessler et al., 1989; Loftus & Marburger, 1983; Means et al., 1989, 1992).

A decomposition strategy involves breaking the question down into parts, answering the parts, and putting together the final answer. When asked to recall information, this heuristic may result in more complete memories (Means et al., 1989, 1992).

With habit recall, when trying to remember certain events, sometimes recalling one's normal habits can help generate a reconstruction based on what the rememberer was likely to have done on a particular day (Lessler et al., 1989).

Guessing may provide the necessary cues to hypothesize about whether something did or did not happen (Lessler et al., 1989; Means et al., 1989, 1992).

In the know-it-all strategy, survey or interview question may be answered despite containing unfamiliar terms because the context and remaining terms still make the intent of the question evident (Lessler et al., 1989).

Landmarking involves being reminded of events that occurred prior to the reference period improves chances of effectively retrieving information (Lessler et al., 1989; Means et al., 1989, 1992).

Minimal thought strategy uses educated guesses to respond to questions because this may be more efficient than answering a question by referring to autobiographical memory (Lessler et al., 1989; Means et al., 1992).

Negative judgment strategy concerning events is when people decide that something did not happen because they cannot recall having the relevant experience (Lessler et al., 1989).

Negative judgment strategy concerning terms is when people decide that something did not happen because they do not know the meaning of a key term in the question (Lessler et al., 1989).

Ordered recall is a retrieval strategy which involves recalling behaviors or events in a reference period in either forward or backward order.

Reconstructing with a calendar in mind is a strategy for remembering which involves using recent events on one's schedule or calendar as markers to retrieve other memories (Belli, 1998; Lessler et al., 1989; Means et al., 1989).

Script based guessing involves searching autobiographical or script information about an event and extrapolating based on the way the event usually occurs for oneself or people in general (Lessler et al., 1989; Means et al., 1989).

Term guessing strategy is when we respond to questions that contain unfamiliar terms because we believe we understand the context presented in the rest of the question (Lessler et al., 1989).

Time reconstruction is when remembering is aided by recalling the time of an event on the basis of relationships with other known events (Friedman, 1993; Huttenlocher, Hedges, & Bradburn, 1990; Huttenlocher, Hedges, & Prohaska, 1988).

Memory for One's Past

Episodic memory is defined as an event that a person has experienced and that is localized in time and space in their memory. In contrast, autobiographical memories are episodic memories that are important to our identity (Brewer, 1994; Conway & Dewhurst, 1995; Hirshman & Lanning, 1999; Schwarz & Sudman, 1994; White, 1989). Until the 1970s there were almost no reports in the research literature on autobiographical memory. Since then many cognitive psychologists have investigated how autobiographical memory is encoded, retained, and remembered (Brewer, 1994; Conway, 1990; Herrmann, 1994; Neisser, 2002; Neisser & Winograd, 1988; Rubin, 1986; Thompson et al., 1997a; Winograd & Neisser, 1992).

Because of their personal nature, it seems likely that research into autobiographical memories might lead to an understanding of factors in adjustment. For example, a better understanding of traumatic memories may lead to retrieval methods that therapists might use to help people come to grips with such memories. Traumatic autobiographical experiences can lead to memories with considerable distortion (Bryand & Harvey, 1998; Niedzwienska, 2003; Safer, Christianson, Autry, & Osterlund, 1998; Wagenaar & Groeneweg, 1990). Repeated recall of traumatic memories improves recall of these emotional events (Bornstein, Leibel, & Scarberry, 1998).

Autobiographic memory consists of different periods, episodes, and moments in life (Brown & Schopflocher, 1998; Burt, Watt, Mitchell, & Conway, 1998; Schooler & Herrmann, 1992; Wright, 1998), Because much of life consists of routine events, autobiographical memory consists of many recurring events (Means & Loftus, 1991; Neisser, 1982). Generally, autobiographical memories have been found to be only approximately accurate (Bruce & van Pelt, 1989; Conway, Collins, Gathercole, & Anderson, 1996; Dritschel, 1991; Edwards & Potter, 1992; McAdams, 2001; Pillemer, 2001; Neisser & Winograd, 1988; Pillemer, 2001; Wynn & Logie, 1998).

Eyewitness Memory

The accuracy of face recognition increases with the duration of exposure to the face (Reynolds & Pezdek, 1992), rehearsal (Read, Hammersley, Cross-Calvert, & McFadzen, 1989), increases in mediators (Groninger, 2000), and decreases with memory load (Podd, 1990). Eyewitnesses, who accurately select targets, are more likely to make their decision more rapidly than those who falsely identify targets (Dunning & Peretta, 2002). In four studies that used multiple perpetrators and lineups, Dunning and Peretta reported that identifications that came within a 10 to 12-second window had a 90% accuracy rate, whereas witnesses using longer identification intervals had accuracy rates of 50%.

Face recognition can be facilitated in various ways. For example, sketches of an alleged criminal have long been known to facilitate face recognition of a felon . Research indicates that procedures that construct a composite of a face from a series of overlays can improve accurate identifications because sketches may help a witness access memory (Levi & Almog, 2000). Evidence also indicates that participants may benefit from "identasketch" drawings (Davies, 1981). Nevertheless, recent research indicates that very frequently the memory of witnesses is not sufficient to develop a useful composite (Levi & Almog, 2000). It is possible that new computer models can present faces in a way that elicits better recall of faces (Gorayska, Cox, Ho, & Roberts, 1998). Nevertheless, in actual police work, sketches rarely lead to the solution of a crime (Levi & Almog, 2000).

The findings about inaccurate autobiographical memory have obvious implications for trials that rely on eyewitness testimony. Historically eyewitness accounts have been considered strong courtroom evidence that can be used to convict criminals. However, if an eyewitness who appears credible is in fact incorrect, an innocent defendant may be sentenced. Because of concerns about the reliability of eyewitness accounts, there are increasing efforts to test the DNA of prisoners, who claim they were wrongfully convicted and compare their DNA to the DNA samples of blood, hair, and skin left at a crime scene. At the time that this book was written, more than 80 convicts, in jail largely because of eyewitness identifications, have been exonerated of their crime (Wells et al., 2000; Wells & Olson, 2003; Yarmey, 1988).

When DNA evidence is not available, psychological evidence of eyewitness inaccuracy has helped exonerate people who otherwise would have been convicted of crimes they did not commit (Wright & Davies, 1999). Certain factors influence eyewitness credibility. Generally, confident eyewitnesses are more persuasive than timid eyewitnesses. However, research has shown that confidence is not always indicative of reliable testimony (Brewer, Potter, Fisher, Bond, & Luszcz, 1999; Gruneberg & Sykes, 1993; Migueles & Garcia-Bajos, 1999; Nolan & Markham, 1998; Perfect & Hollins, 1996; Read, Lindsay, & Nicholis, 1998). Similarly, police are often regarded as having better memory for a crime than civilians; however, this is not necessarily the case (Lindholm, Christianson, & Karlsson, 1997).

Testimony varies in memorability

Testimony that is more detailed and involves imagery may be perceived as more valid (Keogh & Markham, 1998). Similarly an eyewitness' emotional reaction to the crime may help in establishing credibility (Christianson & Hubinette, 1993). In the case of memory for what a witness has heard, the length of what was reportedly heard has been found relevant (Cook & Wilding, 1997). Traumatic memories of events many years in the past may be fairly accurate but key information can be forgotten even from terrible experiences, such as the Nazi prisoner camps (Wagenaar & Groeneweg, 1990). Because of the considerable importance of eyewitnesses in our judicial system, psychologists have made valuable suggestions about how to improve the accuracy of memory reports (Thompson et al., 1997b; Wells & Bradfield, 1998; Wells, Malpass, Lindsay, Fisher, Turtle, & Fulero, 2000).

Interviewing Witnesses

The accuracy of eyewitnesses in court depends on a variety of factors (Marsh, Tversky, & Hutton,. 2005; Woloshyn, Wood, & Willoughby, 1994). The memory of an eyewitness may be affected by when the eyewitness is first interviewed, what experiences he or she had prior to a trial, and how interviewing is conducted during the trial (Cutler & Penrod, 1995). Interviewing should also consider social factors (Wood, Fler, & Willoughby, 1992). For example, witnesses interviewed in the presence of others may succumb to the pressure of supporting the perspectives of dominant group members.

Biased Testimony

Applied cognitive research clearly demonstrates that eyewitness memory, like autobiographical memory generally, may contain inaccurate details. The presence of inaccurate detail raises the serious question of whether such detail arises because eyewitnesses have a poor memory or because the person was influenced to believe details occurred that did not occur. Elizabeth Loftus (Loftus & Palmer, 1974; Loftus, Miller, & Burns, 1978) led the way in examining this issue. In a series of experiments she convincingly demonstrated that leading questions can make witnesses testify that certain aspects of an event happened that actually did not. For example, a leading question can insert a yield sign in a witnesses's memory for a car accident although no sign was present for the witness to have observed.

Since the landmark research by Loftus, numerous investigations have demonstrated that eyewitness memories can be biased in various ways (Narby, Cutler, & Penrod, 1996; Thompson et al., 1997b). Factors that may bias an eyewitness's recall include expectancies (Hirt, Lynn, Payne, Krackow, & McCrea, 1999); stereotypes that apply to a defendant (Loftus, Loftus, & Messo, 1987; Treadway & McCloskey, 1989; Yarmey, 1993; Zaragoza, McCloskey, & Jamis, 1987); scripts for how crimes supposedly occur (Holst & Pezdek, 1992); consequences of an event (Foster, Libkuman, Schooler, & Loftus, 1994); misidentification of a bystander (Read, Tollestrup, Hammersley, McFadzen, & Christensen, 1990); context cues (Parker & Gellatly, 1997); individual differences in susceptibility to misinformation (Tomes & Katz, 1997); and source monitoring (Durso, Hackworth, Barile, Dougherty, & Ohrt,1998; Mitchell, Johnson, & Mather, 2003).

When the events we observe are violent or disturbing, misremembering may occur because we may be less perceptive when fearful (Loftus & Burns, 1982). However, it is important to note that almost all of the "crimes" that have been the object of eyewitness investigation have not been real crimes. When witnesses to actual crimes are interviewed, they may not be influenced by post-event information and other variables (Yuille & Cutshall, 1986). Interviewing 13 witnesses to a murder, Yuille and Cutshall found a high degree of accuracy and little decline over time. Even the color of clothing of the key player was well remembered over time. Neither property nor personal well-being is threatened in the lab.

Implanted Memories/The False Memory Syndrome

Perhaps the most disturbing finding of all this research is the possibility that a witness may be led to believe that an entire event or a series of events occurred when they did not (Loftus, 1997). This question arose because of cases in which children or adults claimed that a parent or a teacher had sexually abused them after being around someone who suggested abuse occurred. No doubt, some children, usually females, are sexually abused by family members or other persons in authority. However, some therapists and clients have accepted the advice provided in a book called *The Courage to Heal* that if you think you have memories of having been sexually abused, you have been and if you suspect you might have been sexually abused, even without evidence, then you probably have been abused. Clearly the costs of being wrong are substantial for either mistake (Polusny & Follette, 1996; Pope, 1996; Pope & Brown, 1996).. As a result, psychologists have been admonished to be careful not to present information that has not been sufficiently researched (Egeth, 1993). On the other hand, therapists and researchers have to be careful not to ignore valid claims of being abused because they do not want to be misled by false memories (Brandon, Boakes, Glaser, & Green, 1998).

Basic research strongly suggests that false memories occur and that they may be common (Lampinen, Neuschatz, & Payne, 1997; Lynn & Payne, 1997; Neuschatz et al., 2001; Payne & Blackwell, 1998; Payne, Neuschatz, Lampinen, & Lynn, 1997; Roediger & McDermott, 2000). However, the commonness of false memories should not be misinterpreted as indicating that memories of traumatic experiences are never valid. Many investigations indicate that distortions increase with time (Intons-Peterson & Best, 1998; Niedzwienska, 2003; Schacter, 1995; Schmolck, Buffalo, & Squire, 2000). Inconsistent information and images can appear to override memories formed initially (Garry & Polaschek, 2000) but post-event information is incorporated in existing memories (Zaragoza, McCloskey, & Jamis, 1987).

Memories of Childhood Sexual Abuse

Applied cognitive psychologists have investigated numerous aspects of child reports of sexual abuse (Goodman & Schaef, 1997; Lindsay & Read, 1994) and have attempted to determine how to identify false memories of sexual abuse (Lindsay & Read, 1994; Ward & Carroll, 1997). While children are more suggestible than adults, children can provide accurate testimony under the right conditions (Coxon & Valentine, 1997; Perner, 1997; Shrimpton, Oates, & Hayes, 1998; White, Leichtman, & Ceci, 1997). Children are more likely to falsely report when anxious (Vandermaas, Hess, & Baker-Ward, 1993), when events are repeated (Roberts & Blades, 1998), when anatomically correct dolls are used to facilitate remembering (Everson & Boat, 1997), and when memories involve medical experiences (Ornstein, Baker-Ward, Gordon, & Merritt, 1997).

Because of problems identified with interviewing procedures affecting the children's reports of sexual abuse, procedures have been developed for interviewing children that elicit more accurate recall (Dietze & Thomson, 1993; Memon, Holley, Wark, Bull, & Kohnken, 1996; Wright, 1993a, b). Summarizing his and others' research Lamb (2004) emphasized the need to use open-ended invitational questions that elicit recall, in circumstances where the child has been trained and empowered to understand their special knowledge (because children are rarely experts). While this seems obvious, Lamb described difficulties with training adults to be competent interviewers because they ask inappropriate, nonleading questions.

Several studies have demonstrated that children and adults may be misled into believing something happened to them that in fact did not. One way to implant a false memory is through hypnotic suggestion (Green, Lynn, & Malinoski, 1998; Spanos, Burgess, Samuels, & Blois, 1999; Whitehouse et al., 1991). However, hypnosis is not necessary to create false memories. A simpler and also effective procedure involves a series of meetings during which a false event is embedded in a discussion of an actual event experienced by the witness. As time passes, a substantial number of witnesses will eventually report that the nonevent actually happened.

Additional research has refined the procedures for misleading witnesses by assessing remember and know judgments of autobiographical memories (Hyman, Gilstrap, Decker, & Wilkinson, 1998). In this research, participants rated childhood memories as having more detail if the memory was one that they remembered relative to memories that were known from another source (such as a friend or family member who told the person about the event). Nevertheless, when people generated images for the memories that they knew about but did not remember, the detail in their subsequent ratings approached that of remembered ratings. Thus, imagining an event that one was only told about, may lead a person to believe that the memory is real. It was initially thought that misleading information simply replaced prior information but research has shown that people keep their prior information and store the misleading information with it (Zaragoza et al., 1987).

Deception/Perjury

Implanted memory results in people believing that something happened to them when it did not. Deception occurs when a person says that their recall of an event or information is true when actually they know their account of the event or information is false (Bond & Less, 2005). Knowingly testifying in courtrooms about false memories is perjury, a punishable offense. Some psychological research has attempted to identify whether witnesses are lying. Efforts have been made to determine cues that may identify deception (Sporer, 1997). Recently, Ekman (2001; 2005) reported that a careful analysis of facial features can help in detecting deception; police departments, who have applied his system, find it useful.

Mugbooks and Lineups

A variety of factors affect face and voice identification in a line up (Roebuck & Wilding, 1993; Wells et al., 1994; Wright & McDaid, 1996; Yarmey, Yarmey, & Yarmey, 1994). Research has shown that certain procedures can bias a witness to identify an innocent person in a lineup whose face was among pictures presented previously to a witness (Deffenbacher, 1996). Also a sequential lineup yields fewer mistakes than a simultaneous lineup (Lindsay, 1999). However, effective procedures for child witnesses differs from those for adults (Dekle, Beal, Elliott, & Huneycutt, 1996). Children are more likely than adults to make incorrect identifications when presented with photos of one possible perpetrator than when viewing a lineup of photos of several possible perpetrators.

Impact

Research on eyewitness memory and testimony by applied cognitive experts has not always been admitted in courts (Kovera & Borgida, 1997). Recently the governments in England and the United States have considered research reports of applied cognitive psychologists on eyewitness testimony (Wells et al., 2000; Wright & Davies, 1999). As a consequence eyewitness interview procedures are now being modified so that witnesses will not be led to unwittingly give false eyewitness testimony (Wells & Bradfield, 1998).

Remembering to do Everyday Tasks

Prospective memory involves remembering actions that we intend to do to meet our goals, duties, or responsibilities. Often a person's best chance to remember an intention is to be reminded by some external stimulus (Baguley & Landsdale, 2000; Brandimonte, Bisiacchi, & Pelizzon, 2000). A prospective memory task that many people do frequently is to water their plants. Unfortunately, people sometimes forget, which may lead to their plant's demise. Recently devices have been developed to help people remember, such as a moisture sensor that is stuck into the dirt. When the moisture evaporates, a beeper is activated (see Fig. 9.2 below). When the plant owner hears the beep, the plant may be rescued.

Reconstructing Memory

Although occasionally everyone may distrust his or her memory, most of the time we place too much confidence in its accuracy. Memories can be incorrect because encoding was unintentionally biased in some fashion. The content of our memories can change because qualitative changes in content occur during

FIG. 9.2 Plant alarm.

the retention period. Although people recognize that less information is retained over time, they fail to realize that memories may change from what was originally experienced and encoded.

Some memory failures are decidedly common, such as forgetting appointments or another person's name (Herrmann & Gruneberg, 1999, in press; Herrmann, Gruneberg, Fiore, Schooler, & Torres, in press). In addition, time it self is not accurately remembered. There is a tendency for people to telescope in estimating the date or duration of an event by reporting that the event happened more recently than it actually did (Rubin & Baddeley, 1989).

As for remembering, different cues can elicit different versions of the memory for a particular event. Lawyers know and capitalize on this fact, but many people do not appreciate how moldable memories can be. It might be supposed that people cannot remember what they never learned in the first place. However, considerable research demonstrates that people do sometimes "remember" events that never happened.

Improving Memory

Memory training techniques can significantly improve memory. Robertson-Tchabo et al. (1980) reported 79% improvement after 5 days of intensive training It was noted that for training to work, initial encoding had to have sufficient depth, and techniques had to be steadily applied. Some researchers broadened memory training to include multimodal elements. For example, Stigsdotter-Neely and Baeckman (1993) compared a 10-week program targeting encoding, attention, and relaxation with encoding training (see also Stigsdotter & Bachman, 1989). The multimodal group showed greater gains at immediate recall than did the encoding-only group.

Other researchers have developed and refined retrieval strategies to improve memory. Geiselman et al. (1986) developed an interview procedure to help people remember. Initially, when trying to remember events, people are asked to recall the context of what they observed. Next they are asked to report everything they can remember about the incident, regardless of its significance. The next step involves describing the incident from some other viewers' perspective. Finally, they are asked to recall the incident in reverse order. In subsequent revisions, the procedure has also included other procedures to enhance recall, such as encouraging the rememberer to relax and clarify the recall commentary (Davis, McMahon, & Greenwood, 2005; Fisher & Geiselman, 1992; Geiselman & Fisher, 1997; Gwyer & Clifford, 1997). Some police departments utilize these procedures.

Parking

The principles of spatial cognition have been used to investigate memory for where they put things (Anooshain & Seibert, 1996), including remembering where one has parked their car (Lutz, Means, & Long, 1994).

Unusual Memory Performances

A number of investigations have examined people with phenomenal memory abilities (Brown & Deffenbacher, 1988; Ericsson, 1985). Such individuals can do amazing feats, such as skim the front page of a newspaper and then recall it word for word. Other individuals can recall complex numbers out to more decimal places than one is interested in hearing (Thompson, Cowan, Frieman, Mahadeeran, & Vogl, 1991). Such fantastic demonstrations of memory are believed in some cases to be due to a physiological disturbance in the brain that somehow enables unusual memory performance. Other memory phenomena are believed to be the result of a life that has favored memory or perhaps the combination of a memory that is somewhat physiologically superior and a favorable life (Ericsson & Polson, 1988; Wilding & Valentine, 1996), or just a favorable life alone (Chase & Ericsson, 1981).

SUMMARY

This chapter addressed retaining and recalling memories. Given that information has been stored, remembering is not as simple as whether we can or cannot remember. We have seen that researchers now believe that there are many ways to conceptualize memory systems, in addition to short- and long-term memory. Many factors make it more or less likely that we will remember when we want. Memory retrieval failures occur for many reasons but people forget different types of information at different rates. Nevertheless, heuristics can help us reconstruct the memory. The amount remembered decreases over time and varies with the kind of information retained, how remembering is attempted (e.g., cued recall, recognition), previous retrieval attempts, as well as the number of cues available that were also present during learning. As has been discussed, the findings of human memory have been found especially influential in how the courts deal with various legal problems.

10

Reasoning, Problem Solving, and Decision Making

It is often wise to not reveal all that we know and prudent to forget when we find we know too much.

— Author unknown

REASONING

Reasoning is thinking that involves certain principles of logic or that requires drawing inferences. Traditionally, philosophy has classified thinking into inductive and deductive reasoning. Inductive reasoning involves drawing appropriate inferences and conclusions from available evidence and is often described as moving from specific information to more general conclusions. If data indicate a certain phenomena occur, then it may be concluded that the phenomena will occur under the similar conditions. Deductive reasoning starts with general information and infers more specific conclusions. In assessing deduction, people are asked to draw conclusions from premises, but typically no rules are provided. For example, we may begin with the premise "All college students like to party" and "Blake is a college student." From these premises we may conclude that "Blake likes to party." In reasoning studies, the typical question asked is, can people think logically? Although reasoning is at the heart of some of the most challenging tasks we face in everyday life (e.g., understanding computer problems, figuring out taxes), many research tasks do not readily translate into everyday reasoning demands (Woll, 2002).

We approach thinking in a variety of ways, with different levels of success, but errors in reasoning are common and systematic. Often we try to bypass a thorough analysis of a problem by using a particular strategy that we believe may yield a correct solution more quickly (Bruner, Goodnow, & Austin, 1956).

Errors in induction involve misperception of valid and invalid instances. Errors in attribution occur because we assume our errors are due to certain situations, whereas errors of unfamiliar others are due to traits or character flaws. Attributing negative outcomes to situations and positive outcomes to skill is another typical way we reason that also contributes to error.

It is crucial that people understand terms properly and orient correctly to the reasoning problem. People often draw conclusions that could be true but need not be true (Pohl, 2004; Oaksford & Chater, 2001). We are likely to erroneously affirm the consequent, while having difficulty correctly denying the consequent (Galotti, 2003). People also frequently accept negative conclusions, especially if they require denying a negative statement (Evans, 1995). Indeed, the majority of categorical syllogism problems do not have valid conclusions. If the premises are not sufficient, a correct conclusion cannot be drawn.

PROBLEM SOLVING

Problems vary in difficulty, involving different mental representations and different kinds of problem-solving approaches (Whimbey & Lockhead, 1999). Determining the actual problem may even be ambiguous. Whenever there is a problem, there is uncertainty and sometimes considerable frustration.

Problem solving involves seeking to achieve a certain goal when you do not know how to accomplish it (Halpern, 1996). Problem solving differs from reasoning. Whereas reasoning requires us to follow one particular logical chain to answer a question problem solving depends, to a great extent, on the nature of the problem.

Problems come in at least three different types. Convergent problems have one solution, that is more efficient or correct than other options. Divergent problems may be solved successfully in a number of ways. When confronted with a divergent problem, a person can try to conceptualize the problem from as many different perspectives as possible. A third type of problem is called creative because it is not amenable to solutions that are readily accepted by others. Creative problems may be convergent or divergent. Creative problems are ones for which standard solutions are seen as not suitable (even if they would work). For example, schizophrenia is a mental disorder characterized by disordered thinking. Some medicines and some therapies help schizophrenics somewhat but others do not. At one time a pre-frontal lobotomy was regarded as an example of a creative solution to the treatment of schizophrenia. This treatment came to be regarded as not creative when it became apparent that the surgery created more problems than it solved.

Convergent problem solving succeeds by following established rules or by relying on shortcuts called heuristics (Kahneman, Slovic, & Tversky, 1982; Tversky & Kahneman, 1973, 1974). Divergent problem solving succeeds by considering a wide range of possibilities not only about the nature of the problem but also about the type of reasonable resolution. Problems are solved in stages: examination, incubation, illumination, and discovery. Although we can use a variety of different approaches to solve problems and be aware of our cognitive limitations, good problem solving requires consideration of many perspectives and options, careful analyses and assessment of solutions.

DECISION MAKING

A special kind of problem solving is deciding what to do about a particular situation or determining what to do once an appropriate solution to a problem has been identified. Decision making involves choosing between two or more alternatives. Decision making takes into account mental representations of related knowledge, expectancies, beliefs or biases, and assessment of potential benefits or costs. Different models have been proposed to account for decision making (Klein, 1997). The quality of decisions we make may be compromised by a number of typical errors, although we often do not know about choices we do not select. Decisions differ in difficulty based on a number of factors, including complexity of the problem, the number of options, the favorability of choices, context, and personal style (Rohrbaugh & Shanteau, 1999). Usually, the goal of decision making is to maximize accuracy and minimize effort, but it depends on the importance of the decision.

APPLICATIONS OF COGNITIVE PSYCHOLOGY TO REASONING, PROBLEM SOLVING, AND DECISION MAKING

Applied cognitive research on reasoning has involved assessing ways people think in real life situations and determining ways to avoid flawed thinking and achieve successful outcomes. Researchers have investigated sophisticated forms of reasoning (Sherman & McConnell, 1996), ways people deal with choices (Houston & Doan, 1996), the over-justification of a position (Tang & Hall, 1995; Wentzel, 1995), and reasoning driven by questions (Graesser, Baggett, & Williams, 1996). Applied cognitive psychologists have even come to the rescue of everyone who completes income tax by studying the reasoning engaged in when people are filling out tax forms (Rupert & Wartick, 1997). The Behavioral Science Research Group of the Bureau of Labor Statistics is regularly asked to evaluate new tax forms developed by the IRS. Using cognitive interviewing methods, inadequate documents that otherwise might be used by the IRS are identified through participants saying aloud their interpretations of instructions and the specific items included on tax forms (Dippo & Herrmann, 1990).

Reasoning in Court by Judges and Jurors

The law is regarded as requiring more reasoning than practically any other problem of everyday life (Treadway & McCloskey, 1989). Consequently, research is needed that identifies the kinds of reasoning used in court. In the case of remembering, the rules for recalling in court are different from rules in other situations, such as therapy or everyday conversation (Engel, 1999; Weinstock & Cronin, 2003). Once better understood, all parties to trials could be acquainted with the kinds of reasoning needed in a trial. Research findings are now available regarding the role of formal and informal reasoning (Bailenson & Rips, 1996), pretrial publicity (Greene & Wade, 1988), size of settlements in lawsuits (Bornstein, 1994), and the language of contracts (Masson & Waldron, 1994). Because cognitive and other psychological characteristics can affect decision making in dramatic ways, lawyers attempt to determine the characteristics possessed by potential jurors and select actual jurors based on whether juror characteristics favor their client (Davenport, Studebaker, & Penrod, 1999; Hastie, 1993; Hastie & Pennington, 1991).

Deciding How Many Children to Have

A calculating device that has become quite common among overseas travelers is a currency converter. Travelers can determine the worth of their money in another currency either by formula or by a rule of thumb. A less common but intriguing extension of these devices is the Chisbo Family Planning Computer which determines the dates of a woman's fertile days. Fig. 10.1 below shows this device.

FIG. 10.1 Family planning computer. A device that determines when a woman is fertile, eliminating the need to compute the fertility period.

Keeping Track of One's Finances

A problem that nearly everyone has is managing finances. Checkbook calculators keep track of your bank balance without having to subtract checks or add deposits. There is no need to worry about arithmetic algorithms or rules of thumb. Figure 10.2 shows such a device and provides information about it.

FIG. 10.2 Checkbook calculator presents the latest balance in one's checking account while adjusting for deposits, withdrawals, and payments. It lessens the memory burden posed by keeping up with ongoing expenses and eliminates the need to make calculations.

Problem Solving in Management.

Management positions in business, government, academia, medicine, and the military require certain cognitive and social skills (Gilliland & Day, 1999). Because effective management is critical to the success of an organization, training in problem solving is widely recognized as necessary for people who assume positions of leadership and authority.

Viewed objectively, clinics and hospitals require medical staff and patients to engage in considerable cognitive processing. Consequently, many aspects of medical management have been subjected to cognitive analysis (Patel et al., 1999). Research has investigated the functioning of medical receptionists (Hill, Long, Smith, & Whitefield, 1995), including medical history intakes (Cohen & Java, 1995) and diagnoses (Clancy, Dollinger, & Hoyer, 1995; Gilhooly, 1990; Patel, Arocha, & Kaufman, 1999; Simpson & Gilhooly, 1997). It makes no sense to have patients explain their condition repeatedly. By preparing hospital staff to take only information necessary for their job, it is possible to speed the process of patient care.

Investigation of problem solving of managers reveals that their problem-solving skills depend critically on the situation and resemblance to situations in which skills were initially acquired and practiced (Healy & Bourne, 1995). A common method for training management skills is the case study approach. Many graduate programs in business administration make use of the case study method, sometimes requiring students to study as many as 1,000 examples of business problems. By learning many examples of problems, a person becomes prepared to recognize critical elements of a problem (Schraw, Dunkle, & Bendixen, 1995) and how to solve on-the-job problems similar to those used in training.

In addition to training aimed at improving general management skills, training also focuses on specific management skills, such as monitoring behavior and supervisory control, planning skills, and production scheduling. Managers must monitor their behavior and their subordinates. They must know when and how to offer their subordinates directions about performing tasks. For subordinates to make good use of their time, the manager must have a clear understanding of appropriate timing of instruction, arrival of materials, and delivery of the output from production. Each of these processes can be improved by carefully considering the limits of human processing and the general approaches people tend to use when solving problems. Improving knowledge of optimizing strategies is especially important for managers.

Cognitive Engineering

Arguably, one of the areas most influenced by cognitive psychology has been problem solving in engineering (Moray, 1999). One basis of the success of cognitive engineering has been a careful and thorough task analysis (Payne, Cohen, & Pastore, 1992; Vicente, 1999). Another way to look at this process is to conceive of it as cockpit analysis. Any job has a workplace, however it is defined. Cognitive engineering considers the effect of stimuli that are critical for job performance, such as all of the lights, dials, and levers in the cockpit of a plane. The goal of the analysis is to place key stimuli appropriately and activate signals in a timely manner. The goal also is to eliminate distracting stimuli. For example, in the first moon shot, the computer screen that the astronauts used to guide the lunar orbiter had a purple button on the screen (Woods, 1995). A cognitive analysis revealed that no one (astronauts, trainers, ground control) knew the reasoning behind that design element. Fortunately, this button did not interfere with astronaut performance but it is possible to conceive of situations in which it might have caused trouble.

Decision Making Faced by Police

Although perhaps less susceptible to ignoring base rates, police (as well as other workers) engage in heuristics that lead to biased thinking (Yoder, 2001). Work conditions are stressful and make noncognitive modes especially relevant as well. Officers work in quickly changing environments that require ongoing analyses of serial or simultaneously occurring events; rapid need to classify and sort information increases the problem of anchoring and adjustment. This bias occurs when our initial assessment of a problem is overvalued and anchors us to certain parameters in our judgment. As a consequence, we fail to sufficiently adjust our judgment when additional information becomes available that logically should cause us to shift our position. Similarly, information that is well-known to us is more available to us when contemplating a problem. If an officer is well acquainted with drug addictions, the officer may erroneously believe criminal behavior is due to drugs rather than, for example, mental illness, because that solution is more available or easy to recall. Although the availability heuristic can speed problem solving in some situations, it may result in error.

The representativeness heuristic provides another opportunity for error. Here events that seem typical are not viewed as critically as they should be, because they are viewed as commonplace. If Carol is a member of gang X, it may be easy to infer that Carol is just like other gang members the officer knows. As a consequence, police may misjudge an atypical occurrence as usual. Another common error is believing that we can exert more control over a situation than we can, which can put officers' lives in jeopardy. As we hope is evident, these thinking errors are not unique to police.

Decision Making Training in Various Professions

People can improve their decision making but improvement comes with study and practice in a single domain. Instead of generalizing principles across situations, decisions are best made if the decision maker has had ample experience with the kind of decision needing to be made. This point is underscored by a study comparing burglars, police, and householders on their assessment of photographed home targets. Logie, Wright, and Decker (1992) found that burglars were more effective than police, who were more effective than householders at remembering physical features of houses. Burglars have more expertise at noting significant changes that were related to attractiveness of a property as a target for burglary (e.g., hedges, fences, occupancy, locks; see also Logie & Decker, 1995).

Another approach to improving decision making is to teach people about the human weaknesses that lead to mistakes. Besides being aware of heuristics, it is also important to be aware that physical, emotional, motivational, and interpersonal factors interfere with decision making. While there is considerable variability in what each of us finds distressing, stress does impair judgement (Cannon-Bowers & Salas, 1998; Kobasa, 1979). When we are experiencing high levels of stress, we should avoid making important decisions. If decisions are to be made appropriately, timing is important. People are likely to make poor decisions if they have been unable to concentrate on the problem, have failed to look at the overall picture, have not been sufficiently analytical, have not been creative in their problem representation, and have failed to follow through on their strengths (Sternberg, 1986).

Fostering Accurate Answers on Surveys

A common heuristic is called satisficing (Simon, 1957; Stolte, 1994). This is where we select the first alternative that satisfies minimum criterion for an acceptable solution. Depending on the importance of the problem we are trying to solve, this may be an acceptable strategy; unfortunately, decisions of some importance should not be solved with the first solution that comes to mind. Some federal surveys encourage people to satisfice because the survey interview lasts many hours, far longer than most people will tolerate. It is clear that interviewing techniques and procedures affect the credibility of answers by respondents (Colwell, Hiscock, & Memon, 2002).

One bad habit that interferes with the accuracy of answers to surveys is seeking information that confirms our views and avoiding information that does not support our views. We may selectively attend to information that supports our opinion while steadfastly disregarding information contrary to our beliefs. Although we should pay close attention to information that disconfirms our ideas, we may not notice or may choose to overlook it. Careful analyses of disconfirming evidence can substantially improve our ability to solve problems. It may also encourage us to consider other information. Sometimes support processes provide new ideas. As previously noted in the comprehension and learning chapter, support processes, such as skimming, careful reading, note taking and detailed examination, can be used to facilitate better decision-making processes.

Reasoning with Palmtop Computers

Probably the first electronic computer that did reasoning focused on arithmetic. Pocket calculators were programmed to follow the algorithms that compute mathematical problems. Since that time, a variety of devices have been developed to carry out certain forms of reasoning.

Today's palmtop devices serve to derive solutions that do not follow algorithmically or by heuristics from the information available. One such device is a road pilot that determines the route you should take to get from point A to point B. Many new cars provide such a device as standard equipment or as an option that the car buyer may purchase.

These devices presumably can calculate a route algorithmically. However, road pilots are unaware of potholes, detours, and accidents and depend on the quality of the initial programming. Hence, they aid problem solving but are not a sure solution to finding the best route (see Fig. 10.3 for an example of one of these products).

FIG. 10.3 A road finder computer determines travel from one location to another, eliminating the need to make spatial calculations with a map.

One of the more entertaining problems a person might tackle is to try to choose the winning horse at a racetrack. Solving such a problem is fraught with all kinds of algorithms that others want to pawn off on a gambler. A horse race analyzer presumably works algorithmically from data about the horses. However, as most gamblers know, a variety of other noncomputational ways exist to help adjust the analyzer's recommendation (see Fig. 10.4).

FIG. 10.4 A horse race analyzer. Based on available statistics about potential competitors, this device calculates the odds that a particular horse will win, place, or show.

Errors

A great deal of work has gone into understanding errors in decision making (Reason, 1988; Rubenstein & Mason, 1979; Schraw et al., 1995; Strauch, 2001; Woods & Cook, 1999). Many of the disasters that have occurred have come under the scrutiny of cognitive psychologists. The nuclear problems at Three Mile Island and Chernobyl have been shown to be due to reasoning and memory errors by operators and not by flaws in the design of equipment.

Detective Work

Solving crimes typically requires reasoning and problem solving. Similar to the process of medical diagnosis, inferences are required (Smyth et al., 1994). Evidence must be noted, identified and handled properly; otherwise, it will not provide useful information. Sherlock Holmes and Dr. Watson are often regarded as the epitome of excellent problem solvers.

Legal Decisions

Police effectiveness depends in part on the cooperation of the citizenry, which may not be forthcoming when the police and citizens differ about what constitutes undesirable behavior (Akehurst, Kohnken, Vrij, & Bull, 1996). Similarly, the execution of crime depends on what potential offenders see as undesirable behavior (Palmer & Hollin, 1999) and with a detainee's or defendant's understanding of the charges (Gudjonsson, 1991).

Judges must make decisions regarding guilt and innocence in all trials at which they preside. Judges have been found to be tougher on defendants than are juries; however, justice in a trial depends on educating jurors in the trial process (ForsterLee & Horowitz, 1997). A great deal of research has been done on how juries arrive at their decisions. As you may know, cognitive and social psychologists are hired to evaluate potential jurors and to advise counsel on evidence and arguments that may persuade certain jurors in a trial (Chapman, Sheehy, & Livingston, 1994).

Applied cognitive psychologists are sometimes called to testify at trials. Expert witnesses are the only kind of witness who are allowed to express opinion. All other witnesses are expected to speak only to matters of fact. The expert witness can express opinion relevant only to his or her expertise. The eyewitness expert testifies whether or not a witness in certain circumstances might be expected to have observed a crime accurately or inaccurately (see Davenport et al., 1999). In other courtroom testimony, experts on comprehension may testify on how certain language in a regulation or in an advertisement is normally understood.

SUMMARY

Mistakes in reasoning, problem solving, and decision making are common. Everyone makes them. This chapter reviewed research and theory that address ways to lessen such mistakes. Sometimes people reason logically but often they do not. Reasoning errors originate from a variety of sources, and the best way to avoid errors is to ensure terms and premises are understood from the outset.

Unlike reasoning, which involves following a chain of thinking, problem solving involves seeking to achieve a certain goal when there is no set path to follow. Success in problem solving may be achieved by following established rules or by relying on heuristics. We described a variety of cognitive applications of reasoning, and decision making that occur in the survey field, the law, business, and other fields. Being knowledgeable about past errors, may decrease our susceptibility to repeating history.

III

Noncognitive Factors Affecting Cognition and Application

11

Social Interaction and Communication

Some people prefer to claim that their memory failed rather than reveal their secrets.

— Author unknown

SOCIAL INTERACTION

Social behavior and expression influence what people perceive, understand, learn, and remember about events, as well as how we reason and solve problems. Friends, acquaintances, and even strangers require us to show that we know who others are and what they do. It is important to recognize the important cognitive tasks that others expect us to remember. Others are more likely to accept memory as valid if it is presented in a confident manner. However, cognitive contrivances, where we manipulate how we provide information, may be used to enhance or detract from self or others' cognitive presentations (Gentry & Herrmann, 1990). For example, to improve the quality of a discussion, a person can attempt to slow the flow of conversation to have enough time to learn and remember.

The importance of social factors to memory was recognized fairly early in research (Bartlett, 1932/1995; Fabrigar, Smith, & Brannon, 1999). When we are in the context of our friends, acquaintances, and even strangers, we frequently have to remember and retrieve information and think. Every social situation requires us to show that we know who others are and what they do. We must make and keep appointments, repay favors, and do chores that others depend on us to do. How well we remember these things affects how others treat us. Clearly, our cognition may potentially affect our social interactions in important ways (Gilbert, Fiske, & Lindzey, 1998).

Increasing awareness of people's expectations, along with modest changes in behavior, show family and friends that you can remember the information important to your relationship with them. As the following list illustrates, cognition failure often occur in one of four ways:

TABLE 13
Social Forces that Interfere with Cognitive Processing

Cognition fails because we may not realize that someone expects us to
   remember something or solve a problem.
Cognition fails because social situations may be too distracting to focus
   on learning, remembering, or thinking about relevant content.
Cognition fails because social interactions interfere with cognitive
performance by diminishing focus and lessening confidence, which
   may in turn decrease one's credibility with others.
Cognition fails when we do not communicate adequately what has been
   learned, remembered, or reasoned due to social distractions.

THE TASK OF REMEMBERING

Our personal life with family, acquaintances, and colleagues can be enhanced considerably if we become more aware of cognitive pacts, which share the burdens of learning and remembering. Pacts are especially common between people who live together because home life requires dividing chores between co-workers who responsibly partition work. People will be inclined to judge your cognitive functioning favorably or unfavorably depending on your relationship with them. The sympathy with which others view your memory or thinking will in part be a function of how you have treated their cognitive performance.

COMMUNICATION

What constitutes effective communication varies with the message topic, context of communication, and characteristics of the audience (Greene & Loftus, 1998). Effective communication requires correct comprehension of the message but how an idea is expressed affects its plausibility. Messages are likely to be believed if people use powerful speech that contains messages that are consistent and salient, use concrete terms, and do not distort the message with overstatements or understatements. In addition, if messages are similar to the beliefs of the listener, seem socially desirable, and elicit a feeling of reciprocity, they are more likely to be believed (Cialdini, 1998). Persuasion can be achieved by either correct logic or attitudinal interventions. Conversational manipulations can be used to keep people from being distracted, to buy time, and to gather information that will enable you to better perform or communicate about the task in class, at work, or at a party. If people couch their recall in language that actively describes their performance with nouns and active verbs, the recall will be regarded as more credible.

The point of many speeches and conversations is to persuade listeners. A variety of strategies are used in the process of getting others to agree to or support the speaker's perspective. Speakers may make their proposal appear much more straightforward than it actually is. In some cases, speakers try to convince you that you have no other alternative by showing the deficiencies of other possible alternatives. Speaking quickly when the listener is unable to fully attend is also effective especially when multiple sides of an issue are presented. Speakers may also force themselves into your space so that you have to listen to them (Cialdini, 1998).

People who receive messages do not have to accept them. Some people actively resist messages. In court, such a person might be called a hostile witness. Receivers can be led to increase their resistance by inoculation, which involves presenting a person with part of a negative message, which renders the person better prepared to reject a message (Hovland, Janis, & Kelly, 1953; McGuire, 1964). For example, in trying to convince someone that Ralph Nadar is an unsound choice for president, a person doing the persuasion might begin by recounting a negative fact about Nadar that prepares the person to resist any positive claims that he or she may hear about his candidacy. Persuasion is most effective in changing attitudes with an incremental approach (Eagley et al., 2001).

Indeed, our preexisting attitudes affect how we remember. Although we are all aware that we tend to remember information that supports our opinion, Eagly et al. (2001) did a meta-analysis of studies of memory for material consistent or inconsistent with attitudes. Inconsistent and consistent information was retained equally well using immediate and delayed recall and recognition. Although memory was better with immediate recall, it was also better when respondents had more intense attitudes and were more verbal. Messages inconsistent with attitudes were remembered equally well because they elicited more reflection, differentiation, and counter arguments. In contrast, consistent messages validated opinions and therefore were not elaborated. Inconsistent messages elicit active resistance if recipients have the capacity to defend their attitudes and they may be remembered well.

The way we communicate is affected by the channel used for communication. Whether the channel of delivery is face-to-face, e-mail, phone, written, or signed may diminish or enhance its impact. For example, communication over standard phones does not permit a person to see someone else's reactions to what is said in a conversation. Indeed, some research indicates that people will not discuss sensitive and secret topics face-to-face but will do so on the phone (Hamilton & Parker, 1992) or by e-mail.

To be convincing, the content of a message should be internally consistent. The people with whom you interact will invariably discount what you recall if it contains obvious inconsistencies. Your recall will tend to be better accepted if you have a corroborating source, such as newspapers, books, or memos or another individual whose memory is trusted, who can back up what you say. If a person does not recall the source of information, the information itself may be doubted (Lampinen, et al., 1999; Marsh & Bower, 1999).

Being able to remember where information was learned is important for everyday life; this is called source monitoring. Remembering the source of information may affect how we use it. While we may not often be told information in confidence, when we are unable to recall a source, it may be unwise to cite or use that information. Monitoring our sources of information can be critical in making good decisions and managing problems and people (Johnson, 1993). Research by Marcia Johnson and others (e.g., Johnson, Hashtroudi, & Lindsay, 1993) focused on factors that influence our ability to identify the source of information. Plausibility, coherence, and consistency of information with general knowledge as well as motivation, cost-benefit analyses, and social context all influence ability to monitor sources (Johnson, 1997). Similarity in content, speakers, or timeline complicates our ability to judge who said what. As we get older, we are less efficient at binding or integrating source and content memory (Chalfonte & Johnson, 1996) although attending more to factual features in information (Hashtroudi, Johnson, Vnek & Ferguson, 1994) and being more personally engaged (Brown, Jones & Davis, 1995) may compensate.

COMMUNICATION IN CONVERSATION

Conversations between people typically involve a steady, complex exchange of information that is quickly processed and responded to by each individual, in coordination with other participants. Whereas cognitive psychology has primarily focused on information processing in conversation, social psychology has looked at more interactive elements. Some aspects of conversation routinely require us to draw inferences, some of which depend on attributions. Attributions are our internally generated description and explanation of why others and we behave as we do. Although these internal hypotheses about behavior may occur automatically, other times they are more likely to receive our conscious attention. In Weirner's (1985) review of expectancies, negative events and unexpected outcomes triggered more attributions about others.

Other work on social interactions notes that people have a general tendency to certain biases. For example, we are likely to underestimate how much situations influence behavior, whereas we overestimate personal determinants for ourselves and those we know well. We also have certain expectations that we try to confirm and we under use data that is available to us. When we process social situations in more depth, bias and error is lessened (Klayman & Hay, 1987).

APPLICATIONS OF COGNITIVE RESEARCH ON SOCIAL INTERACTION

Socio-economic Status and Cognition

Reviews of the literature show that memory performance is directly related to socio-economic status (Guadagno & Herrmann, 1998; Herrmann & Guadagno, 1997; Richardson, 1991; see also Bentley, Kvalsvig, & Miller, 1990). People who are higher in socioeconomic status score better on memory tasks than people who are lower in socioeconomic status. The reasons for this correlation remain to be further investigated, but some possibilities are better health and education (Wright, 1999).

Collaborative Recall

Sometimes people help each other in recalling information. When people take a trip, they tend to chip in with relevant information about how to stay on the correct route. Recall that involves the collaboration of two or more people can be facilitated (Graesser, Person, & Magliano, 1995; Kahl & Woloshyn, 1994) or compromised (Johansson, Andersson & Ronnberg, 2000; Stephenson & Wagner, 1989). Meudell and associates (Meudell, Hitch, & Kirby, 1992) found memory was better on a range of memory tasks when conducted in collaboration with other people and another study showed that collaborative recall can facilitate the eliciting of eyewitness reports from children (Greenstock & Pipe, 1997). On the other hand, groups of people may be less effective than individuals at remembering. Johansson et al. (2000) found that married couples were less effective than paired strangers, who in turn were less effective than individuals, at recounting episodic information that occurred on a visit to a college campus. This poorer memory may be a consequence of disrupted retrieval of individuals working with others to reconstruct events. Basden, Basden, Bryner and Thomas (1997) compared individuals and two-person groups and found that deficiencies can be offset when retrieval strategies are organized and interference minimized or when individual testing is done.

APPLICATION OF COGNITIVE RESEARCH ON COMMUNICATION

Applied cognitive research has contributed to knowledge about communication skills. Research has shown that effective communication requires an appropriate degree of confidence, correct use of vocabulary, an avoidance of overstatement or understatement, completeness with appropriate inclusion of detail, internal consistency, and supporting arguments with corroborating evidence.

Warnings

Warning signs are posted in public areas, on highways, and on many products that we buy. It is crucial that the wording in a warning be clear and the graphics, used to underscore the wording, be effective. If a warning is not effective, those responsible for communicating the warning may be sued or brought up on criminal charges (Peters & Peters, 1999) or both. Some researchers have identified the importance of color, font, and the role of keywords in signs (Edworthy & Adams, 1986). Others reported that compliance with instructions for pesticide use was improved when warning information was presented in directions for use and when personal pronouns were used, On the other hand, probabilistic warning statements decreased compliance (Yamagishi, 1997; see Teigen & Jorgensen, 2000).

Pretesting of Surveys

One procedure that turned out to be very effective in the survey industry was protocol analysis applied to pretesting or interviewing participants about survey questions (Ericsson & Simon, 1993). Respondents were asked in applied cognitive laboratories to think aloud as they read and answered potential questions for surveys (Ericsson, 1999; Willis, Royston, & Bercini, 1991). What respondents said eliminated some questions from the survey and conferred legitimacy on other questions. This procedure allowed researchers to modify the survey more rapidly than could have occurred in a field survey. Other methods were also tried on surveys with some success, but nothing was as influential as this type of cognitive pretesting interview (Forsyth & Lessler, 1991).

Forms Design

Modern life abounds with printed forms that people must fill out. There are good forms and bad forms. Good forms make sense. You know what information they call for. Bad forms are confusing. Income taxes are paid after completing a barbaric complicated form. Research has shown that shading sections of forms dispose people to ignore the instructions in shaded areas. Forms that present text in capitals are harder to understand than forms that present text in lowercase.

Instructions are critical to making a form interpretable to people (Meissner, Bringham, & Butz, 2005). Research has sought to identifying communicative properties of instructions (Wright & Hull, 1999). Formal instructions are understood better than narratives (Bekerian & Dennett, 1990). Information about risk (Halpern, Blackman, & Salzman, 1989; Natter & Berry, 2005; Yamagishi, 1997) and public health information (Hux, Reid, & Lugert, 1994; Wright, 1999) is best understood if it is presented in a conventional manner. Similarly, spoken information, such as radio news, is best understood if it follows the conventions of broadcasting (Berry, Scheffler, & Goldstein, 1993).

Interpretation of Survey Answers

When a person generates answers, he or she can provide some information, but it may not be clear whether this information meets the requirements of the question (Jobe & Herrmann, 1996; Tourangeau, 1984). Consider, for example, a question that asks, "In the last 7 days, how many times did you drink coffee?" Most people are not able to remember this information exactly. In such cases people estimate their answers ("If I drink about 3 cups a day, I must drink 21 cups a week"). People also may satisfice by answering a question incorrectly or briefly to avoid searching out a time-consuming and mentally taxing response (Krosnick, 1991).

Some researchers may prefer that respondents explain what they know or indicate when they are unsure. Whether people feel that they know enough to comment accurately on their performance of a cognitive task may affect their response (Hippler, Schwarz, & Sudman, 1987; Suchman & Jordan, 1990). Research intended to lead to the development of products or services requires accurate data from potential customers. Nevertheless, many of the topics that bear on the psychological effectiveness of products and services may elicit less than honest responses. For example, people may not want to report on their poor exercise habits, the amount of alcohol they drink daily, or how much life insurance they carry. Applied cognitive psychologists should be sensitive and careful in planning how they obtain data relevant to products and services (Bradburn, Rips, & Shevell, 1987).

Providing Escape Hatches for Respondents

Psychologists often ask open-ended questions at the end of an experiment. If a participant seems not to say much in response to questions, the researcher may assume the participant does not have an attitude one way or the other. When the participant is offered such a response, it acts as a filter. This allows people to not provide their own response. A full filter allows participants to say they know nothing about a topic before the question is even asked. A quasi-filter presents a "do not know" response as a legitimate answer to the question, as indicated in the earlier example. In other cases, the "do not know" option is not explicitly stated, but the researcher accepts it when it is used (Schuman & Presser 1981). Allowing people to respond that they do not know an answer could increase errors of omission. That is, participants may not provide an answer when they could. Alternatively, pressuring people to come up with an answer when they have little basis to do so could inadvertently encourage meaningless responses, increasing errors of commission.

Thus, the wisest way of surveying people is to be as explicit as possible in defining the level of precision that qualifies as an adequate response (Ayres & Wood, 1999). Instructions indicating that a person's "best estimate is acceptable" or "if they can't remember exactly, just say so" may be quite useful. Additionally, researchers can maximize truthful communicative intent by scrupulously following recommended procedures for collecting data on sensitive topics (Willis, Sirken, & Nathan, 1994)

Response Bias

How people respond to questions is framed by the way questions are asked and the manner of the questioner. Wording is critical (Miller & Herrmann, 1997). Whether we are trying to find out what a friend thinks or alternatively how well new scheduling software works, we should carefully consider how we introduce and ask questions. Closed questions, requiring only a yes or no, are more likely to elicit a response, even to an unanswerable question, for the majority of children and a significant proportion of adults (Waterman, Blades, & Spener, 2001). Generally, open-ended free-recall questions elicit accurate but less complete information from children as compared to adults; children's responses are more accurate when given "Wh-" questions. Regardless of age, leading questions that suggest a particular response should be avoided.

Many times information is collected about a product or service by surveying people's opinions and attitudes. When people are told that any response is fine, implying that "don't know" responses should be avoided, people often report in the final questioning that their responses to some questions were based on a wild guess (Beatty & Herrmann, 2001; Beatty, Herrmann, Puskar, & Kerwin, 1995). Carefully considering the potential for bias in regards to certain issues or topics is also critical. When asking people to respond to sensitive topics or questions, such as health care or ethics, there is a greater chance of inaccurate responses. Individual concerns about risk and loss, and concerns about embarrassment or disapproval, influence respondents' willingness to answer accurately. Eliciting concerns before obtaining responses to sensitive questions increases truthful responding.

Fact versus Opinion

It is important not to confuse fact with opinion. If someone is labeled as a "bum" or a "jerk," the label is not factual in that these terms do not convey a fact. To convey a fact, words must be clear in their denotation. For example, calling someone an arsonist may indicate that the person has torched buildings. Calling the same person a "ne'er do well" would simply reveal lack of respect (Herrmann & Rubenfeld, 1985).

The issue of fact and opinion is important to the crimes of libel (written defamatory statement) and slander (spoken defamation). If someone has been convicted of arson, then calling him or her an arsonist is factual. The law protects fact but not opinion. Alternatively, if someone has not been convicted of arson and there is no evidence the person committed arson, then calling that person an arsonist is risky because the term is factually defined. Alleging facts that are untrue may lead to being sued for libel or slander.

Almost all libel and slander cases are based on sentences rather than individual words. It is easier to establish the truth or falsity of sentences than individual words. Nevertheless, some cases have come down to words. The word Nazi was judged to be factual in a libel case in the United States years after World War II. The court held that calling someone a Nazi was tantamount to calling someone a person who participated in awful crimes against humanity.

SUMMARY

Many human enterprises fail because social behavior interferes with developing the necessary cognitive skills to be successful. This chapter reviewed some of the ways that the social environment affects our cognitive processes. Cognition fails because we may not realize that someone expects us to remember something, because social situations are sometimes sufficiently distracting that we do not attend or encode information properly, because social interactions interfere with obtaining the necessary information to manage the task, and because a person does not communicate adequately what one knows. Taking account of how social behavior affects cognition is essential to many applications.

12

The Physical Environment

A notebook knows more than the mind.
— Author unknown

Knowing how to make the best use of the physical environment is essential to improving memory and cognition. Great detectives, such as Sherlock Holmes and Colombo know the superiority of physical stimuli. Super spies like James Bond, Austin Powers, and even Inspector Gadget also recognize that witnesses will be most effective when in the appropriate environment. When witnesses are unable to recall details of a crime, the great detectives and super spies have them return to the scene of the crime. Good students of every generation have found that it pays to study in the room that they are to be tested.

Other environmental cues help us remember as well. The physical environment is a powerful aid to cognition because physical stimuli elicit attention more easily than do ideas about the stimuli. You can use your memory and other information-processing abilities to do your cognitive work, or you can make good use of the environment. Arranging the environment to help you work more effectively or using prosthetics, robotics or correctors, and several other kinds of aids to do some of your work can be quite useful. The theory behind the effects of the environment on cognition is straightforward. There are at least seven phenomena concerning the influence of the environment and cognition.

First, the physical environment affects how people feel. If the physical environment is not comfortable, a person may become frustrated and fatigued, leading to difficulty in optimizing cognitive performance (Hedge, 1994). Second, physical stimuli remind us of other stimuli and of things we intend to do. Third, physical stimuli that change over time are especially powerful in eliciting memories, behaviors, and intentions. Such stimuli have been described as active

139

whereas physical stimuli that do not change have been called passive (Harris, 1980a, 1980b, 1984a, 1984b). Fourth, physical stimuli that are not normally found in an environment are more powerful in eliciting memories, behaviors, and intentions than stimuli that are typically part of the environment. Fifth, physical stimuli must be placed where people will see them to be effective. Sixth, people will remember a stimulus better if they create an image of the stimulus. This effect may be greater when people create interactive or bizarre imagery (Higbee, 1988a, 1988b). Seventh, people generally remember smells better than visual stimuli. If a smell is associated with information or upcoming events, the smell may be especially dependable cue in reminding one of the needed memory (Chu & Downs, 2000).

APPLICATIONS OF EXTERNAL AIDS

Commercial Cognitive Devices

There are many different kinds of cognitive devices sold commercially, which differ according to the kind of assistance they provide. Because physical stimuli are naturally so powerful, people have devised ways to use natural objects to stimulate memory. In principle, a cognitive aid may be developed naturally or commercially. Different types of commercially availables aids are listed below.

TABLE 14
Different Kinds of Commercial Cognitive Aids

Cognitive prosthetics - objects and devices that can be used to facilitate memory performance

Cognitive robots - objects and devices that carry out a memory task for an individual

Cognitive corrector - objects and devices that remember something forgotten or
    solve a problem that a person could not solve

Cognitive assessors - objects and devices used to evaluate a person's memory capability

Cognitive trainers - Objects and devices that provide instruction on maximizing
    cognitive processes

Cognitive sources - objects and devices that maintain knowledge or records

Cognitive art - visual displays that either guide a person's use of memory or a
    person's attempts to solve a problem

Cognitive organizers - ways to organize possessions and papers spatially so that one
    remembers where they are

Cognitive symbols - objects and visual displays that remind a person of memory and
    cognitive tasks to be performed

Cognitive superstitious possessions - objects and devices that facilitate cognition
    because a person believes they affect cognitive processes memory and cognitive
    tasks to be performed

Many entrepreneurs and psychologists have created commercial external aids that purport to aid memory and cognitive processing (Harris, 1980 a, 1980b; Herrmann & Petro, 1990; Hersh & Treadgold, 1994; Intons-Peterson, 1997; Kapur, 1995; Lynch, 1995; Parente' & Anderson-Parente', 1991; Parente' & Herrmann, 2003; Yoder & Herrmann, 2004). No single aid helps people with all cognitive tasks. Instead, different commercial aids address different cognitive tasks. For example, the memory aids used for shopping (such as a credit card alarm) differ from the aids used to control one's finances (such as an electronic checkbook that records purchases) or those that remind us of social obligations (alarms for appointments). Because different types of memory are used for different cognitive tasks, different aids are available.

Partly because of increasing demands to manage information, many cognitive aids have been developed in the last decade. It is likely that many more will be invented in the next decade. The following sections describe the many examples of the external cognitive aids that are commercially available.

Cognitive Prostheses

Just like a physical prosthesis, an artificial device that replaces a missing part of the body, cognitive prostheses are designed to assist cognitive functions such as memory, attention, and problem solving. Cognitive prostheses particularly augment the abilities of those who are cognitively disabled. Although these products facilitate cognitive performance, they do not guarantee performance will be perfect. For example, a memo written on a pad of paper is a prosthetic aid. The message on the pad reminds us if we look at the message. Of course, you still might look away and forget to do it. Checklists of groceries can be used to purchase items most people buy regularly. Almost everyone needs to be aware of when they have scheduled appointments and events in their lives. For many people, the primary record system is an appointment book, planner, or diary (Lipman, Caplan, Schooler, & Lee, 1995). There are dozens of different kinds available. Other people keep sticky notes or an erasable board or record their schedule on a computer. All of these aids passively remind us.

The standard clock-radio is so commonplace that we don't even think of it as a memory aid but many people use it to remind them of things to do. A shopping calculator or a checkbook calculator can make it easier to keep track of money. Of course, like paper records, these devices require that all proper entries be made to work correctly.

A variety of products have been developed to help people remember to take medicine. You can buy plastic pill boxes labeled for the time of day and day of the week that medication is to be taken. High-tech pill boxes have an alarm that can be set to the times that pills must be taken (Park & Kidder, 1996).

Most alarms provide acoustic alerts that cue without requiring that the user look at or localize sound. In the kitchen or rooms nearby, many people use a mechanical or electronic windup kitchen timer to remind them of numerous chores that arise during the day. Timers are useful also in work situations. For example, when someone calls and asks you to come to the office or meet for coffee in 10 minutes, you can set the timer to ensure you remember to go.

Computerized alarm systems are also available for employers to use to remind employees or clients of work responsibilities. For example, phone systems have been developed that remind people of doctor's appointments and other intended tasks (Leirer, Morrow, Pariante, & Sheikh, 1991; Leirer, Morrow, Tanke, & Pariante, 1991; Leirer, Tanke, & Morrow, 1993).

One of the most challenging everyday cognitive tasks is remembering to do chores, meet appointments, and manage obligations that must be done at a certain time (Walbaum, 1997). A variety of products are now sold that beep to remind the owner of appointments, which are also shown on a tiny display screen. These products include watches (Naugle, Prevey, Naugle, & Delaney, 1988) that trigger an alarm at the appropriate time. Some watches store appointments taken off a personal computer via a cable or infrared transmission, and along with related information, such as phone numbers, flight schedules, and other information.

Similarly, there are electronic diaries in the form of palmtop computers that provide people with personal data when they need it. For example, these "personal data assistants keep in memory phone numbers, addresses, and one's daily schedule. In addition, they remind a person of the appointments and chores that they intend to do on a particular day (Herrmann, Brubaker, Sheets, Wells, & Yoder, 1998; Walker & Andrews, 2001, 2004).

Cognitive Robots

A robot carries out a memory task for an individual. A programmed thermostat "remembers" to turn a furnace on and off. VCRs can be programmed to record shows. Lighting can be programmed to turn off and on. Many coffeemakers can be programmed to start brewing coffee at a certain time in the morning. When the automatic coffeemaker starts making the coffee at the set time, it has been a good robot because it has performed the task for you. Any device that performs a cognitive task for you is a cognitive robot. People can even act as someone else's robot when they remember something or solve a problem for them.

Cognitive Corrector

This aid can be thought of as special kind of robot that helps a person correct a memory error. Some examples of cognitive correctors are key chains that beep when you clap, correcting the cognitive failure of having forgotten where you put the keys. Once you hear the key chain beep, you can find your keys easily. Credit card alarm wallets signal an alarm if one or more credit cards have not been returned to the wallet within a brief period of time (e.g., two minutes). Another memory corrector is a toilet seat that when left in the vertical position (almost always by males) automatically returns to the ho rizontal position (saving many marriages and other significant relationships). If someone attempts to help another person find something, then that person is acting as a corrector.

Cognitive Assessors

If you decided to evaluate your cognitive powers, there are various ways you can do so. You may enjoy trivia game shows, anagrams, or puzzles. Some people use the electronic game called Simon as a test of the current cognitive functioning. Recently, software called the *Memory Monitor* was developed by Herrmann to guide people to rate various aspects of their memory functioning; the ratings in turn can be used to predict a person's memory functioning at a particular time (Herrmann, Plude, Yoder, & Mullin, 1999). Computerized assessment systems have also been developed to assist clinicians in conducting a thorough assessment of a client's cognitive functioning. These programs present simulations that provide a real-world assessment of various everyday cognitive tasks (Larrabee & Crook, 1989; Poon, 1980). For example, the programs present pictures of people on a computer screen, while a speaker says their names, simulating introductions.

Cognitive Trainers

In addition to accessing their memories, some people are interested in trying to improve their cognitive functions. A variety of tapes have been produced that promise the listener an improved memory (Rebok, Rasmusson, Bylsma, & Brandt, 1997). Videos have also been produced with the same objective (West & Crook, 1992; West, Yassuda, & Welch, 1997). More recently computer programs have been developed that promise to improve a person's memory, by training specific skills and strategies for learning and remembering names and faces, facts and figures, and intentions to complete activities (Baldi, Plude, & Schwartz, 1996; Plude & Schwartz, 1996a, 1996b). Because the software is the only method devised so far that is interactive, it most nearly approximates what it would be like to be trained by a personal memory trainer. One recent review of the approach taken on these disks indicates that they may be more effective than prior means of memory training (Rybash, 1998). In addition, software may be useful in helping to retrain people who have diminished memory function due to neurological impairment (Parente', 2000).

Knowledge Sources

Because we recognize that our memory is imperfect, we keep external knowledge sources on topics that otherwise might be forgotten. For example, many people keep at least some of their books from college for future reference. We do not really expect to remember many of the things we learned in school or on the job. Instead, we learn how to efficiently look things up. Similarly, we do not expect to remember all of the details of experiences that were once fresh in our minds. Nevertheless, we sometimes need information that we just cannot recall.

A number of objects and devices maintain knowledge or records that can be used to support memory and thinking about hard-to-remember topics. It is often advisable to keep standard sources including dictionaries, encyclopedias, thesauri, the Guiness Book of World Records, Farmer's Almanac, and atlases. It is also helpful to retain work-related professional books, manuals, disks, and catalogs. These knowledge sources keep facts readily on hand that otherwise might not come immediately to mind. Of course, they also provide us with information that we may not have known in the first place. The internet provides another highly accessible record but here the user must carefully discriminate the quality of source.

Cognitive Records

Personal records provide a special type of information. When students take notes in class, a secretary takes minutes from a meeting, or a court stenographer records a trial, records are kept because unaided memory often fails. A backup record of information or intentions is very helpful whenever a person forgets the details of an event or information. People can record their thoughts with portable voice organizers or transcription. Additionally people can connect a recorder to their phone to check some of the details of a message later. However, such recordings can only be for personal use. For example, recordings made without someone's knowledge are inadmissible in court. Research indicates that there is a tradeoff between storing information in memory and external storage of information (Schonflug, 1986). Very successful people have been found to keep more backup records and external knowledge sources than less successful people (Hertel, 1993). Therefore, it is likely to be helpful to keep and carefully organize notes from meetings, readings, and lectures.

Most of us have thought about how we could learn names more efficiently. One activity that could help is to write down the names of people met and an analysis of each name learned. People sometimes use tape recorders to help them rehearse. One award-winning teacher we know takes photos of all her students and places their names on the back so she can associate each name with salient characteristics of the individual. Many students create a deck of index cards with vocabulary or concepts on them that they use as an external aid.

Cognitive Art

People sometimes exhibit paintings, objects, drawings, and sketches in their home or at work that remind them of past experiences or particular knowledge. During the Renaissance, artists created paintings that were intended specifically to help people use the mnemonic called the method of loci discussed earlier. People used this method to learn lists by mentally placing each item on a list in different spots on the painting (Yates, 1966).

Visual displays that either guide a person's use of memory or attempts to solve a problem are common in many occupations. Doctors' offices are typically covered with diagrams of the body and the internal organs. Those posters are not there just to impress patients. They provide the physician and staff with a constant reminder of knowledge they need to know. Nowadays many professions use posters to refresh and remind people of critical information.

Cognitive Organizers

Losing things is one of the most annoying memory problems we face. All too often when we put an object down, we do not pay attention to our behavior. The simplest way to avoid losing things is to be organized. The ease with which people learn and remember depends in part on the organization of the environment and a person's familiarity with this organization.

To avoid forgetting to take necessary items, it is a good idea to reserve a place in your office or home where you put your take-aways. As the day goes on, stack things in that spot. When you prepare to leave, you will not have to remember what you need to take. Some people like to reserve a shirt pocket or section in a purse to serve as a portable take-away spot for putting certain things one does not want to forget, such as concert tickets, checks, and important papers.

Another way to avoid losing things is to simply make them harder to lose. Hotels often attach a large object to each room key because guests accidentally walk off with keys on smaller keychains. When a foot-long piece of metal is attached to the item, a person is more likely to remember to return it.

Another way to avoid losing one's keys is by keeping them with you at all times. Key chains may fasten to one's belt or some other part of one's clothing. Small metal boxes are made that attach under a car. Similarly, hollow stones are sold to hide keys while blending into the garden. Give a duplicate to your neighbor, that is if you have a neighbor you don't mind having the run of your house.

When people work under pressure, time is precious. We do not want to waste time trying to remember the forgotten location of a misplaced folder, contract, or other piece of information. To avoid this problem, people arrange their desk or workspace so that it is memory-friendly. Items that are used every day, pens, stapler, and tape are put on top of the desk or in a drawer that is handy. Similarly, people organize desk drawers and files. They carefully store less frequently used items in a closet or in a cabinet in another room.

A variety of products are sold solely for the purpose of organizing one's possessions. For example, there are fishing tackle boxes and sewing boxes that are essentially identical. Portable offices are sold to use on car trips, which provide a desktop, storage area, and a variety of supplies and devices commonly needed in the office. Many stores and mail order catalogs sell labels to be put on clothing and other possessions. Also labels can be made for files, drawers, and containers so that the contents can be identified at a glance.

Cognitive Symbols

In everyday life people employ a variety of objects to remind themselves of memory and cognitive tasks that need to be performed. For example, some people put a rubber band on their hand to remind them of what they have to do. If a person must meet an appointment or do a certain chore by a certain time, he or she can avoid forgetting that intention by doing any one of several things. Perhaps the easiest thing to do is to put one's purse over the other shoulder or put one's wallet in a pocket not usually used. A person can switch one's watch from the usual wrist to the other wrist. Another ploy to ensure being reminded is to dress differently. For example, wear memory jewelry, such as a bracelet or a disgusting tie that leads others to make comments that remind the wearer that he or she has an important task to do. Of course, if you use this strategy often, people may not comment because they have decided you have bad taste. Alternatively, cues can sometimes interfere with remembering an appointment or deadline (Cook, Marsch, & Hicks, 2005).

Positioning objects in an unusual manner may also provide an effective reminder. Placing an object in an unusual place may symbolize that something needs to be remembered. Some day planners come with stickers that are intended to remind people of things to do (such as a man digging represents work, a pile of money indicates the bank, an image of milk, eggs, and bread symbolizes the grocery).

Cognitive Motivational Aids

Baseball, football, and basketball teams sell hats and tee-shirts with the hope that fans will wear these at games to encourage their team to win. The teams feel this is so important that they will periodically give away items with their logo on it. Some psychologists have taken on to this custom. Parente' (1998) produced tee-shirts that bear images related to memory with the goal of motivating people to practice their memory tasks (see also Payne & Wenger, 1992, 1995).

COGNITIVE FRIENDLY PRODUCTS

There are many products that serve important functions in our everyday life and are cognitively friendly. For example, many cars today come with several buzzers that remind the driver to perform chores required by law (e.g., using seatbelts) or to keep the car in running order (e.g., turn off the headlights when the car is turned off). Some cars automatically turn off the headlights when the key is removed from the ignition. Thus, the car is programmed to turn off the lights for the driver. Table 12.1 contains a classification of the usefulness of some products according to task and the age of a user.

TABLE 12.1

Mean Usefulness Ratings for Commercial Memory Aids

According to the Age of the User

	Memory Aid	Age of the User		
		Elderly	Middle	Young
1.	Iron-With Memory	3.6	4.2	4.1
2.	Tape-Recorder	2.5	3.6	4.1
3.	Whistling Teapot	4.0	3.3	3.6
4.	Car Memo-Pad	2.1	3.0	3.3
5.	Parts Cabinet	4.1	3.6	3.5
6.	Electronic Memo-Pad	1.8	2.5	3.0
7.	Coffee-Maker	3.8	2.1	3.8
8.	Bookmark	4.0	2.6	2.9
9.	Plant Alarm	4.2	2.8	2.9
10.	Memo Stickers	2.7	3.9	3.8

Note: Rating of 1 indicates not useful, and a rating of 7 indicates that the item was perceived as extremely useful (Petro, Herrmann, Burrows, & Moore, 1991).

DRAWBACKS OF COMMERCIAL COGNITIVE AIDS

Some people argue that use of cognitive aids lessens cognitive ability because a person no longer practices remembering the task. Yoder and Puga (2004) found that palmtop users were less effective at encoding verbal information than people who used other memory methods, such as planners and lists. However, in spite of this potential limitation, given all the demands on our time and energy, external aids can simplify at least some aspects of our lives.

People differ in the kind of aids they prefer. In some cases, this is a matter of personality, preference, and personal experience. For example, technophobes avoid the use of electronic devices to solve their problems. Age may also be a factor (Morrell, 1997) as young, middle-aged, and older adults rely on different kinds of aids (Petro, Herrmann, Burrows, & Moore, 1991: see Table 12.1). For example, young people tend to use electronic devices, whereas elderly people prefer to use nontechnical aids that perform specific tasks. It will be interesting to see if this holds up as more technologically sophisticated users grow older.

SUMMARY

The physical environment is a powerful aid to cognition because physical stimuli elicit attention more easily than do ideas about the stimuli.   Cognitive performance can be enhanced in many applications simply by altering the physical environment to make people feel better, remind people of things to be done, and make them aware of stimuli that they might overlook. In addition, devices can be used to enable a person to avoid using their mind altogether. You can use your memory and other information-processing abilities to do your cognitive work, or you can make good use of the environment. Arranging the environment to help you work more effectively and using prosthetics, robotics or correctors, and other kinds of aids to do some of your work can be quite useful.

13

Physiological and Emotional States

Drink and self pity may help people cope
with their misery but drink and self pity
also prevent getting out of misery.
- Author unknown

PHYSIOLOGICAL STATES

Memory and other cognitive processes are sometimes subtly and other times powerfully affected by our physiological condition (Weingartner & Herrmann, 1992). Physical states, chemical states, and overall health status may separately or collectively interact to influence consolidation of memory and learning (Weingartner & Parker, 1984). Some changes in physiological state may have positive effects (especially the cognitive enhancing nutrients, drugs, and other agents); however, most changes are negative (Rosenzweig, 1998). Virtually every kind of medicine has side effects, and some of these interfere with memory and cognitive performance. Physical fitness and exercise are related to better memory and cognitive functions. On the other hand, personal habits such as smoking lessen the beneficial effects of exercise on memory (Bruce, Hays, & Pring, 2004).

A person's physical state may affect ability to perform cognitive tasks. Several factors influence a person's physical state. First, physical state depends on a person's health and fitness. A person who is in good physical condition will do better when performing a cognitive task than when that person has not had enough exercise (Blumenthal & Madden, 1988; Chodzko, Zajko, 1991; Clarkson-Smith & Hartley, 1989; Emery & Gatz, 1990; Etnier et al., 1997). Other things being equal, a person who eats proper amounts and types of nutritious food can expect better cognitive performances compared to someone who does not eat well (Kolakowsky, 1997). Similarly, physical states depend on adequate sleep. When we are fatigued, we become less flexible, more perseverative, and take longer to plan, even though simple memory may not be affected (van der Linden, Frese, & Meigman, 2003).

Changes in physiological condition also occur because of disease processes, emotional responsivity, and environmental factors. Because changes in physical condition may be due to changes in standard of living, a person's physical condition may covary with sociological variables, such as income, educational background, or the nature of one's job. Such changes in physical condition may contribute to individual differences in cognitive performance.

EMOTIONAL STATES

Emotions have been defined as "internal, mental states focused on affect " (Clore, Ortony, & Foss, 1987). Emotions are likely to be temporary states that often involve appraising different situations or other external circumstances (Morris, 1992). As a consequence, our cognitive interpretation of events is an important part of emotion. Learning how to modulate emotion to organize and manage cognitive effects may include teachable skills that parents could use to maximize their children's development).

In general, emotional-type responses are forgotten more slowly. Selective attention, meaningfulness, and rehearsal are part of the reason why this occurs. Our brains may also process this information differently. One general explanation is that emotional events cause greater cortical arousal than neutral events, which can affect the memory trace created by the event. More emotion creates more activation or reverberation along the pathway and stronger consolidation of the memory, and results in better permanent memory (Hebb, 1949; Gold (1986) speculated that stress releases epinephrine, which in turn increases circulating glucose. As you may recall from chapter 6, circulating glucose enhances memory. In a series of interesting studies, McGaugh (1992) has showed that the effects of epinephrine are dose dependent: a low dose of epinephrine enhances retention, whereas a high dose impairs memory.

Sometimes when an event arouses extremely threatening emotions, or when trauma is repeatedly experienced, we may develop defensive reactions, which can even include amnesia. Emotions influence what we attend to and how we interpret what occurs. It is important that we recognize the impact emotions can have on our ability to process information and learn ways to use and harness the power of emotion in the most effective ways.

On the other hand, material that is irrelevant and spatially peripheral to the emotional event is not remembered as well. Emotions often have little or no influence on accomplishing simple cognitive tasks, but they are more likely to exert an influence on more complex and difficult tasks. Research has firmly established mood congruency, where we selectively take in information that fits with our mood. We can use this to our advantage by matching our activities with our mood state. It is easier to be slower, more methodical and systematic when we are experiencing negative mood states; conversely, when we are feeling good, we can use this to generate ideas and consider problems from more global perspectives. With mood dependence, memory can be enhanced by reinstating the same mood or emotional state as when we initially learned or were exposed to the incident. Although this is not a particularly strong memory aid, it can sometimes help us remember what we need to know.

APPLICATIONS OF COGNITIVE ASPECTS OF PHYSI-OLOGICAL MODES

Identifying Disease that Impairs Cognition
Until recently many people did not recognize that physical illness can impair cognition, that is except for those who were ill, aging and pathology researchers, and some medical personnel. Even most of the major textbooks on cognition say nothing about the effects of illness on perception, memory, problem solving, and communication. Thanks to research in epidemiology, a catalog of illnesses that impair cognition has been collected, such as shown in Table 13.1.

TABLE 13.1
Major Conditions of Ill Health That Impair Cognition

Physical diseases

Addison's disease	anoxia hypotension	AIDS
arthritis	brain tumors	cancer, most kinds
chronic fatigue	chronic pain	encephalitis
epilepsy	head injury	heart attack
hypertension	hyperthyroidism	learning disabilities
migraine headaches	multi-infarct	multiple sclerosis
sensory disorders	stroke	syphilis
surgery, major	toxic exposure	

Psychiatric disorders

ADD	anxiety disorders	bipolar disorder
dissociative disorders	dyssomnias	
schizophrenia	stress disorder	

Gerontological diseases and disorders

age-related memory impairment	dementia	sensory loss
Alzheimer's	Korsakoff's disease	Parkinson's disease

It is no surprise that people who are frequently ill have significantly more cognitive problems than people who stay in good health (Weinman, 1994). If a person is ill, it is advisable to avoid important mental tasks whenever possible. Especially complex tasks become more difficult when we are ill and we are more prone to error. Most illnesses cause some discomfort, which makes it hard to attend. A bad cold or an upset stomach slows remembering (Matthews, Davies, Westerman, & Stammers, 2000; Smith, 1992).

Confusion and disorientation are common when pain is extreme. Arthritis impairs registering and retrieving information because of the distracting pain. Cardiovascular diseases cause permanent difficulty in short-term memory because of neurological damage caused by insufficient blood flow. In addition, Matthews et al. (2000) report some people experience discontinuous amnesia for events before surgery but even trivial health events, such as a boil, can cause an occasional cognitive failure because of the distraction of discomfort.

Cognitive Impact of Neurological Diseases

Some illnesses severely impair memory. Alzheimer's disease is the most widely known memory illness. Korsakoff's syndrome, often caused by excessive alcoholic consumption over a prolonged period, involves a severe loss of the ability to register new memories. Strokes also impair memory in that a blood clot in the brain disrupts memory, often permanently. Mini-strokes send many tiny clots to the brain, impairing memory, but usually not permanently. Very low blood pressure, which is a life-threatening condition, also impairs memory because it lessens one's ability to pay attention. Severe depression can impair memory, particularly with regard to the ability to encode and organize information

TABLE 13.2
Cognitive Problems Due to Neurological Impairments

Forgetting something that was said to you (even after being reminded)
Getting lost on a route that you knew previously
Forgetting appointments that you feel are very important.
Having trouble naming common objects
Forgetting enough information regarding your job that you no longer
    can do certain tasks that you have been accustomed to doing
Repeating actions without realizing it
Purchasing things you already just bought
Being confused as to time of day or your location
Being unable to keep track of your money or checks you have written
Losing an ability at which you were proficient
Taking on a sudden change of personality

(Niederehe & Yoder, 1989); fortunately, the effects of depression are not permanent. The cognitive problems presented in Table 13.1 may be indicative of the beginning of a serious neurological disorder (Campbell & Conway, 1995; Mark & Mark, 1992).

A controversial but potentially helpful new method has evolved to help the severely physically disabled. People who cannot speak or write have been found able to guide a cursor through a device that uses brain waves and small ocular muscular responses (Metz & Hoffman, 1997). Researchers found paralyzed individuals can communicate by answering yes/no questions and in some cases compose sentences after years of paralysis (Doherty, 1999).

Medications that Facilitate or Impair Cognition

In years past, some people claimed that amphetamines ("speed," "uppers") enhance cognition. Although amphetamines keep a person awake for a cognitive task, these drugs are highly addictive and dangerous. Also, stimulants are not a good way to rouse you for a cognitive task. They may keep you awake, but they also make you more distractible. What often helps cognition the most is motivation. Researchers continue to develop drugs for people whose cognition is neurologically impaired (Rosenzweig, 1998), but they have side effects that are worth tolerating only if a person has a true neurological disability.

Substances or medicines that make a person jittery or sleepy interfere with cognition. Medicines can be quite effective at treating some troubling problems or symptoms, but most medications have side effects, and some of these interfere with cognitive performance. Any medicine that makes you sleepy impairs cognition. Most antihistamines and cold medicines have this effect as do most tranquilizers, some antidepressants, and sedatives. Any medicine that makes you jumpy, such as stimulants and many diet pills, can impair cognition (Brown & Larson, 1993). Even some antibiotics have been found to impair cognition.

TABLE 13.2
Sample Substances and Events that May Impair Cognition

Internal Medicines - amphetamines, analgesics, antibiotics, antiemetics,
    antihistamines, glaucoma eye drops, scopolamine
Psychiatric Medicines - anxiolytics, antidepressants, antipsychotics,
    lithium, sedatives
Treatments that impair cognition briefly or permanently - surgery,
    electroconvulsive shock, transcutaneous stimulation)
Substance Abuse - amphetamines, illegal drugs, alcohol, caffeine, nicotine
Experiences - emotional trauma, fatigue, lack of sleep, hypoglycemia,
    individual criases, societal chaos, malnutrition, overeating

If you are taking medication, check the insert that came with the medication. Unfortunately, many cognitive problems that arise may not be described on these inserts. Consequently, you should call your doctor or pharmacist if you suspect that a medicine has side effects that hinder memory or other cognitive functions. Table 13.2 shows some medications, substances, treatments and experiences that are some that are known to impair cognition (Brown & Larson, 1993; Carren, 2002).

Commonly Ingested Chemicals can Interfere with Cognition

Although people usually do not think of coffee, tea, soda, and alcoholic beverages as chemicals, they are. Coffee, tea, soda, and tobacco contain chemicals that act as stimulants. If stimulants are not used in the right amount, they will not facilitate cognitive performance. Too little of a stimulant leaves one less capable of cognitive performance because of diminished attention. Too much of a stimulant makes one jittery and easily distracted.

Cognition is also affected by use of, and addiction to, controlled substances, such as alcohol (Birnbaum, Taylor, Johnson, & Raye, 1987; Hashtroudi & Parker, 1986), cannabis (Block & Wittenborn, 1984; Schwartz, 1991), cocaine (von Gorp, Hull, Wilkins, Hinkin, Plotkin, Moore, & Horner, 2000), opiods, and PCP. Alcohol depresses the central nervous system. Alcohol is sometimes called amnesia food because it impairs working memory (Ambrose, Bowden, & Whelan, 2001); and, with many years of use, it slowly destroys tissue in the brain stem and cortex. As tissue is destroyed in the brain, learning ability is reduced. With enough alcohol-induced damage, a person can become incapable of learning. This tissue loss stops when alcohol intake stops, but the lost tissue does not regenerate and cannot be restored by medical intervention. Some of the memories that disappear due to alcohol use involve semantic knowledge, some involve procedural knowledge, and some involve past experiences combining these types of information. With such losses, people become less competent, less adept, and less interesting.

People remember information better if they abstain from mind-altering substances. Some people say that these substances relax them and that being relaxed helps them learn better. But research evidence refutes this claim. Alcohol, marijuana, and other mind-altering drugs impair cognitive performance immediately after use and possibly indefinitely. If relaxation is the goal, there are safer ways to relax than use of mind-altering drugs.

From time to time, the public hears that a certain medicine enhances cognition. However, all cognitive medicines developed thus far do not help cognition in a normal person. This is because the medication has been developed to correct deficiencies. Unless you have the disease the medicine has been made to treat, you will not benefit from the medication because these medications are typically designed to stabilize a chemical imbalance. Also, these medicines can cause serious (even fatal) side effects and drug interactions if not properly prescribed.

Self Care

Individuals need to take care of themselves, if not consistently then at least before a situation where optimal cognitive performance is important. Besides appropriate nutrition and exercise habits, keeping doctors' appointments is part of self-care. Many health centers now have given up on expecting individuals to remember their appointments and routinely call to remind people (Gates & Colborn, 1976).

Driving

One important application of cognitive psychology has been in the investigation of drivers' health. Recent research showed that people make as many errors in driving when sleep deprived as they do when they are drunk (see Walker & Herrmann, 2004).

Sleep Loss

It is very clear that sleep loss and fatigue interfere with all manner of cognitive performance (Blagrove & Akehurst, 2000; Chmiel, Totterdell, & Folkard, 1995). A number of studies investigated the effects of rotating sleep cycles, such as people who do shift work. It is clear that shift work leads to impaired cognition.

Health Interviews

When people are ill, getting a careful history of past events may be extremely useful in diagnosis and treatment. Some cognitive research revealed that health histories may be in error. Certain ways of interviewing people about their physical fitness foster greater accuracy in reporting (Cohen & Java, 1995). For example, people are more likely to recall prior health problems if they first recall major milestones of their lives.

Clinical Assessment

In the past two decades, understanding of neurological impairments on cognition has expanded considerably (Lewkowicz & Whitton, 1995; McCarthy & Warrington, 1990; see also Nilsson & Markowitsch, 1999). To narrow the range of possible diagnoses, efforts have been made to develop screens to assess various high-probability problems. A screen is a quickly administered test that detects whether a person is impaired but does not indicate the specific nature of the problem. A well-known screening test is the Mini Mental Status Exam (Folstein, Folstein, & McHugh, 1975), in which a person answers a series of routine questions (such as "Where do you live?"; "Who is President of the United States?").

People with serious neurological impairment may have difficulty answering these elementary questions. This test has been enormously helpful to many clinicians, but the test provides little specific diagnostic information. Because of such difficulties, research has tried to develop more efficient, sensitive, and specific measures. One such test is the Memory Impairment Scale (Buschke et al., 1999; Gifford & Cummings, 1999).

As a result, a new treatment area has emerged in the past several years to help people who have suffered neurological impairment, often because of head injury or disease (Baddeley, 1995; Gianutsos, 1991; Solberg & Mateer, 1989). The specialists who work in this area belong to the Society for Cognitive Rehabilitation, an interdisciplinary organization consisting of cognitive psychologists, clinical psychologists, speech pathologists, and other health care professionals. A variety of treatments for cognitive impairment have evolved. Initially, cognitive rehabilitation efforts focused on individuals sustaining head injuries due to accidents (Caprio-Prevette, 1999; Gianutsos, 1991; Hux et al., 1994; Parente,' 1998; Parente' & Herrmann, 2003). Subsequently, findings from cognitive psychology have been applied to helping people with neurological impairments of other origins, such as stroke and epilepsy (Baddeley, Wilson, & Watts, 1995; Crook & Longjohn, 1993; Wilson, 1987; Wilson & Moffatt, 1992; Wilson & Patterson, 1990). More recently, cognitive methods of rehabilitation have been developed for people with dementia, a group of people once believed to be beyond rehabilitation (Camp & Foss, 1997; Camp et al., 1996) or avoidance (Fotuhi, 2003; Mark & Mark,).

Empowering Neurologically Impaired People to Use External Aids

There is considerable evidence that people with neurological impairments can benefit from external aids, including reminding devices (Baddeley, 1990, 1993; Bourgeois, 1990, 1993a; Camp et al., 1996; Cockburn, 1996; Fowler, Hart, & Sheehan, 1972; Jones & Adam, 1979; Kim, Burke, Dowds, Boone, & Park, 2000; Kurlychek, 1983; Naugle et al., 1988; Sandler & Harris, 1991; Skilbeck, 1984). Most reminding devices that have been investigated are prosthetics (Parente' & Herrmann, 2003; Wilson, 1987). For example, pill boxes with alarms that signal when medication is to be taken increase the chances of taking the medication on time, but they do not guarantee it. A person can get distracted after the alarm sounds.

Forgetting to take medication can have serious consequences. If the failure to take medication can threaten a person's life, extra procedures have to be taken to make sure the person does not forget to take the medication. Devices may be carried that signal an alarm when medication should be taken (Park & Kidder,

1996). A person's health care provider or phone service may take the responsibility to call when medication should be taken. Research has shown these interventions can dramatically increase compliance with a medication regime.

Improving the Accuracy of Diagnoses

Cognitive psychology can be used to facilitate diagnosis and treatment of disorders, diseases, illnesses, and injuries (Kohn, Corrigan, & Donaldson, 2000). Signal detection theory, which has been very successful in the investigations of perception and memory, has been found useful in developing diagnoses (Swets, Dawes, & Monahan, 2000). Through careful consideration of symptoms present, inconsistent symptoms, and symptoms not present, it is possible to generate mathematical estimates of the likelihood that a person has a certain disease or disorder.

Improving the Accuracy of Treatment

For a person to recover in a timely fashion, or even recover at all, it is important to take medication as prescribed. External aids have been developed to remind patients to take their medicines on time (Park & Kidder, 1996) and to record whether or not a patient has completed treatment as prescribed (Cramer, Mattson, Prevey, Scheyer, & Ouellette, 1989).

Prison Life

Although some research has focused on expertise of inmates (Logie et al., 1992), most research on cognitive functioning in prisoners and inmates focused on cognitive distortion around a prisoner's sense of blame and responsibility. Gudjonsson and Sigurdsson (1996) determined that confabulation or creative nonfactual responses to questions by prison inmates was related to their memory, intelligence, suggestibility, and personality. Other research determined that the proportion of people with head injury is greater in prison than among the general population (Miller, 1996). Many of the people with head injury in regular prison populations were injured before going to prison and sometimes prior to their first encounter with the law (Sarapata, Herrmann, Johnson, & Aycock, 1998).

APPLICATIONS OF COGNITIVE ASPECTS OF EMOTIVE MODES

Flashbulb Memories

Flashbulb memories are formed at or after an important and often unexpected event occurs. For example, people may have flashbulb memories for important national or international events, such as the London subway bombings or the airline attacks on the World Trade Center and Pentagon. People often report what they were doing, wearing, and feeling at the time when they first learned of or experienced the event. Several decades ago Brown and Kulik (1977) polled people about a number of events. Most of the people they interviewed had flashbulb memories of President Kennedy's assassination. In contrast, although 75% of African Americans polled had flashbulb memories for the assassination of Martin Luther King, fewer than one third of the Whites interviewed had that memory. It appears that events that have important consequences for us are more likely to be stored as flashbulb memories. Although flashbulb memories do become increasingly distorted over time (Neisser & Harsch, 1992) they may be more accurate than most other memories because of their emotional content (Schacter, 1995; see also Chu & Downes, 2000; Mace). On the other hand, although the roles of mood and emotion have been established in autobiographical memory (Christianson, 1992; Walker, Vogl & Thompson, 1997), research has also shown that other memories regarding the same event can interfere with accuracy (Brown & Kulick, 1988; Wright, 1993b).

Eyewitness and Trauma Memory

Eyewitness research and eyewitness observations provide another source of information about how we process emotionally laden information. Eyewitness memory has to do with the study of memory for personally experienced episodes that emphasize accuracy of the report, particularly as it relates to possible misinformation encountered after the event. Many of these events have strong emotional components. In general, we tend to focus on what we perceive to be the most important information and exclude information that appears to be more peripheral and less important.

Research suggests that as emotion increases, there is an increasing restriction of cues that can improve or diminish cognitive performance (Easterbrook, 1959). This narrowed attention and heightened focus on the emotional event has been called tunnel memory. When people are exposed to extremely traumatic incidents, the individual most often thinks about and reacts to the event. Intrusive thoughts about the event also preoccupy thinking. At other times some individuals are completely unable to remember anything about it. Freud (1901) long ago identified defense mechanisms that protect us from perceived threats. Sometimes repression occurs, in which events are simply not recognized or acknowledged; those events are pushed out of conscious awareness. Although repression is an interesting phenomenon, there is limited empirical support for this construct (Eich & Schooler, 2000; Erdelyi, 1996; Loftus & Ketcham, 1994).

At other times information is distorted during initial registration or later during storage or retrieval to make it consistent with our self-image, our assessment of others, or our judgment of situations (Greenwald, 1980). On other occasions, as in the case of sexual abuse, some victims may be unable to remember anything about the event for long periods of time. They experience amnesia for related events. Christianson and Nilsson (1989) reported on a case study of a woman who had been brutally assaulted and raped and as a consequence experienced psychogenic amnesia. Several weeks afterwards, police escorted her to the place where she had been found after the assault. She grew increasingly anxious as they moved toward the place where the rape occurred (according to the rapist). On location, she became sick and cried. Forgetting life-threatening events may not be uncommon. In a group study of women with past histories of documented trauma, Williams (1994) found that 38% of women who had been treated for rape or sexual abuse prior to 12 years of age did not initially remember the abuse or treatment 17 years later when they were interviewed about it, even though hospital records provided clear documentation. Occasionally, traumas are so threatening that people experience psychogenic fugue states where they forget their identity and past life and wander around aimlessly.

Making Judgments

Not only is memory both enhanced and impaired by emotional events, but also our ability to judge and evaluate information is also affected. Our mood does influence our assessment of people, objects, and events (Bower & Forgas, 2000). In one study participants were asked to evaluate a job applicant for a management position based on a face-to-face interview using a series of standardized questions. In this study the applicant was really a confederate who gave the same responses to each interviewer. Before the interview began, the interviewers' moods were manipulated by providing positive, negative, or neutral feedback about their performance. What they found was that the interviewer's mood was important. Happy interviewers rated the confederate as having good potential, whereas interviewers who experienced negative feedback rated the candidate much more negatively and felt they were unlikely to recommend hiring. One small point of consolation to remember when you don't get the job offer you want is that your interviewer's mood can be very important, and that probably has nothing to do with you.

Besides judging people, we make determinations about what we read or hear (Bower & Forgas, 2000). One study induced students to feel angry or satisfied before they read a newspaper review of a restaurant. The review they read contained an equal number of positive and negative statements. Later, after the mood state was neutralized, they rated the restaurant and tried to remember what had been reported in the review. People who read the review when angry rated the restaurant more negatively than those who read the review when satisfied. In another study, Bower and Forgas reported that angry readers reacted more negatively to anger-provoking comments, whereas disgusted readers reacted more intensely to disgust-provoking comments in the review. The more intense the reaction during reading, the more negatively the restaurant was rated and the more mood-congruent comments were recalled. Just as we tend to remember mood congruent information, we also tend to judge information in ways that are congruent with our mood. Induced moods affect our judgements and evaluations.

Unrelated Events Affect Mood and Judgments

Forgas and Moylan (1987) interviewed people before and after going to the movies. Using a public opinion survey as a cover for the study, movie patrons rated their mood, their satisfaction with personal and work circumstances, politics, the future, and their opinion about the severity of penalties for violations of the law like drunk driving and drug trafficking. People who had viewed a comedy were more optimistic about events, compared with people who had seen a sad drama. Interestingly, movie patrons who had seen a violent movie were more likely to recommend more severe penalties for crimes compared with other moviegoers.

Similarly, decision making may also be impaired as well when we are experiencing stress, happiness, depression, or other emotional states. Positive moods often lead to fast, simple, and superficial processing of information (Fiedler, 1991; Hertel & Fielder, 1994; Isen, 1987; Mackie & Worth, 1991). People who are feeling good tend to rely more on intuitive rather than analytical heuristics, and they tend to be more inclusive and less discriminating in their approach to tasks. When we feel good, we may not feel compelled to engage in certain actions (like studying for the big test), and often we see little need for detailed and systematic effort. For example, Martin and associates (1993) asked happy and sad subjects to generate a list of birds and to stop once they felt their performance was satisfactory. Sad subjects worked longer and remembered more bird names than happy subjects. Feeling good allows us to engage in tasks more superficially and with less deliberation. Depending on what needs to be done, this can help or hurt us.

Isen (1987) hypothesized that positive affect is more interconnected to our other knowledge, so more associations are triggered under these conditions. Many other competing thoughts can come to mind as we try to accomplish things when we are happy. In solving problems, people experiencing natural positive moods may come up with a higher number of proposed solutions (Vosburg, 1998), or they may simply perform more poorly relative to people experiencing negative or neutral moods (Kaufmann & Vosburg, 1997). Negative mood states are related to slower, more systematic strategies.

Information Management

A number of different factors explain why negative mood states affect cognition. Ellis, Ottaway, Varner, Becker, and Moore (1997) presented students with a variety of text passages and asked them to detect inconsistent information. They found people who experienced induced depressed moods were less able to comprehend information and were less effective at critically evaluating information. They were also less adept at recognizing contradictory information. People who were stressed were less able to effectively remember information and less able to note contradictions in presented material. Stress diminished ability to recognize inconsistent information. As Gilbert (1993) noted, the first information presented is uncritically absorbed under demanding circumstances. When people experience altered mood states, such as stress or depression, they are less able to sort out false or misleading information and may have more trouble recalling other information. Recognizing and remembering false information requires more effort than accepting information as true (Gilbert, 1993).

Coping and Emotional Intelligence

In recent years, there has also been interest in emotional intelligence. This involves our ability to perceive emotion accurately, to understand it, and to express it (Mayer & Salovey, 1997) as well as modify it when necessary (Goleman, 1995; Mayer & Salovey, 1997). Parents can help their children develop emotional intelligence by encouraging them to identify their emotions and understand how emotions influence their behavior and by modeling appropriate emotional behaviors. If parents fail, therapists can be quite effective at helping people understand and manage their emotions and behaviors. Figuring out how to read emotions and cope with them is important for successful living. Even when we are feeling low, we may engage in mood repair to try to offset bad feelings. Mood repair involves deliberately not allowing oneself to think bad thoughts. Some of us are better than others at regulating negative moods. Ruminating about distressing thoughts often helps maintain the negative mood state, whereas actively doing something or reframing one's thoughts can improve negative moods. People who engage in active mood repair use deliberate strategies to search for pleasant ideas and memories to offset a recently induced negative mood (Teasdale et al., 1995). Teasdale et al. also found that mood repairers had higher self-esteem and showed fewer or reversed mood-congruent memory for information. In any event, some evidence suggests that unpleasant memories are forgotten faster than pleasant memories are forgotten (Walker, Skowronski, & Thompson, 2003).

Definition of Mental Illness

Although cognition and emotion are often regarded as unrelated (Panzarella, Alloy, Abramson, & Klein, 1999), cognitive well-being and mental health have been synonymous with emotional health. The World Health Organization defines cognitive disorders as a subcategory of mental illness. Applied cognitive psychologists have been investigating the emotional basis of cognitive dysfunction (Panzarella et al., 1999). In addition, research by Sprock & Herrmann, (2004h) as sought to identify what aspects of cognition have been targetd for investigation of different mental illnesses, as defined in the Diagnostic and Statistical Manual IV (American Psychatric Association, 2000). The results of this research suggest that cognitive dysfunction is associated.

In addition, cognitive research established new understandings of the differences between real events and experiences a person imagined (Destun & Kuiper, 1999; Johnson & Raye, 1987). Much of this research has also focused on the process of monitoring how people distinguish between actual intentions, anticipated intentions, and imagined events (Carroll, Mazzoni, Andrews, & Pocock, 1999). Delusions represent a related problem. Delusions are false beliefs that are highly resistant to change, even in light of contrary evidence. Common to a number of mental illnesses and physical diseases, people suffering from delusions may be biased to process threatening or negative information more readily than other information (Miller & Karoni, 1996). This type of dysfunctional thinking is characteristic of persons suffering from schizophrenia and major depressive disorder.

Depression

Major depression is often regarded as a cognitive disorder, both in terms of its etiology and in its effects (Beck, 1976; Brewin, 1998; Channon & Baker, 1996). Very depressed people often experience memory problems, which interfere with adjustment as well as everyday problem solving (Channon & Baker, 1996). One basis of the recurrence of depression is intrusive memories (Baum, Cohen, & Hall, 1993; Berntsen, 1996; Miller & Karoni, 1996) that distract the individual from focusing on the task at hand.

SUMMARY

Cognitive processes are affected by our physiological condition. Physical states, chemical states, and overall health status may separately or collectively interact to influence consolidation of memory and learning. Every kind of medicine has side effects, and some of these interfere with memory and cognitive performance. Physical fitness and exercise are related to better memory and cognitive functions. Changes in physiological condition also occur because of disease processes, general health status, emotional responsivity, and environmental factors. Similarly, cognitive processes are affected by our emotional state, affecting our interpretation of events and what we remember of them. This chapter reviewed a variety of ways that physiological and emotional states affect assessment and cognition in personal and professional lives.

14

Responding

It is better to check and be right than to be
confident and eventually in error.
                                    -Author unknown

We judge how people think based on how they respond. If a person is asked a
question, such as "Have you received the flu vaccine?," the answer is taken as a
report (yes I did; no, I did not), as a belief about whether the person was vacci-
nated, or as a fabrication to satisfy the questioner. To develop products or services
or to properly evaluate policies, an applied researcher must be able to assess responses that participants give in research studies. This chapter reviews findings
detailing some of the factors that affect responding and the kinds of inferences
that can or cannot be made about responding.

Responding may require more than just determining the appropriate
cognitive performance. Task performance may depend on other factors. In many
social contexts, people may intentionally misrepresent their response. In other
cases, people may unintentionally generate misleading responses because
of response bias or because they are trying to respond correctly to the task
regardless of their knowledge or feelings. Certain procedures or instructions
may encourage people to respond to demand characteristics cued by the
experiment or method used. Alternatively, people may also generate sound
responses that are beneficial in developing products and services. Ideally, a
cognitive response to a task is appropriate and accurate.

RESPONSE COMPLEXITY

At the simplest level, people may be asked to verify that they saw or heard or remember an event. Verification responses are made to some criterion. Often these
experiments are set up so that *yes* responses are as equally likely to occur as are

'No' responses. However, some respondents may be biased to say 'Yes' because of cultural bias to respond positively. Generally people say 'Yes' faster than they say 'No' (Woodworth & Schlosberg, 1954). Almost as simple as verification, sometimes a limited selection of responses is offered. When we are expected to select a response from three or more choices we must demonstrate our knowledge of certain content. Choice responses are given to tasks using a form that specifies, for example, "Did you remember [or perform any specific cognitive process] content *A, B, C?*" Thus, choice response allows people to report whether they attended to, perceived, understood, learned, or remembered *A, B,* or *C.* Another common type of response format is to ask participants to rate a property of a task on a Likert rating scale, which might range from strongly disagree to strongly agree or other appropriate contrasting descriptors.

COMMUNICATIVE INTENT

Previously in this text we have reviewed research that has demonstrated that people sometimes misrepresent what is known in various situations and that characteristics of what they say (gaps, inconsistencies) provide clear evidence. Also, we previously discussed that people sometimes lie in court when the stakes are very serious (such as childhood sexual abuse). Some people lie about someone else's cognitive performance to manipulate others. Sometimes people who attack others blame victims to exonerate attacks against them (Wright & Davies, 1993; Johnson, 1992). Given that we know misrepresentation occurs, it may not be surprising that research participants sometimes lie in research.

Cooperation

Obviously cognitive psychology needs truthful data to derive conclusions about the phenomena it investigates. It has been commonly assumed that research participants speak truthfully about the cognitive content they know as well as the cognitive processes they use. For example, when participants perform a cognitive task, we assume they are trying to perform the task properly. We also assume their answer reflects what they really know. Nevertheless, some participants report deliberately providing false answers to sabotage a study they did not want to participate in.

Pressure to Deceive

People lie by omission and commission in everyday life, often for good reasons such as to maintain confidentiality and privacy (Singer, Thurn, & Miller, 1995). Participants can say that they do not know when they do (Beatty & Herrmann, 2001; Beatty et al., 1998; Hasher & Zacks, 1979; Reder, 1987a, 1988). The likelihood of lies is affected by feedback (Elaad, 2003). Thus, when developing, marketing, or selling a product or service, extra effort may be necessary to arrange the conditions of a study so that a participant wants to respond accurately and truthfully. Otherwise the findings of a study may not get to the truth of what makes a product or service meet people's needs.

APPLICATIONS OF COGNITIVE RESEARCH ON RESPONDING

Games

The game of chess was regarded for centuries as the means for training generals and kings (World Book, 1995). Winning was regarded as the result of cunning and strategy. In 1966 DeGroot published a book on how people play chess. His research demonstrated that chess experts possess an extensive memory for patterns of pieces on a chess board. Subsequent research showed that this memory gave the chess expert the edge against less experienced players (Chase & Simon, 1973; DeGroot, 1966). Thus, study of chess playing revealed that winning was not simply based on strategy but also on memory for prior patterns and the moves that worked best. Instead of simply unusually high intelligence, large amounts of practice made the chess player an expert. Research showed that the average amount of practice time to develop chess expertise was 10,000 hours (Simon & Barenfeld, 1969). These investigations into the basis of chess mastery revealed that expert responding is often based on plain hard work -- practice makes perfect.

Sports Psychology

Athletes have long been respected for their physical appearance and athletic skill. However, applied cognitive psychology has shown that effective performances are also based on cognitive processes. Research has conceptualized skilled athletic performance as a multidimensional function of perception, attention, knowledge, and practice (Bisacchi & Starkes, 1999; Helsen & Starkes, 1999; Zeitz & Spoehr, 1989). This approach has been applied to basketball (Allard & Starkes, 1991), gymnastics (Ste-Marie, 1999), cycling (Wierda & Brookhuis, 1991), rock climbing (Smyth & Waller, 1998), volleyball (Borgeaud & Abernathy, 1987), snooker (Abernathy, Neal, & Koning, 1994), and football (Rutherford & Fernie, 2005). Sports researchers have increasingly applied cognitive psychology in recent years. For example, research investigated the nature of the cognitive abilities that constitute expertise for a sport. For example, soccer players are not necessarily faster at information processing than novices, but they possess greater and more comprehensive domain knowledge of the sport (Anderson, Beveridge, Conway, & Dewhurst, 1999).

Timeliness of Responding and Time Management

Time waits for no one. Modern society recognizes the value of time. Businesses teach time management to executives and employees so that people will respond accurately and efficiently. People engage in activities to carry out a plan, such as meeting project deadlines (Engle & Lumpkin, 1992). In today's world, scheduling computers take over much of a person's time management (Burt & Forsyth, 1999; Norman, 1993). Research has shown that the duration of an activity is associated with the likelihood a response is executed. Remembering intentions to make a response, like remembering an appointment or completing a chore, depends on a variety of factors (Kvavilashvili, 1992). Keeping track of how time has been spent is also necessary to respond properly in the future. Unfortunately, even this does not guarantee we will always respond accurately or at all.

Making Computing Artifacts Motorically and Cognitively Compatible

One of the earliest applications of cognitive psychology was the design of computer interface systems. Considerable research found that the layout of letters on the now antiquated typewriter keyboard could not be improved to increase efficiency because of mechanical properties of the key strike patterns (Norman & Fisher, 1982; Rinck, 1999). The design of databases required considering known properties of the human cognitive processing system (Lansdale & Cotes, 1999). Research also played an important role in the development of the mouse (Card, Moran, & Newell, 1983). Before the mouse, there was only a screen and keyboard arrows to reposition the visual display; moving around was cumbersome and time-consuming.

Driving

Cognitive processes are essential to safe driving (Groeger, 2000), Because driving a car can result in injury or death, the governments of many nations have developed programs to investigate both safe driving practices and the basis of accidents. Research has shown that one factor that affects safety is poor driving conditions, especially the degree of highway lighting (Steyvers, Dekker, Brookhuis, & Jackson, 1994). The likelihood of accidents has also been attributed to speed and other factors (Groeger & Chapman, 1996). Not surprisingly, accidents often occur because the driver fails to act or to remember hazards that are known to be present (Kruysse, 1992; Wagenaar et al., 1990).

People also differ in the capacity to recognize dangerous traffic situations as they develop. Errors in driving may occur if the driver is not fully aware of his or her sensory deficits and cognitive deficits (Holland & Rabbitt, 1992). However, getting information about the actual causes of an accident may sometimes be difficult because drivers may fail to report details that show they were at fault (Underwood & Milton, 1993).

In many instances people get behind the wheel of a car when they are not prepared to fully attend to road conditions. Research by Strayer, Drews, Crouch, and Johnston (2004) clearly demonstrated drivers' response is impaired during phone conversations. In recent years, considerable attention has been focused on the use of cell phones while driving. Did you know that the chance of an accident is greater when you are talking on a cell phone than when you have consumed alcohol? Having others in the car or listening to books on tape is not nearly as disruptive as phone conversations while driving. Apparently, in these other conditions, when difficult driving conditions emerge, we either fail to attend to environmental stimuli or other passengers stop talking; the other cell phone partner is unaware of the necessity for these adjustements.

One of the frustrating problems that occurs to nearly every diver sometime is getting lost in new or infrequently traveled areas (Martin & Jones, 1997). People make a variety of errors in everyday route finding (Smyth et al., 1994). One reason for getting lost is receiving poor directions because people and GIS software differ in their ability to provide directions. Another is that the layout and traffic patterns in some cities are irregular and consequently harder to navigate than others (Denis, Pazzaglia, Cornoldi, & Bertolo, 1999).

SUMMARY

Developing knowledge about effective and ineffective cognitive functioning and creating applications that facilitate cognitive processes require capturing representative participant responses in a variety of different situations. While the complexity of a task routinely influences our performances, people can intentionally and unintentionally respond in inappropriate ways. Certain procedures that emphasize the need for honest feedback may encourage people to respond in the most appropriate manner. This chapter reviewed some of the factors that lead people to generate sound responses that may be beneficial in developing products and services.

15

Cognitive Assessment

People who need someone to do a
challenging job for them will seek
someone with good cognitive skills.
– Author unknown

Individual differences have to do with variations in how we process information, think about issues, and solve problems. Individual differences in cognition are assessed today using a variety of self-report, behavioral performance, neurological, and pharmacological methods depending on the kind of information sought. People differ in the speed and accuracy of their cognitive functions. For example, people who score higher on intelligence tests spend more time encoding a problem and less time executing a response, relative to poorer performers (Sternberg, 1986). Cognitive assessments may be used to measure a student's capability to learn, to refine or substantiate a physician's diagnosis of a medical problem, to identify areas for rehabilitative training, to match cognitive skills with employment position, or to provide a guide to self-improvement. However, until fairly recently cognitive assessments were not designed to make predictions about everyday functions, even though they have been used to draw these types of inferences.

Historically, individual differences in cognitive performance have been assessed for a number of traditional tasks, such as a person's recall for digits, verbal comprehension, and memory for word lists, prose, and drawings. In the 1970s and 1980s research found many tasks used in traditional assessments did not generalize to all other situations as had been assumed (Underwood, Boruch, & Malmi, 1978; see also Herrmann, Schooler, et al., 2001). Poor performance on the traditional tasks was found not to necessarily generalize to everyday life. For example, a deficit in digit recall was found not to necessarily indicate a deficit in other types of learning, such as words or prose. In addition, not remembering digits during the assessment did not necessarily mean people were poor at remembering phone numbers or digits in other real life circumstances. The lack of correspondence presented a challenge to the assessment of individual differences and, at the same time, to cognitive theories about performance. This chapter reviews approaches to cognitive assessment currently used in business, medicine, and other fields.

APPLICATIONS OF COGNITIVE RESEARCH TO ASSESSMENT

Brain Imaging Measures

Today's imaging techniques allow us to see how the brain works in ways never before possible. Computerized axial tomography (CAT) and magnetic resonance imaging (MRI) make it possible to identify with precision the location and amount of brain injury. For example, anatomical atrophy in the hippocampus of patients with Alzheimer's disease can be observed with MRI. Similarly, CAT scans can reveal the ventricular enlargement associated with impaired short-term cognitive performance in Alzheimer's patients. Positron emission tomography (PET) can detect ongoing neural activity that in turn reflects regional metabolic decreases in glucose use corresponding to poor cognitive performance in Alzheimer's or stroke patients (Posner, 1992; Posner & Raichle, 1994). Functional MRI is a modified version of magnetic resonance that measures hemoglobin molecules and then determines brain areas receiving greatest supplies of blood and oxygen. These scans have good spatial resolution and are less expensive and safer than PET scans; however, they require at least two scans to compare activity when doing the target task versus an appropriate comparison task.

Even though it sounds straightforward, interpreting patterns of increased and decreased activity can be challenging. Individual differences further complicate the interpretation because different people may use different brain areas to do the same task. For example, specific brain areas may be highly active when most of us select the next move on the chess board, but the same areas might not be active for chess masters or people with special expertise in the task. Instead, experts may simply recognize the pattern and recall the appropriate move (Amidzic, Riehle, Fehr, Wienbruch, & Elbert, 2001).

In addition to comparing responses of different groups of people, advances in neuroimaging allow us to see the brain activity associated with different stages of memory function. For example, Stebbins et al. (2002) explored frontal lobe activation during word encoding by presenting young and older adults with word lists that manipulated level of processing. This procedure resulted in the composition of group maps of brain involvement which the authors suggest might predict better or worse adaptation to aging.

Cognitive Scales

Most cognitive scales available today provide specific indices of reasoning or memory performance. These scales often do not measure metacognitive beliefs and typically do not assess physiological variables. Nevertheless, these scales do provide a detailed assessment of cognitive performance for some particular tasks. These types of scales will continue, in one form or another, to make up the core of cognitive performance assessment and provide the basis of inference about cognitive processing and components' overall functioning. Increasingly they are also combined with imaging techniques to get a more comprehensive view of cognitive functions.

Wechsler Scales.
Following traditions initiated by Binet, David Wechsler led the way in developing measures to assess intelligence. These scales are probably better viewed as measuring a person's academic competence around the time the test is administered (Herrmann & Cadwallader, 2000). The Wechsler Memory Scale (WMS; Wechsler, 1945) was developed using a format similar to the widely used Wechsler intelligence scales. It contains performance tests of memory, such as the digit span task, paired associate and prose learning, and memory for geometric figures. Although other memory scales have been developed in recent years that have better characteristics than the revised WMS, it is still frequently used today.

Mini-Mental Status Exam.
This screening scale (discussed in the chapter on physiological states) asks a person is widely used. It consists of a series of routine questions ("What day is it today?"; "Where are we located?"). Answers to these questions permit rapid detection of dementia or other serious neurological damage (Rebok & Folstein, 1993) that may not be immediately evident in casual conversation.

Halstead-Reitan Neuropsychological Battery (HR).
This neuropsychological battery, developed by Halstead and extended by Reitan (1955), has been used extensively to assess a person's potential cognitive functioning. This assessment battery includes a mix of cognitive measures, which assess sensory input, attention and concentration, learning, language skills, visual spatial skills, executive functions, and motor output. In that the HR attempts to sample a broad range of cognitive functions, it is necessarily limited in how completely it can measure cognitive performance. For example, standard cognitive measures, such as paired associate learning or story recall, are not included in the HR. Because cognitive performance is combined with other kinds of performance in certain scoring schemes, the HR does not provide a complete measure of cognition. Nevertheless, the HR is useful when the objective of an assessment is to address general cognitive functioning.

Luria-Nebraska Neuropsychological Battery (LN). Reflecting the theories of Alexander Luria, this battery includes tasks to assess performance on immediate verbal and nonverbal cognitive tasks. However, it does not assess long-term cognition. Norms are provided for scoring that account for education and age. This battery is useful when the objective of an assessment is to address not only memory but also other cognitive functions.

Rivermead Behavioral Memory Test (RBMT-E). This revised battery was developed with the explicit purpose of crossing the laboratory-real world gap in cognitive assessment research (de Wall, Wilson & Baddeley, 1994). Designed to screen problems for people with non progressive brain injury, the RBMT-E consists of a series of tasks fashioned after everyday cognitive tasks, such as remembering to do something when an alarm goes off, remembering a person's name, tracing a short route, and responding to orientation questions (similar to the Mini-Mental Status Exam). The virtue of the RBMT-E is that it monitors change over time and generates an assessment that generalizes more readily to everyday life than any of the previously described scales.

Computerized Test Batteries. A variety of software products have been developed in recent years to assess cognition. Initial research suggests that the computerized test battery has some advantages over person-delivered assessment, in part because it ensures comparable stimulus presentations across assessments. The program scores and prints the results with normative data for comparison. Presently, no assessment device has emerged as the leader. Nevertheless, a variety of cognitive tasks, including those with ecological validity (such as remembering a chore), are difficult to include in a computer assessment. Such software is likely to become increasingly popular, but only as a part of standard assessment. Efforts to develop new methods of assessment continue (Rabbitt, Maylor, McInnes, Bent, & Moore, 1995; Sunderland, Beech, & Sheehan, 1996).

Self-Reports about Cognitive Performance. Personal reports about performance are commonly solicited to measure metacognition. Metacognitive reports simply reflect what people understand and believe about their cognitive skills and deficiencies. Two methods are commonly used to obtain these self-reports: questionnaires and diaries.

Cognitive questionnaires typically ask about a person's cognition in a variety of everyday cognitive tasks. These questionnaires provide a good procedure for taking stock of what a person believes about his or her cognitive abilities. However, questionnaire responses provide only a partially accurate index of how frequently people successfully perform actual cognitive tasks (Cavanaugh, Feldman, & Hertzog, 1998; Herrmann & Neisser, 1978; Hertzog, Park, Morrell, & Martin, 2000; Stone, Turkkan, Bachrach, Jobe, Kurtzman, & Cain, 2000), partly because the nature of the question affects the nature of the response (Schwarz, 1999).

Keeping a cognitive diary typically involves recording certain thoughts, memory failures or behaviors as they occur. When diary entries are faithfully recorded, they can provide a more systematic and representative account than that provided by questionnaires.

APPLICATION RESEARCH ON COGNITIVE ASSESS-MENT CATEGORIES

Every person has a cognitive style, a unique way of approaching and dealing with cognitive problems (McKenna, 1990). Such variation appears to be the combined influence of attitudes, cognitive skills, and characteristic emotional states. We also have an array of attitudes about people, activities, objects, and cognitive tasks. These attitudes affect our inclination to perform cognitive tasks and the amount of effort expended when a cognitive task is attempted. Each of us also possesses a unique set of cognitive skills and unique pattern of physical characteristics, such as susceptibility to fatigue or illness. A variety of cognitive abilities or styles have been identified by cognitive research. The best-known characteristics are described in the following sections.

Gender

Some research indicates that males and females differ on some memory and cognitive tasks (Crawford & Unger, 2004; Matlin, 200). Based on group averages, females show some superiority for anagrams, speech production, and general verbal ability (Hyde & Linn, 1988) whereas males demonstrate more efficient visuospatial abilities (Loring-Meier & Halpern, 1999) and better quantitative reasoning (Benbow & Stanley, 1983). Such differences partly reflect gender differences in environmental experiences (Crawford et al., 1989; Herrmann et al., 1992). However, Levy and Heller (1992) reported that females tend to have less hemispheric lateralization than males. This means that males have greater asymmetry in cerebral functioning, which translates into greater specialization with more brain area dedicated to the task at hand. On the other hand, this differential specialization makes females more able to adapt in the case of left hemisphere damage than males.

Age

Many people maintain cognitive performance with increased age. Some skills may sharpen with age, but those that rely on fluid intelligence decrease gradually as we get older (Evers et al., 1997; Mantyla, 1994; McDaniel & Einstein, 1993; Petro et al., 1991;). Cognitive functions deteriorate in part because of disease processes (Terry et al., 1999); however, memory and cognition deteriorate with normal changes in aging as well (Crook et al., 1986; Yoder, 1984; Yoder & Murray, 1989) in part due to failure to practice. Applied cognitive psychologists have been at the forefront of this research (Rabbitt, 1990; Rabbitt et al., 1995; Rybash, 1996). Cognitive function deteriorates with age for certain kinds of tasks, such as unfamiliar tasks involving memory (Rybash, 1996; Tenenbaum et al., 1999). Age has been linked to differences in the processing demands of visual inspection (Dollinger & Hoyer, 1996), memory for order in a routine (Tenenbaum et al., 1999), speed and accuracy of everyday memories (Sunderland et al., 1996), attributions in memory strategies (Devolder & Pressley, 1992) and the influence of mood on memory (Yoder & Elias, 1987, 1991). However, there seems to be no change in ability to inhibit unconsciously processed information (Holley & McEvoy, 1996).

Alternatively, cognitive function may increase in accuracy for certain domains, where we have particular expertise, such as one's occupation or hobbies. In recent years, numerous researchers have applied knowledge of aging characteristics to everyday problems (Rabbitt, 1990). Because the older population is growing faster than other age groups, cognitive products and services need to be particularly designed for seniors (Morrell, 1997; Rowe & Kahn, 1997).

Research advances regularly inform the development of better ways to train older people to perform memory and cognitive tasks more effectively (Poon, Rubin, & Wilson, 1991; West, 1988). A series of products have been developed at the behest of the government and foundations to enhance cognitive skills (Plude & Schwartz, 1996a, 1996b) and assess memory more accurately (Rebok, Rasmusson, & Brandt, 1996). Initial evaluations of the software training have indicated that it may be superior to training using books, classes, or videotapes (Rybash, 1998).

Occupational Expertise and Avocational Skills

People who are good at their job carry in memory a great deal of work-related knowledge (Scribner & Beach, 1993). Such people are more able to learn and remember occupational information than people who have not invested effort in their job (Cooke, 1999). Practice and thoughtful reflection leads workers to acquire skills at the cognitive tasks emphasized by the occupation (Ericsson, 2005; Goldman, Petrosino, & Cognition and Technology Group at Vanderbilt, 1999; Hoffman, Shadbolt, & Burton, 1995; Weber & Brewer, 2003; Bertrand, Cellier, & Giroux, 1996; Charness & Schultetus, 1999).

Many people invest their effort in avocations and hobbies. Thus, they appear average at work but exceptional in the community of those who share interest in their hobby. When these people hear information pertaining to their hobby, they retain the information much better than people who are novices or who have other hobbies.

Mnemonists and Memorists

An mnemonist is a person who has developed exceptional memory abilities through the use of classical image mnemonics, such as the loci or peg word methods. Chase and Ericsson (1981) described an undergraduate, who was eventually able to remember eighty-digit number spans after practicng one hour every day for two years. Another famous mnemonist could recall 31,811 digits of the constant *pi* (Biederman, Cooper, Fox & Mahaderan, 1992).

A mnemonist's skills are specific and directly related to practiced study strategies. In contrast, a memorist is not interested in performing exceptional cognitive feats. Instead the focus is on using memory efficiently (Neisser, 1982). In short, these are people, such as you, who simply remember certain things well.

PERSONALITY

Personality can influence how people interpret aspects of the environment as well as how they think and approach cognitive tasks (Brunas-Wagstaff, 1998). Nevertheless, in the quest to identify principles of how information is represented, cognitive psychology has not paid enough attention to how individual differences affect outcomes. More research is needed because much of the research that has been conducted has been problematic and equivocal.

Levelers and Sharpeners

Early in the previous century, Wulf (1922) presented people with drawings and then subsequently asked them to recall these drawings. In recall, individuals were found to either sharpen turns in a line or to smooth or level these turns.

Subsequent research showed that this difference in recall corresponded to the way other material was recalled, with levelers blurring and merging memories and sharpeners magnifying distinctions. However, measurement problems have been noted that confound interpretation of these findings (Tiedeman, 1989; Vick & Jackson, 1967).

Field Dependence

Witkin demonstrated that people vary in the extent that their perception of a line is affected by the field or background that contained the line (Witkin & Tenenbaum, 1983). That is, people who are more field independent correctly perceived a line in a frame without being influenced by the position of the frame. People who depend more on the field indicated a different position for the line with each change in the frame. Subsequent research showed that this difference in perception corresponded with the way other cognitive tasks were performed.

Internal and External Control

Some people feel they are in control of events in their lives, whereas other people feel that the events are determined by factors other than themselves. Belief in internal or external control of one's life influences how we approach cognitive tasks. For example, internally controlled individuals take more time to complete cognitive tasks than externally controlled people (Searleman & Gaydusek, 1996). For example, internally controlled people use more time to search short-term memory than externally controlled people (Searleman & Herrmann, 1994).

Need for Cognition

Some people make use of nearly every cue in the environment whereas other people do not. There is some reason to believe that those who make use of external aids are more productive than the external aid-free person (Hertel, 1988). Interest in complexity is another related individual difference variable that affects cognitive processing. Cacioppo and Petty (1982) described this distinction as the need for cognition or the desire for information and intellectual challenge.

People with a high need for cognition derive more satisfaction from completing complex cognitive tasks than people who are less interested in obtaining information. Need for cognition is not related to overall cognitive ability, although it is related to real life decisions such as staying in college (Stanovich & West, 2000).

Driven Personality versus Relaxed Personality

Highly organized individuals remember intended acts in time more than less organized individuals (Reason, 1988; Searleman & Gaydusek, 1996; see also Wichman & Oyasato, 1983). This distinction is sometimes called the Type A personality, characterized by an urgent, time-centered approach to getting tasks completed, versus the Type B person who works at a more relaxed and graceful pace. Searleman and Gaydusek (1996) found that Type A personalities tended to make use of external aids more than the Type B personalities (see also Wichman & Oyasato, 1983; Yoder & Herrmann, 2003).

Suggestibility

People sometimes remember events that never happened (Payne, Elie, Blackwell, & Neuschatz, 1996; Roediger & McDermott, 2000). One explanation of this phenomenon is that people vary in suggestibility (as found in hypnosis research), with highly suggestible people being more likely to recall events that have not occurred (Paddock et al., 1998; Saunders & MacLeod, 2002).

APPLICATION RESEARCH ON THE USE OF ASSESSMENT CATEGORIES

Human Resources

Human resource specialists decide whether to hire a person for a particular job, especially supervisory and executive positions. For these decisions, they use knowledge about individual differences in cognition. Certain individual differences represent a barrier to management unless people learn to manage how they come across to others.

Development of New Training Methods

Developments in training systems continue (Plude & Schwartz, 1996a, 1996b; Rebok et al., 1996; West, 1988). Several software programs have been created to train or improve memory, by providing instruction, detailed examples, opportunities for practice, and response feedback. Typically, the focus is on trying to remember names and faces or to improve attention.

Individual Differences in Autobiographical Memory

In the case of autobiographical memory, people vary in their susceptibility to memory illusions (Eisen & Carlson, 1998; Platt, Lacey, Iobst, & Finkelman, 1998). Not only are there marked differences in ability to uncritically absorb information, research has shown that people are more suggestible and field dependent when deprived of sleep (Blagrove, Alexander, & Home, 1995; Blagrove, Cole-Morgan, & Lambe, 1994). One method, that has been used in psychotherapy to aid remembering, is guided imagery, where people are given specific step-by-step instructions on imagining certain hypothetical events. One problem with this approach is that it can lead to false memories (Hekkanen & McEvoy, 2001; see also Wilkinson & Hyman, 1998). While guided visualization procedures *may* help in reconstructing real events, research demonstrates clearly that it can result in recovering memories for events that never occurred.

SUMMARY

Cognitive assessment varies with context, such as business, the professions, government, and others. The knowledge, skills, and abilities that are needed in one context are not necessarily what are needed in other contexts. Even the approach used to assess cognitive abilities in clinical contexts depend on a variety of factors, such as a person's age, socioeconomic status, and potential prognosis. Similarly, assessment in everyday life will vary with the kind of cognition under consideration.

16

Occupational Experience

Do what your job calls for and you will
enjoy prosperity and peace of mind.
                    – Author unknown

Thousands of occupational choices are available from which we can choose how
to spend our work life (e.g., Holland, 1994; Peterson, Mumford, Borman, Jeanneret, & Fleishman, 1999). While we recognize that much professional work
places difficult demands on memory and cognitive processes, many low-pay-
ing jobs also place considerable cognitive demands on workers. Experience and
practice are usually beneficial in mastering necessary job skills for all manner of
occupations.

This chapter points out how different cognitive processes may be emphasized in different occupations. Applied cognitive psychologists, whose job is
to facilitate the project operations within specific occupational groups, attempt to
determine the cognitive skills of the ideal worker and then develop ways to improve these skills in other workers. Although there may be considerable overlap
in cognitive demands across different job categories, understanding the required
tasks may help people develop the requisite cognitive skills (Anderson, 1981;
Healy & Bourne, 1995).

Different occupations make use of different cognitive processes or at
least place different emphases on certain skills (Holland, 1994). On-the-job experiences tend to increase expertise on those occupational tasks (Patel, Groen,
& Frederiksen, 1986; Schoenfeld & Herrmann, 1982). The employment categories used by the Department of Labor are presented in Table 16.1.

TABLE 16.1

Employment Categories
Agricultural business
Business/Office work
Communications and media
Construction
Domestic science
Environment
Government
Humanities/The arts
Health
Industry/Manufacturing
Marketing and advertising
Personal Services
Recreation
Transportation

If we want to understand what cognitive processes are necessary, we must analyze the skills required in a particular job. Such an analysis requires considering what actions are required to complete the task, the necessary components or parts of the process, and when the task has been adequately completed (Anderson, 1981; Colley & Beech, 1989; Patrick, 1994). After analyzing the steps, components, and general strategies that are involved, these actions are cataloged so they can be used for training. For example, work in industry commonly requires the operation of complex machinery and automated systems.

A task analysis in industry examines the planning and scheduling of work to be done, the monitoring of operations required by the work, constraints on this work, the demands made on workers by the operations of machines, necessary communication among workers, and factors that motivate workers. Operators of machines and systems have to develop mental models of the machines and systems they control. They also must acquire a keen understanding of how the machines and systems malfunction (Moray, 1999; Vicente, 1999).

In trying to understand how we acquire cognitive skills necessary to complete certain tasks, Carlson (1997) summarized 16 tasks necessary for cognitive skill acquisition. Most of these tasks are pertinent to specific occupations; they include arithmetic, mathematics, geometry, device trouble shooting, computer programming, computer text editing, device control, rule-based puzzles, games, video games, diagnoses of X-ray pictures, decision making, social science word problems, physical science word problems, and medical problem solving.

An appreciation of which skills are required for a particular job will prepare you to better understand the cognitive demands made by careers in general and in the career you choose for yourself. The job descriptions in the following sections illustrate some of the cognitive demands required of workers.

EXAMPLES OF JOB DESCRIPTIONS

Air Traffic Controllers

Air traffic controllers have very demanding jobs (Vortac et al., 1996). They are expected to guide pilots through a crowded sky with many potential obstacles and through all kinds of weather to a safe landing. Air controllers study screens that show all aircraft detected by radar in a region. Each plane is shown by a bright dot or blip on the radar screen. Perhaps the most difficult situation to confront an air controller is when two planes appear to be headed on similar trajectories. Because airplanes travel at high speeds, often several hundreds of miles per hour, the controller must quickly determine and communicate what to do to avoid a collision.

During World War II research found that an air controller could track only a limited number of planes at one time. The airspace is constantly changing, which makes safely guiding pilots a complex working memory task. Not only are working memory demands heavy, but the air controller must also have a strong knowledge base in long-term memory that can be quickly and flexibly retrieved so that dangerous developing patterns in the sky are noted and preemptively offset.

Anesthesiologists

Among the medical profession, anesthesiologists probably have one of the most critical jobs. The anesthesiologist must give patients undergoing surgery the right combination of chemicals to ensure the absence of pain. However, taking people from consciousness to unconsciousness requires crossing a fine chemical line. Too much anesthesia can cripple or kill a patient, and too little is ineffective.

Administering anesthesia requires considerable knowledge. Anesthesiologists must memorize what kinds of chemicals mix best for patients with different diseases and disorders, while also keeping in mind individual characteristics of each patient. Thus, administration of anesthesia relies a great deal on long-term memory. However, a patient's reaction to anesthesia may change during the course of an operation, requiring anesthesiologists to keep track of many details (pulse, temperature, color, etc.), which make additional demands on working memory. Obviously, if an anesthesiologist forgets some of the signs and symptoms of problems during an operation, the appropriate adjustment in anesthesia may not be made.

Assembly Line Workers

The job of an assembly line worker may be regarded as difficult because it involves so much repetition. For example, an assembly line job might involve securing a certain bolt on a certain part of a car, such as bolting the dashboard above the steering wheel. At one time, this job was seen as undesirable because doing the same thing repeatedly was regarded as very boring. In recent years, the challenges of assembly line work have been recognized; with many companies these jobs are well paid with better work conditions, which include rotating assigned tasks regularly.

The primary challenge to assembly line workers is that the boredom leads to mistakes. Depending on the task or product, such mistakes can be especially serious. Many of these procedures are critical to the safe operation of the car.

Bartenders

The job of a bartender is more complicated than many people suspect. Some bartenders are self-taught, but many go to a bartending school to learn what they need to know. Bartenders must know the ingredients of drinks, how to mix them, and what kind of glass to put a drink in. In addition, bartenders must know social skills, especially those necessary to manage someone who is drunk. They must know how to judge the quality of various forms of alcohol and how to maintain the stock of alcoholic beverages needed by a bar (Beach, 1988).

Also, bartenders nowadays must know laws that pertain to them. Several court cases have found bartenders responsible for allowing people to get drunk and then drive away, whereupon they got into an accident. As a consequence, bartenders are expected now to keep track of how many drinks that they have served. Thus, the bartender must maintain in long-term memory how to make alcoholic drinks as well as laws and social conventions. In addition, the bartender must maintain in short-term memory which drink should be made and for whom, while also maintaining in both short- and long-term memory who has had which drinks in the span of an afternoon or evening.

If you have the occasion to watch a bartender at work in a busy and crowded bar, it is truly impressive. They almost seem superhuman in being able to do so many things at once. Research has shown that bartenders are not born being able to handle so many tasks. Study and practice are the key. At bartenders' school, student bartenders are expected to memorize the ingredients and the steps of preparation for 100 or more drinks. They practice making different drinks repeatedly. In addition, they practice taking several orders at one time and making all of the ordered drinks flawlessly.

It might appear that practice alone is what makes a bartender successful. However, another critical factor is the environment (Beach, 1988). Recall that different kinds of glasses are used to hold different drinks. Fig. 16.1 illustrates some of the shapes of these glasses.

Brandy   Champaige   Sherry   Whiskey Sour

FIG. 16.2 The shapes of cocktail glasses for mixed drinks remind bartenders what drinks were ordered.

If a bartender is forced to make all drinks in a glass with the same shape, he or she is likely to make an error. Under normal conditions, the glass provides a cue as to which drink should be made. If bartenders are forced to make all drinks in metal, cardboard, or Styrofoam cups, where the liquid is not very visible, they make more errors. Being able to see the color of liquids in a glass also gives the bartender cues about which drinks are being made.

Lawyers

Administering the law depends a great deal on memory and reasoning. Court cases are adjudicated through application of a series of rules, either in the form of laws or in the form of precedents of prior court cases. Success in law school involves a a great deal of memorization of laws and precedents. Practicing law requires seeking appropriate cases and determine how the law applies to these cases.

Learning how to apply laws and precedents is also very important, which gives the legal profession its reputation for skillful reasoning. Lawyers must also be familiar with the practice of law, such as how to present information to juries (Davenport et al., 1999; Greene & Loftus, 1998; Hastie, 1993). Lawyers generally ave extensive vocabularies so that they can explicitly describe their cases.

Nurses

Nurses bear the brunt of responsibility for treating patients. Although physicians diagnose and assign treatment, it is nurses who administer medicine and other treatments. That requires considerable knowledge. Nursing school requires memorization of anatomy, pharmacology, and disease processes so that symptoms can be recognized and treatment efficacy can be assessed. Nurses must also depend heavily on their procedural memory to recall how to monitor patient functions and operate medical equipment. Nurses must know the legal restrictions that pertain to ethical medical care.

Over a career, nurses develop and use a variety of cognitive skills (Patel et al., 1999). The need for rapid remembering of extensive knowledge renders their memory automatic. Expertise in nursing is related to fast remembering and problem solving in a range of situations. They must also be capable of instructing patients about self-care (Wright, 1999).

Nurses often work under extremely stressful conditions, which may adversely affect memory, learning and ability to resolve problems (see Chap. 13). For example, nurses who work in intensive care often deal with patients who are near death. Nurses bear considerable responsibility when attempting to help these patients. Research has shown that nurses' memory and cognitive performance are better on normal wards than in intensive care units (Broadbent et al., 1982).

Marines

To survive, a marine must develop certain cognitive skills. Marines need to be well informed about their field equipment and know how to maintain and repair their equipment. For example, the first and most important piece of equipment for marines to be familiar with is their rifle. Marines must be able to take the rifle apart and put it back together in a matter of seconds. Doing so requires not only coordination but also rapid sight recognition of the different parts and rapid procedural remembering of how they fit together. Combat situations require rifles to be disassembled and cleaned, so they can be fired safely. As a result of this experience, Marines become adept at working and maintaining machines.

Marines routinely stand guard in peacetime and in wartime. Guard duty in peacetime is necessary to ensure equipment is not stolen and security is maintained. In wartime the need for guards is obvious. To be an effective guard, a Marine must be able to recognize common sights and sounds in the area (Dollinger & Hoyer, 1996). More important, the Marine must detect any new sight or sound in the immediate environment and then investigate the origin of sight or sound. The area the Marine is responsible for must be systematically examined. In other words, the Marine must continually and vigilantly attend while on watch. Vigilance tasks are difficult for humans.

During peacetime, failing to be alert may result in a court martial. During wartime such a failure may result in execution. Thus, there is considerable motivation to do a good job as a guard even when tired. Guard duty skills are often retained after leaving the military.

Police Officers

Police officers learn a great deal of information about the law. Continually remembering the law, or consulting aids with legal information, makes a police officer extremely facile with knowledge of how the law applies in a variety of situations. Police officers are trained in interviewing procedures, observing, recording and maintaining evidence, and using mug books and lineups. In recent years these procedures have been automated for some police forces (McAlliarwe, Rearden, Kohlmaier, & Warner, 1997).

     Learning how to manage different, and often difficult situations is also important. With experience, police officers become expert at recognizing signs that a crime may be occurring or has occurred. They also become expert at recognizing people who might be involved in crime. Both of these skills require refining sensory and perceptual abilities as well as developing better strategies for remembering information. These skills most likely stay with a police officer for years after retiring from the police force.

Physicians

The medical profession is arguably regarded as one of the most important in our society. Practicing medicine requires an accurate memory (Patel et al., 1999), involving an enormous amount of knowledge, such as the memorization of anatomy, diseases and disorders and their symptomology, treatments and their use with diseases and disorders, legal criterion for malpractice, and management procedures. Diagnosis and treatment relies a great deal on long-term memory (Smyth et al., 1994). However, some diagnoses rely on many details (pulse, temperature, color, etc.) that can also make diagnosis and treatment a short-term memory task. Obviously, if a physician forgets some of the signs and symptoms while examining a patient, the appropriate diagnosis and treatment may elude the physician. Besides needing superior information selection and integration skills, good problem-solving skills are also required because of the ambiguity and noninclusiveness of symptom information. In addition, we hope physicians exercise excellent decision-making skills in assessing the most appropriate interventions.

Pilots

One of the most complicated occupations is that of a airplane pilot. As a result, pilots are highly respected for their impressive skill and professional knowledge.

Just a look at a cockpit (shown in Fig. 16.2). It illustrates how challenging the process of flying can be (Sarter & Amalberti, 2000). A pilot must acquire skilled motor movements to control an aircraft and interpret the many dials that indicate aspects of a plane's flight status (Durso & Gronlund, 1999; Wickens, 1999). Successful air travel depends, of course, not only on what pilots do, but also on the entire aviation system (Wickens, 1999).

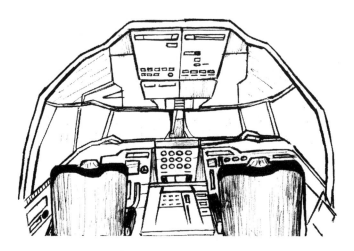

FIG. 16.3 The cockpit of a plane attests to the cognitive Challenge of flying and to the amazing cognitive capabilities of pilots.

Errors in flight obviously can be catastrophic (Reason, 1988). Research has examined how errors depend on what people notice visually (Jentsch, Barnett, Bowers, & Salas, 1999; Larson & Perry, 1999; O'Hare, Wiggins, Batt, & Morrison, 1994; Wiegmann, & Shappell, 2001; Smith, Chappelow, & Belyavin, 1995;), their feeling of knowing (Koriat, 1993, 1994; Nelson, 1996; Schraw, 1995; Wright, 1996), workload (Parkes, 1995), cognitive style (Jelsma & Pieters, 1989), cross-cultural influences (Baddeley, Meeks, Gardner & Grantham-Mc-Gregor, 1995), and other factors (Dekker, 2002).

Secretaries

Secretaries learn how to prepare, file, and find documents. Customs for preparing documents depend on the particular workplace, Experienced secretaries learn general schemas for office procedures and for creating documents. As a result of this experience, secretaries are able to spot errors that other people never notice.

In filing and reorganizing information, secretaries acquire mental organization of which most people are unaware. As a result, an experienced secretary can often find documents that would be lost to others (Rabbitt & Abson, 1990). They also can recall small (but important) details that most people forget. Secretaries tend to keep their skills at mental organization throughout their careers.

Restaurant Servers

The job of server challenges memory and cognition as much as most jobs today (Stevens, 1993). Research has shown that waitresses and waiters manage an incredibly large memory load by organizing their memory tasks spatially, temporally, and conceptually (Ericsson & Polson, 1988). They are expected to know a great deal about food in general, to know which meals on a menu taste the best, and to know which kinds of food and drink go together. Servers must keep track of which meals must be delivered to each table and to whom the different meals at a table must go (customers do not appreciate being served the wrong meal). In addition, the server must remember which orders have been sent to the kitchen for preparation. As if that is not enough, the waiter has to remember at what stage in a meal a customer is at for all the tables that he or she is responsible. Special orders and customers who change their requests place additional demands on a server's memory. If the waiter fails to show up when the main course is finished to take dessert orders or provide a check, customers may get irritated.

Although many people try work as a waitress or a waiter, many find the task too strenuous and seek other kinds of work. Career servers are highly practiced because they are survivors with a history of challenging serving jobs. If you have had occasion to work as a waitress or waiter or to watch food servers at work in a busy and crowded restaurant, it is readily apparent that they must be very effective at remembering to do many things at once. As noted earlier, bartenders face comparable problems (Bennett, 1983).

SUMMARY

Occupational demands challenge cognition in a variety of ways. This chapter showed how different occupations rely on different cognitive processes to successfully complete the job at hand. Applied cognitive psychologists seek to identify the cognitive skills of the ideal worker in an occupation and then develop ways to improve these skills in other workers. Although there may be considerable overlap in cognitive demands across different job categories, understanding the required tasks may also help our society be more productive and lead our citizens to find more satisfying work lives.

17

Careers of Applied Cognitive Psychologists

Do work that you love and you will always love your work.

— Author unknown

Another excellent way to understand applied cognitive psychology is to examine the nature of the work that applied cognitive psychologists do (Herrmann, 1994). By studying how the careers of applied cognitive psychologists vary, you will acquire a concrete understanding of many of the abstractions touched on in this text. If you are interested in becoming an applied cognitive psychologist, the information presented in this chapter will increase your appreciation of what this career is like. Even if you are not going to become an applied cognitive psychologist, some knowledge of this career will give you a better understanding of how different kinds of scientists interact and collaborate in our society.

In the United States there are nearly as many basic researchers employed as there are employed applied researchers (basic, 61,615; applied, 71,697; National Science Foundation, 1994). Over the course of a professional career, there are a number of differences in basic and applied researchers' career paths.

CAREER PREPARATION DEVELOPMENT

Applied scientists begin their careers with similar background and training, but different foci in their work create differences over time. Applied researchers eventually become knowledgeable about all kinds of research topics because they are constantly shifted from one research topic to another. Basic researchers tend to be specialists while applied researchers are more likely to be generalists.

Applied research is more interdisciplinary than is basic research (Schonflug, 1993b).

The work environment of a scientist is in the laboratory, the field, and the institution in which the scientist conducts research. Where basic research is largely conducted in colleges and universities, applied research is largely conducted in government and industry (Chapanis, 1986; Cochran, 1994; Gruneberg & Morris, 1992a, 1992b; Gruneberg, Morris, Sykes, & Herrmann, 1994; Hoffman & Deffenbacher, 1993; Leirer, Morrow, & Tanke, 1994; Vicente, 1994).

Basic and applied researchers differ somewhat in the professional organizations to which they belong. In the memory and cognitive field, basic researchers belong to the American Psychological Association (APA) or the American Psychological Society (APS). and the Psychonomic Society, and to Division 3 of the American Psychological Association, Applied researchers are less inclined to belong to APA or APS but are more likely also to belong to application-specific organizations. For example, cognitive psychologists involved in survey research may join the American Association for Public Opinion Research or the American Statistical Association. Both basic and applied psychologists belong to the Society for Applied Research in Memory and Cognition (SARMAC).

For the most part, ethical issues are the same in both applied research and basic research (APA, 1987; Sigma Xi, 1991); however, in applied research, secrecy is often a matter of policy, regardless of a researcher's desire to share his or her work. For example, business and industry often insist on secrecy to deny their competitors the chance to steal a creative idea. Government administrators often insist on secrecy to maintain the public good and sometimes national security (Fiore, Jentsch, & Rubenstein, 2004; Fiore, Rubenstein, & Jentsch, 2004). Thus, it is more likely that a basic researcher reports findings publicly, not because of ethical standards but because of employment policy.

CUSTOMS CONCERNING ACTIVITY

Nature of Employment. Basic researchers devote most of their work efforts to the research process, although teaching and academic administration also play a major part in their work lives. Applied researchers spend much more time in their workday on other activities that are peripheral to research. Considerable time is spent in drumming up business and in convincing potential clients that the applied research unit can render a useful service (Alba & Hutchison, , 1999) . Once clients are identified, considerable time is also spent in establishing and maintaining trust, cooperation, and acceptance. Basic researchers do something analogous when they apply for grants (Miller, 1995); however, there is a fundamental difference. When basic researchers apply for a grant, their goal is to convince other experts in their field of the value of their intended project. When applied researchers attempt to recruit a client, the client usually knows little or nothing about the scientific specialty of the researcher. Thus, the applied researcher must employ approaches and communication skills that differ from those preferred by basic researchers. The applied researcher must be concerned with translating technical matters into simple language accessible to a wide range of professionals. Because basic researchers focus on a problem for much longer than is true of applied researchers, basic research is not usually interdisciplinary. When basic research is interdisciplinary, it usually engages disciplines that are conceptually (but usually not practically) close to the discipline of the basic researcher who heads a project. In contrast, applied research is often interdisciplinary because application goals typically involve broader aims that embrace a spectrum of needs or concerns, that, in turn, necessitate specialists prepared to address different dimensions of the problem. For example, health research often involves more than one kind of physician, an epidemiologist, a sociologist knowledgeable of health matters, a bio-statistician, a computer expert familiar with medical statistics, and sometimes a psychologist who is knowledgeable about the health topic.

Management

The applied researcher works in the world of 'bossdom. ' The boss (or the boss's boss) chooses the topic of research, determines partially or totally how to conduct the research, and exercises a veto power over whether the work is ever published (Wilson, 1952). In contrast, the basic researcher in academia chooses the topic of research, decides how to conduct it, and how to publish its findings.

Research teams are a common feature of applied research. The size of a team tends to be larger in applied contexts than in basic research because more pragmatic issues must be addressed by applied research along with the theoretical issues of concern to basic research. In academia the research team is composed of specialists whose background focuses on relevant elements of the research project. The team is headed by a basic researcher, usually the most senior researcher or the most knowledgeable researcher for the topic under investigation.

In the applied world, the composition of teams is usually heterogeneous. Administrators who are not specialists often head the teams. Because of the differences in composition and goals of teams, decision-making about research is typically very different between basic teams and applied teams. In particular, the decisions about how applied research should be conducted hinge less on substantive theoretical issues and more on how the research meets the needs of constituencies represented by team members.

Clients

The clients of applied research are typically those who commissioned the research or those who might be served by the application at which the applied research is targeted. Basic researchers do not have clients per se. Instead, the basic researcher produces research articles that will, ideally, elicit the respect of other basic researchers. Applied researchers attempt to convince their clients on the basis of not only the persuasiveness of research findings but also on how the findings fit in with pre scientific notions of the phenomena and how the phenomena is seen to affect special interest groups. Basic researchers attempt to convince clients on the basis of the persuasiveness of research findings and relevance of the application to society.

Different Reward Systems. Applied researchers tend to work for raises, bonuses, and prizes that may accompany an application that increases profits, leads to a publicly obvious success, or improves understanding of a production process (Leirer et al., 1993). In contrast, basic researchers tend to work for publications, grants, prizes, and promotion.

Basis of Advancement

In applied research, advancement depends on the degree to which one's research is seen as having solved the designated problems by clients and by management. Over the long term, applied researchers have a better chance of career success if an upper level manager monitors them. Although this may help basic researchers determine their priorities as well, advancement in basic research depends on the amount and quality of research. Additionally, the more topical the research is to current scientific interest, the sooner the basic research community accepts the researcher.

Who Conducts the Research

In the applied world, the applied researcher is often not the one who conducts the research. Instead, the applied researcher contracts with commercial specialists for appropriate kinds of research. Most government research is done under contract, and a good deal of research in business and industry is done in a similar way. The advantages of contract work to the applied world are that the institution does not have to maintain a variety of specialists. In academia and in basic research institutions, the basic researcher conducts the research.

Firing Practices

Applied research is conducted at the will of the institution. Basic researchers work by contract before tenure; after tenure, as long as their institution is solvent, they may work as long as they do not do something blatantly immoral.

Differences in Content and Style of Professional Writing

Basic and applied cognitive researchers tend to publish in different journals (Gruneberg et al., 1995; Herrmann & Gruneberg, 1993; Johnson & Field, 1981). Applied researchers publish their work in journals when possible but typically they publish their work in technical reports. Technical reports are intended to provide a rapid response to a technical problem; moreover, the technical report is expected to become outdated more rapidly than basic journal articles because of continuing applied work.

Authorship

In applied research, researchers are authors but the authors also may include key administrators or other individuals within or outside of the organization who helped make the research possible. Many labs in government and industry routinely give an authorship to the lab director. Some lab directors require that they be listed first on publications, regardless of the amount of input given to the particular project. In basic research, authors listed on a publication are those individuals who have played an important role in the research. Conceptual direction of the research usually guarantees authorship, and in psychology the first author is generally the one who was most responsible for the ideas guiding the research.

Importance of Publication and Presentation

The applied researcher is concerned about where to publish to achieve the most commercial good. Furthermore, there are often pressures not to publish in places where it might either give competitors information on a researcher's recent advances or provide benchmarks against which competitors could design competitive products. In contrast, basic researchers usually face the demand to publish or perish where the prestige and rejection rate of the journal is considered in evaluation. Applied researchers worry about the content and the manner of presentation, whereas basic researchers worry mostly about the content of their presentations.

A CASE STUDY IN WORK CUSTOMS

This section of the chapter provides examples of the kinds of jobs applied psychologists might have in academia, business, and the government. Each case study addresses the origin of research topics, the kind and degree of specialization, the commitment to research, the qualifications for a research job, the special problems that confront a researcher, financial compensation, the personal attributes characteristic of researchers in the job, and the range of opportunities for each kind of applied research employment.

An Applied Cognitive Psychologist in Academia

Origin of Research Topics. The most striking aspect of being in academic research is individual freedom. Academic researchers generally have full control over the topics they investigate. The topics of research are typically conceived by professors who then direct or do the research. Many academic research projects stretch over many years.

Specialization. Because research projects are protracted, academic researchers almost always become specialists as they often devote many years to intense study of a particular cognitive process.

Love of Research. Academic research attracts and retains people who love research in their specialty area. They commonly become intrigued with a selected set of phenomena early in their career and stay with those phenomena for their career.

Qualifications for a Job in Academic Research. Academic researchers generally must have obtained a Ph.D. They go through similar periods of time before promotions to associate and full professor, typically 6 before promotion to associate professor and another 3 to 7 years to full professor. The criteria for advancement are very similar across four or five bands of colleges and universities: highly selective, selective, and somewhat selective, and nonselective. The opportunities for research decrease across these bands and responsibilities for teaching and service increase.

Special Problems of Academic Researchers. Applied research is often regarded as not sufficiently theoretical to be respected in some institutions. Sometimes, applied researchers become frustrated because their basic research colleagues do not appreciate applied research. In addition, some researchers have difficulty finding sufficient time to complete research projects because of other demands on their time.

Financial Compensation. Salaries in academia are often reputed to be low, but surveys indicate that academic salaries do not differ greatly from government or business salaries (NSF Study of Doctorates, 1992). Despite stereotypes about the poor professor and the rich corporate employee, basic and applied researchers receive roughly comparable salaries (basic, $56,800; applied, $60,800; National Science Foundation, 1994). Additionally, an academic researcher can make additional money by obtaining a grant, writing books, being an expert witness in court, and consulting. Academic work hours are the most flexible of any profession. Also, the availability of time for vacation during students' time off and in the summer can seldom be found outside academia.

Attributes of Academic Researchers. Academic researchers are often stereotyped as absentminded professors. Whether or not the stereotype is true, academic researchers characteristically have an insatiable curiosity for phenomena in their field. A second important attribute of an academic researcher is a desire for rigorous and logical thinking. A third important attribute of an academic researcher is sensitivity to the dominant research themes in one's field. Much academic research is done solo or by a team of assistants who carry out the work of a professor who leads the team. As a result of such concentrated effort, it is often the academic researcher who makes breakthroughs in the major problems of a particular field.

An Applied Cognitive Psychologist in Business

Business research addresses a wide range of issues. The most striking aspect of engaging in research in business is that the questions under investigation frequently change with the market's demand for certain products and services. Many business research projects are brief, lasting just a few months, but many other projects can last years. It is also not unusual for a business project to be terminated prematurely because fears about real or imagined market forces (Alba & Hutchinson, 1999) lead upper executives to decide to terminate a current project.

Origin of Research Topics. In business, high-ranking executives generally decide on research topics, often based on studies that reveal which products or services are selling well. Once a topic has been handed to the researcher in business, the business researcher must determine how to investigate the relevant psychological phenomena in ways pertinent to the potential product or service. In the case of big corporations, researchers sometimes are assigned to investigate fundamental psychological processes.

Specialization. Although research in business may shift frequently, some business researchers become specialists for the research topics assigned to them if they get to work in that area for some time. Unlike most situations in academia, there is a strong tradition of secrecy surrounding business research. The whole point of business research is to devise new or better products that competitors do not have and that will generate a profit. Without secrecy, competitors could develop similar products and services, reducing or eliminating chances for profit and making funds invested in research a waste.

Different businesses tend to emphasize the development of certain kinds of products that will appeal to a targeted market. A company's marketing goals dictate which type of research and product development is pursued.

Within a business setting, organizational forces strongly influence how research is conducted. Researchers often work as members of teams that have specific goals in terms of product development, production, or merchandising.

Business research occurs within a social context in which researchers often have to answer to individuals outside of their discipline and ultimately to stockholders or to owners of the company for which they work. This type of situation sometimes promotes political infighting about how a product should be developed. The solution that one team develops may interfere with the processes proposed by the other team in solving its problems. Researchers in business strive to be assigned to successful operations and will seek reassignment if a project appears to not be working well. Once a researcher is associated with a successful project, promotion tend to follows.

Love of Research. Business research attracts and retains people who love research on certain topics and who like the chance to be part of important, sometimes sensational, and profitable discoveries. They commonly are assigned to investigate a selected set of phenomena early in their career and may stay with that work for much of their career.

Qualifications for a Job in Research in Business. Applied cognitive researchers in a particular business generally have a very similar career path to each other. However, they may have radically different career experiences from researchers in other companies.

Special Problems of Business Researchers. The secret nature of business research often makes research difficult. It is hard to ask colleagues in other businesses, academia, and government for advice on a research project that one is not allowed to discuss. Thus, business researchers sometimes feel cut off from other researchers. Alternatively, if business research makes a scientifically important finding, the researcher may be unable to share the findings with colleagues, present papers at conferences, or publish the finding in journals because doing so would violate corporate security.

Financial Compensation. Salaries in business are often reputed to be high. However, there is great variation in salaries across individual researchers in a business and across different businesses (NSF Study of Doctorates). An applied cognitive psychologist who works in business can make additional money by writing books, being an expert witness in court, and by consulting, but often this requires permission from upper level management.

Attributes of Business Researchers. Business researchers are generally oriented toward practical issues in a field, especially those fields that are relevant to the products or services their employer provides. Also, business researchers are usually interested in engaging in ground breaking research and product development.

An Applied Cognitive Psychologist in Government Research

In government research, the questions under investigation sometimes change more frequently than in business and much more frequently than in academia. In government research many projects are brief, lasting just a few months, though some projects can last years. It is also not unusual for a government research project to be terminated prematurely.

Origin of Research Topics. The topics of research in government are formulated repeatedly at different levels. In the United States, the Congress or key members of the Executive Branch establish policy and broad research objectives to meet the problems facing the country (Fischoff, 1990; Miller, 1969). Then upper executives in research agencies conceive of the specific topics within the broad objectives established by Congress or the Executive Branch. Then the specific topic is handed to a government researcher or a team of government researchers.

Specialization. Because of the volatile nature of politics, the problems before the Executive Branch and the Congress are continually changing. Much government research addresses psychological phenomena that have not received systematic attention before. The novelty of much government research often seems like basic research in its focus on investigating fundamental psychological processes. However, research projects are always applied in that this research must address particular problems in society.

Because legislative priorities are constantly changing, government researchers are continually being shifted from one research project to another. Thus, government researchers often become involved with more research projects than researchers in academia or business. As a result, applied researchers in the government inevitably become generalists.

In certain cases, a government researcher will work on a project that lasts for a longer period of time than projects last in academe and business. This occurs when the public remains focused on a particular issue for a while. Examples of such issues include the problems of the unemployed and the treatment of Alzheimer's disease (Aronson, 1988).

Research projects are more likely to extend for even longer periods in the military (Driskell & Olmsted, 1989) because security concerns preclude having researchers in the private sector conduct investigations. However, specialization is the exception in government research. Those that do specialize for a while are eventually shifted to other projects and rarely return to the specialty they acquired.

Love of Research. Government research attracts and retains people who enjoy research for research's sake. Researchers in academia and in industry typically develop and maintain a wide range of interests.

Qualifications for a Job in Government Research. Most government researchers have a Master's degree or a Ph.D. Unlike academia, it is possible in the government to pursue a research career with a Bachelor's degree.

Special Problems of a Government Researcher. Applied cognitive researchers in government are aware of the particular mission of a project. Sometimes the need to maintain confidentiality about projects requires that researchers not take work home at night.

Financial Compensation. Salaries in academia and government are comparable (NSF Study of Doctorates). In the government, outside employment is possible but you have to get permission before you can do such work. If there is a potential conflict of interest between outside employment and your government work, it may be impossible to get permission. Consequently, most government researchers do not do outside work.

Attributes of Government Researchers. An applied cognitive researcher in the government requires an open mind and curiosity to adjust to the continual change in research projects (Herrmann, 1997b). Because government researchers must be able to explain a research project to another expert, to a member of Congress, to an official in the Executive Branch, or to a citizen. Government researchers conducts research for the overall good of society.

Range of Opportunities for Employment in Government Research. A wide range of research jobs exist in the government although most government researchers serve as analysts. However, most government research is conducted by businesses that contract with the government to do the necessary research. An exception to this arrangement is the military, which often does its own research to ensure security for the product or service being developed.

SUMMARY

Applied cognitive psychologists experience somewhat different careers depending on whether they work in academia, industry, or government. Many of the differences in career paths have to do with the type of organization for whom you work. Another basis of choice has to do with your tastes for specialization. If a person is interested in many different phenomena, then government research may be a good career choice. If specialization is more to one's liking, then a career in academia or business may be more appropriate.

18

The Future of Applied Cognitive Psychology

Prepare well and the future is yours.
— A fortune cookie

BREADTH OF SUCCESS

This text has demonstrated that applied cognitive psychology has become enormously successful. In the past several decades, a wide range of real-world problems have been tackled and solved by applied cognitive psychologists. Products, services, and procedures have been devised that facilitate a broad range of cognitive abilities necessary for managing the everyday world. A careful reading of the previous chapters indicates that many different cognitive applications have been developed in the areas of trauma intervention, cognitive assessment, cognitive improvement strategies, survey technology, cognitive rehabilitation strategies, devices that aid prospective memory, artifact and software design improvement, police interviews of eyewitnesses, legal resolution concerning trademark infringement, and numerous other cognitive-support products and services. It has been predicted that the applied cognitive approach will make inroads into many other areas as well (Nickerson, 1992, 1997).

More than 40 companies employ cognitive psychologists in the development of memory products or services. In addition, many applied cognitive psychologists are employed by government. Encouraging further growth of applied memory research and stronger links between the applied and basic research communities will result in better, more comprehensive understandings of cognition, which in turn will lead to more useful products, services, and training methods.

IMPORTANCE OF APPLIED COGNITIVE PSYCHOLOGY

Although the role research plays in creating technological advances is sometimes under appreciated, society can judge the value of products and services. The more useful a product or service is, the more valuable the public judges a field of science. Thus, as cognitive psychology gains in stature as a discipline by providing useful applications and technologies, society will become more willing to support grants for basic research and for the projects of applied researchers (Herrmann & Yoder, 1998). Applications need to be publicized because of their use to society and to enhance the reputation of cognitive psychology and the fundability of our research (Esgate & Groome, 2004; Smith et al., 1996).

Basic research places a premium on controlling all but the targeted variables and consequently attempts to isolate effects of independent variables. Although this emphasis on scientific rigor has provided important understandings of how cognition functions, other approaches are necessary to ensure progress. The more cognitive applications that are developed and successfully implemented, the more society will be willing to support cognitive research. To demonstrate the power and use of basic research, basic researchers need the applications and technologies developed by applied researchers. If the application or technology cannot be easily marketed and sold, the researchers should do as George Miller (1969) said many years ago, "give psychology away."

DEVELOPING APPLICATIONS

We recognize that not everyone is interested in pursuing doctoral training in cognitive sciences and committing their career to the pursuit of research. However, after some reading and probably some serious thinking you may have some ideas that you think could be translated into useful products or services. Earlier in the book we discussed ways to generate ideas for applications. We hope that you have made some notes for potential copyright at this stage. You will recall that a potential application should work, be unusual (deviant, innovative), and be very plausible to others.

For example, suppose a person is interested in how false memories are created. Developing procedures to encourage people to ask critical thinking questions that distinguish facts supported by evidence (e.g., records, corroborating sources) as more credible and meaningful than nonverified information might be useful. Repeated application of these procedures might even enhance the ability to distinguish real memories from false memories (Johnson & Raye, 1981; Schooler, Gerhard & Loftus, 1986). With practice, the individual improves in making these distinctions without necessarily being able to fully articulate what has been learned (Shiffrin & Schneider, 1977); unfortunately even experts can have difficulty explaining how decisions are made (Hoffman, Shadbolt, Burton & Klein, 1995). Such procedures might help individuals, as well as therapists and legal professionals, gain insight into the state of recalling a valid memory and a false memory, while increasing awareness of the malleability of memory. Practice with such a memory discrimination procedure could be helpful to victims, relatives, and professionals who struggle to manage false memory allegations.

The new neuroimaging brain scanning technologies enable a look at differences in activation patterns when retrieving actual as opposed to only imagined memories. A possible product that could be developed is software (Neuhoff, 2000; Niccaise, 1998) that compares activation patterns of real versus imagined events. Repeated trials comparing actual versus imagined events could result in distinctive patterns across individuals. Such hypothetical software might eventually provide a useful tool in distinguishing subtleties between real memories and false memories as researchers develop more sophisticated understandings of meaningful activation differences.

Applied cognitive psychologists often engage in the design of products, services. To develop all facets of a product or service, an applied cognitive psychologist needs to take into account physical, psychological, and social factors that may influence how a task may be approached. We believe that the design process is most likely to be successful if the designer considers all the modes of the multimodal model (Mullin, Herrmann, & Searleman, 1993; see also Newell, 1990) that a product or service affects. If a product or service development is approached in this manner, the product is more likely to be usable. Extensive pretesting of the product or service or parts of the product or service is beneficial for long-term success. The following factors make up a framework for application design.

TABLE 18.1
Framework of Application Design

Information processing
Mental manipulations
Physical environment
Social environment
Strength
Physical state
Chemical state
Health
Attitudinal state
Emotional state
Motivational state
Expertise
Cognitive competence
Personal style

Teamwork

In the future applied cognitive research will increasingly make use of teamwork. As the technological basis of cognitive products and services grows, different kinds of professionals will be called to work on a product. Even after a worthwhile product or a service has been developed, a team is needed to help develop the concept further. Besides specialists, the team might include a potential user of the product. Such a member will invariably introduce an atmosphere that encourages thinking about the product or service in realistic ways.

It has been suggested that applied cognitive research should be conducted in academia. However, it is customary in academia to concentrate primarily on basic research. Although this situation is not likely to change soon, there is merit to considering the advantages of encouraging more technology research in academia (Gruneberg, 1996; Gruneberg, Morris, Sykes, & Herrmann, 1996).

The most important reason for having more applied cognitive research in academia is that it would expedite communications between the two camps. Basic researchers will learn sooner of applied research that challenges the assumptions of basic research, and applied researchers will learn sooner of important developments in basic research. Also, when applied research investigates controversial issues, there are advantages to investigating these topics in academia because academia is usually more independent of external pressures than are researchers in the government or business.

NEW CONCEPTIONS OF THE BASIC-APPLIED RELATIONSHIP

Bacon's conception of basic and applied research still dominates thinking about the relationship between these two kinds of research: basic research creates knowledge (Buschke, Sliwinski, & Luddy, 1998), whereas applied researchers determine how to apply this knowledge (Dubin, 1976; Marx & Hillix, 1963; Pressley, as cited in Gruneberg et al., 1996; Wilson, 1952). In addition, the applied researcher sooner or later gives feedback to the basic researcher about inadequacies in the basic view of some phenomena.

Nevertheless, several researchers have found Bacon's (1620/1905) model insufficient. Instead, they have sought to modify Bacon's model or even devise a model to replace it. Here are the several latest competitors to the standard relationship advanced by Bacon.

The Cultural Model

This model assumes that the basic research culture is different from the applied research culture (Herrmann & Raybeck, 1997; Semmer, 1993). Thus, communications between these two camps often involves misunderstandings. This model predicts that successful communication between basic and applied research leads to the most effective basic-applied relationship. Accordingly, successful communication requires basic and applied researchers to increase their understanding of their respective approaches to science, their work environments, their scientific languages, and the prejudices they have toward each other.

As mentioned earlier, researchers who investigate basic and applied research belong to different professional cultures. Consequently, cultural variables affect substantially the social cognition of basic and applied researchers (Kuhn, 1962; Thagard, 1993). Differences between basic and applied researchers in their understanding of science, their customs of work, and their prejudices about the other camp can strongly influence the outcomes of investigations and how they are publicly described.

A Bi-directional Conception of the Bacon Model

Some modern versions of Bacon's (1620/1905) basic-applied model argue that the cycle does not go in one direction: basic to applied, then applied to basic, and so on. In addition, the cycle may begin with the application, either with a product or a service. When a product or service is especially compelling, researchers seek to derive the basic principles that made the product or service useful in the first place (Landy, 1993; Levy-Leboyer, 1993; Schonflug, 1993a, 1993b; Suigman, 1993).

Sometimes the speed of the adoption of a product has far exceeded psychological understanding of its effect, such as in the case of the cell phone. Now psychologists are trying to identify the cognitive processes that enable best and worst uses of the cell phone. For example, it is well established that drivers of automobiles are more likely to get into an accident if they are using a cell phone while driving (Strayer et al., 2004; Strayer, Drews, & Johnston, 2003; Strayer & Johnston, 2001;). It is only recently, well after the development of the product, that the basic principles governing safe and unsafe use of this product are being developed (Walker & Herrmann, 2004).

The Noise Variant of the Standard Model

A common model of statistical inference is the signal detection model. Experimental effects, if real, add to or subtract from normal variance whereupon inferential statistics identify effects as significant (Green & Swets, 1966). The standard model can also be characterized in terms of signal and noise, wherein basic research reduces ignorance by eliminating noise (confounding variables). By this account, applied psychologists gain greater control of phenomena in applying basic principles because they work to further eliminate noise in real-world settings (Banaji & Crowder, 1989; Gruneberg & Morris, 1992a. 1990b).

The Situational Model

Some researchers argue that the only critical difference between basic and applied research is where research is implemented. Presumably, all research consists of measures of phenomena and hypotheses about how these phenomena occur. Thus, the critical factor in determining the usefulness of so-called basic or applied research is how well the research situation matches the situation of application. If there is a good match, then manipulations of variables should lead to clear inter- pretation of findings.

Theoretical Perspective Underlying Basic and Applied Research

It has been proposed that basic and applied researchers follow different theoreti- cal traditions as they infer different interpretations of research findings (Koriat & Goldsmith, 1996; Payne & Blackwell, 1998). For example, for about three decades many basic researchers relied on a storehouse model of memory. In con- trast, applied researchers focused on the correspondence between applications and performance. One reason for this difference in approach may be explained by differences in how theory is used. On the other hand, this difference in use of theories may be the result of basic and applied researchers having different mis- sions - that of discovering basic principles versus creating usable applications.

The Dimensional Model

This model characterizes basic and applied research according to ecological and epistemological dimensions. Basic research is assumed to be high on the epistemological dimension in that it contributes to knowledge; applied research is high on the ecological dimension in that it ostensibly taps real-world issues. However, because different instances of research vary along these two dimensions, it is possible to have research that contributes substantially to epistemology and real-world issues. It is also possible to use a dimensional approach that contrib- utes substantially to epistemology but little to real-world issues. Alternatively, there may be little contribution to understanding (i.e., epistemology) but some contribution to real-world concerns.

Thus, the dimensional model assumes that basic and applied scientists are both contributors to the knowledge creation process and to the research pro- cess (Herrmann, Raybeck, & Gruneberg, 1997). Instead of two types of research (basic and applied), there are many instances of research that may be characterized both in terms of enhancing understanding and contributing practical worth (Vi- cente, 1994).

The Essential/Common Process Model

Some processes are common to many phenomena in the world. Common processes provide the fundamental explanations of natural phenomena. They are evident across a set of tasks, situations, and subjects. For example, a process that is common to virtually all learning is that of rehearsal. Thus, in fulfilling their role in the basic-applied cycle, basic researchers have traditionally employed what might be called a common process strategy (Herrmann, Raybeck, & Gruneberg, 1997). Because basic research is dedicated to elucidating principles that are common to all phenomena, including applications, this research fails to address processes essential to a particular application.

Certain processes only occur in certain applications. A common process becomes essential when it has been appropriately modified to be applicable in a specific context. Thus, applications are best developed by applied research through the use of an essential processes strategy. To make a common process such as rehearsal useful, applied research must identify how to modify the practice of rehearsal to be most effective in a certain situation. For example, the procedures for rehearsing names are different from the procedures for rehearsing faces.

The role of the essential process strategy is evident in a great deal of modern application research. For example, researchers and therapists who applied established methods to improve an individual's cognitive functioning found that traditional mental training did not help some people. Consequently, these researchers decided to also investigate the effects of particular extrinsic variables, such as the use of stimulants, on cognitive performance. Thus, the essential process strategy was useful to develop the nature of processes that are essential to cognitive improvement (White, 1998), a method that was more effective than that previously used (Parente' & Herrmann, 2003).

The essential process strategy was useful in developing procedures for training people with head injury, reported by Parente' and Herrmann (2003). This strategy has also been useful in showing that people may fail at memory tasks even when their memory is otherwise functioning satisfactorily. For example, for a person to succeed at remembering, he or she must possess at least a normal level of arousal or activation. Extreme fatigue or emotional upset makes memory failure almost inevitable. Thus, a normal level of arousal, which can be improved with a stimulant for individuals who are underaroused, is a factor that can be essential to effective memory performance.

Basic research derives its power from discovering processes that are useful to the full range of applications. However, when it comes to a particular application, essential processes may likely account for a greater percentage of variance than common processes (Herrmann, Raybeck, Gruneberg, Grant, & Yoder, 1998). For example, one essential process in cognitive improvement and rehabilitation is skill learning. Variables identified by applied research as affecting skill learning are critical to whether any improvement or rehabilitation is ever achieved in particular cases. Knowledge of common processes does not bear on improvement or rehabilitation per se. For example, basic research has shown that recall generally is enhanced if the conditions are similar to conditions when learning occurred (Tulving, 1983). People with cognitive impairments can be taught to apply this encoding specificity to maximize retrieval. Generalization strategies, which originated with essential processes, must be adapted systematically through essential processes to create effective skill training across different circumstances and situations.

FUTURE APPROACHES TO BASIC AND APPLIED RESEARCH

Most basic researchers support the standard model. Thus, they assume that applied research is never truly a theoretical enterprise, a fact that applied researchers must contend with when they interact with basic researchers. Alternatively, applied researchers identify essential variables critical to applications and disregard secondary variables that are not necessary to the overall application. In essence, many applied researchers base their activities on their theoretical view of a problem. Basic researchers who subscribe to the standard model must contend with applied researchers' focus on essential variables, which may or may not correspond with their interests. However, utilization of this information could result in better basic research models.

SUMMARY

Applied cognitive psychology is growing. Results from cognitive research have infiltrated more domains of professional and personal lives, from daily activity scheduling to manipulating someone's memory for something. Developing a more comprehensive understanding of how people think and remember is obviously important for optimizing how we live today. Creating new and better products and services is also necessary to advance knowledge and to promote better living. Clearly, the development of an applied cognitive psychology that aids people in their everyday cognitive functioning can improve the quality of our lives.

EPILOGUE

THE AIM OF PRACTICAL PSYCHOLOGY

Hugo Munsterberg: "The Present Situation of Practical Psychology. "
We take a narrow view of scientific knowledge if we claim that it has a right to
exist only when it can serve our practical interests and can be applied to the tasks
of life. Truth must be respected as valuable in itself. Like beauty, it fulfills an ideal
demand, and we ought to devote ourselves to the discovery of truth without asking
how far the truth can be used to bake our daily bread. But our view is certainly
no less narrow, if we take the opposite stand and are indifferent to the practical
usefulness of our scientific results.

The admirable eagerness to contribute to and to spread theoretical
knowledge has often led to unwillingness to link theoretical psychology with
the practical needs of the community. Some have the feeling that psychology
loses its dignity when it becomes the handmaid of routine life. Nobody imagines
that physics and chemistry are desecrated by being harnessed for the technical
achievements of society. We could not imagine the laws of electricity or of steam
power being known in the laboratories and not being applied for transportation, for
lighting our houses and for cabling our news. It is no less fitting and natural that the
progress of psychology, too, should become helpful to the community wherever
mental life is involved in its affairs, and it is evident that the mind takes a characteristic part in every domain of social interest, of education and of religion, of
politics and of law, of commerce and industry, of art and of scholarship, of family
life and of practical intercourse, of public movements and of social reform.

To be sure, the history of mankind shows that the greatest technical
triumphs were always won through the work of scientists who did not think of
the practical achievements but exclusively of theoretical truth. The work of the
engineer has always followed where the physical truth seeker has blazed the path.

It cannot be otherwise with applied psychology. The results of psychological technique must remain superficial without a solid foundation of theoretical psychology, and this must be laid without any side-thought of practical usefulness. But as soon as such psychological knowledge is really secured, we have simply no right to disregard it, when the needs of society are so evident. (Munsterberg, 1914, pp. 341-343).

Without communication from basic research to applied research, applied researchers operate separately from basic researchers. Without communication from applied research to basic research, cognitive psychology may never achieve its potential. Cognitive psychologists, basic and applied, need to create channels of communication with other groups in society. Through communication, cooperation, and collaboration, basic and applied researchers can make their greatest contribution to the solution of the world's problems.

Published by Hugo Munsterberg in 1914 as Part I. Principles of Psychology, Chapter XXVII in Psychology: General and Applied (pp. 341-343), New York: D. Appleton and Company. For more informationon Munsterberg's ideas and career, see M. Munsterberg (1922).

GLOSSARY

KEY TERMS FOR
APPLIED COGNITIVE PSYCHOLOGY

Accessibility. The likelihood of being able to retrieve a memory with sufficient cues.

Applicability of manipulations. The range of tasks for which mental manipulation will be effective: generally applicable manipulations facilitate most or all cognitive tasks, whereas specifically applicable manipulations facilitate just certain tasks.

Applicable research. A study whose results are relevant to a group of products. Contrast with applied research.

Application. The development of a product, procedure or service on the basis of basic, ecological, or applicable cognitive psychology.

Assessment of cognition. Identification of individual differences in performance of cognitive tasks in general as revealed by self-observation or by formal testing.

Attention. The process or orienting to, and observing, the world around us and the contents of working memory.

Attributes of a trace. One facet of the meaning of the information in a trace.

Availability. Works from the assumption that information was learned, this refers to whether or not information is currently represented in memory

Basic model of basic-applied research. Assumes that basic research has the responsibility for identifying the fundamental principles of nature, after which applied research has responsibility for practical uses of these fundamental principles.

Bi-directional conception of the Bacon model. Some modern versions of Bacon's basic-applied model argue that the cycle does not go in just one direction: basic to applied, applied to basic, and so on. In addition, the cycle may begin with the application, either with a product or the service.

Central processor. A component of the cognitive system that selects and implements manipulations of any type to facilitate cognitive performance.

Cognitive aids. An object or device that facilitates cognitive performance.

Cognitive contrivance. A deliberate distortion that portrays someone else's cognitive performance as better or worse than it actually was to achieve certain social goals.

Cognitive science. Interdisplinary field that draws from cognitive psychology, computer science, neuroscience, philosophy and other related fields.

Cognitive stereotypes. Beliefs people hold about the cognitive performance of others, based on group characteristics (gender, race, physical appearance, or occupation).

Cues. Aspects of the environment that may facilitate remembering.

Cultural model of basic-applied research. Assumes basic research is high on an epistemological dimension in that it contributes to knowledge; applied research is high on the ecological dimension in that it taps the real world.

Decay of a memory. The physiological erosion of a memory.

Demand characteristic. A property of some experimental tasks that is instrumental in altering the participant's response, apart from the intended manipulation

Distortion of a memory. An alteration of a memory trace, in which inaccuracies are usually undetected.

Ecological validity. Research focus corresponds to real world events.

Encoding. Intentional or incidental registration of information.

Encoding specificity. Later ability to retrieve is dependent on the intial context of learning.

Episodic memory. Thought to hold memories of specific vents, with which the learner has had direct experience.

Essential/common process model. This model assumes that basic researchers employ a common process strategy, which is dedicated to elucidating principles that are common to all phenomena, including applications. Applied researchers imply an essential process strategy, which is dedicated to identifying the process that are essential to only the application under consideration.

Experiment. A test of scientific theory where independent variables are manipulated and dependent variables measures; random subject assignment to condition is required.

Heuristic. A shortcut or rule of thumb that can be used in problem solving, reasoning, and decision making.

Information processing approach. Uses computer metaphor to understand and explore human cognitive processes

Interference between traces. A source of forgetting in which the primary memory trace to be remembered is confused with one or more other memories.

Learning. An intentional form of registration.

Long-term memory. A component of the memory system that holds information indefinitely.

Memory processes. Includes the registration, retention, and remembering of information.

Memory trace. The mental representation of stored information.

Mental manipulation. A mental activity or behavior that orders and organizes thoughts to assist paying attention, perception, registration, retention, remembering, reasoning, problem solving, decision making, and communication.

Mental representation. An internal depiction of information.

Mnemonics. Strategies which facilitate information retention and retrieval.

Noise variant of standard model of basic-applied research. Characterized in terms of signal and noise, wherein basic research reduces ignorance by eliminating noise (confounding variables); applied psychologists work to further eliminate noise in real-world settings.

Priming. The increase in trace strength that results from familiarizing one with the material to be learned or retrieved.

Procedural memory. Though to hold memories related to actions or behaviors or sequences of these activities.

Quasi-experiment. An empirical research approach that involves incomplete experimental control, typically because of nonrandom subject assignment to manipulated conditions.

Recall. Retrieval of information based on generating information without cues or aids.

Recognition. Retrieval of information where th learner must decide whether information was previously presented.

Retrieval. An intentional form of remembering.

Semantic memory. Thought to hold memories of general knowledge.

Situational model of basic-applied research. Some researchers argue that the only critical differences between basic and applied research is where research is implemented. Applied research matches the situation of application well, whereas basic research does not.

Social context manipulation. A technique that identifies social factors harmful to performance or that alters social behaviors to maximize cognitive performance.

Source monitoring errors. An inability to remember the original source of particular information.

Symbolic cognitive tasks. Tasks whose performance, successful or unsuccessful, affects the state of a personal relationship between people.

Task situations. Broad categories of daily life in which cognitive tasks occur including home life, work, obligations, and recreation.

Task-specific manipulation. A behavior that is especially effective for a particular kind of cognitive task.

Test anxiety. Fear and nervousness that inhibits cognitive performance, especially for a topic of particular importance to the individual.

Warm up. The increase in speed and proficiency at performing a cognitive task that results from initial attempts at the task.

Working memory. A hypothetical limited-capacity workspace thought to consist of a central exeutive, phonological loop, and a visuospatial sketchpad

Weschler Memory Scale (WMS) The oldest and possible best known memory battery which assesses and individual's "personal and current information, orientation, mental control, logical memory, digit span, visual reproductive memory, and associative leaning."

Whole report procedure A test in which the recall of an entire stimulus array is attempted.

Word fragments Test in which one attempts to recall the word that corresponds to segments and parts of the letters making up the word.

Word-stem completion Test in which one attempts to recall the word that corresponds to some of the letters making up the word.

Working memory The components of the memory system (phonological loop, visuo-spatial sketch pad, central executive) that holds information for approximately one minute.

Yerkes-Dodson Law The relationship between arousal and performance, i.e. that performance increases from low to intermediate levels of arousal, but decrease at high levels of arousal.

References

Abernethy, B., Neal, R.J., & Koning, P. (1994). Visual-perceptual and cognitive differences between expert, intermediate, and novice snooker players. *Applied Cognitive Psychology, 8*, 185-211.

Adams, J. A. (1987). Historical review and appraisal of research on the learning, retention, and transfer of human motor skills. *Psychological Bulletin, 101*, 41-74.

Adams, R. Mc., Smelser, N. J., & Trieman, D. J. (Eds.). (1982a). *Behavioral and social science research: A national resource. Part I.* Washington, D.C.: National Academy Press.

Adams, R. Mc., Smelser, N. J., & Trieman, D. J. (Eds.). (1982b). *Behavioral and social science research: A national resource. Part II.* Washington, D.C.: National Academy Press.

Akehurst, L., Köhnken, G., Vrij, A., & Bull, R. (1996). Lay persons' and police officers' beliefs regarding deceptive behaviour. *Applied Cognitive Psychology, 10*, 461-471.

Alba, J. W., & Hutchinson, J. W. (1999). Applied cognition in consumer research. In F. Durso (Ed.), *Handbook of applied cognition.* New York: Wiley.

Allard, F. & Starkes, J. L. (1991). Motor-skill experts in sports, dance, and other domains. In K. A. Ericsson and J. Smith (Eds.). *Toward a general theory of expertise: Prospects and Limits* (pp 126-152). New York: Cambridge University Press.

Ambrose, M. L., Bowden, S. C., & Whelan, G. (2001). Working memory impairments in alcohol-dependent participants without clinical amnesia. *Alcoholism: Clinical & Experimental Research, 25*,185-191.

American Psychiatricl Association. (2000). *Diagnostic and Statistical Manual of Mental Disorders* (4th ed.). Washington, DC: : American Psychiatric Association.

Amidzic, O., Riehle, H. J., Fehr, T., Wienbruch, C. & Elbert, T. (2001). Patterns of focal-bursts in chess players. *Nature, 412*, 603.

Anderson, J. A. (1990). Hybrid computation in cognitive science: neural networks and symbols. *Applied Cognitive Psychology, 4*, 337-347.

Anderson, J. R. (1981). (Ed.). *Cognitive skills and their acquisition.* Hillsdale, NJ: Erlbaum.

Anderson, J. R. (1983). *The architecture of cognition.* Cambridge, MA: Harvard University.

Anderson, J. R. (2000a). *Learning and memory: An integrated). approach* (2nd edition New York: Wiley.

Anderson, J. R. (2004). *Cognitive psychology and its implications.* New York: Worth.

Andersson, J., & Rönnberg, J. (1995). Recall suffers from collaboration: joint recall effects of friendship and task complexity. *Applied Cognitive Psychology, 9,* 199-211.

Anderson, J. R. & Schooler, L. (2002). The adaptive nature of memory. In E. Tulving and F. I. M. Craik (Eds.). *The Oxford Handbook of memory.* Oxford University Press: New York.

Anderson, J. R., Conrad, F. G., & Corbett, A. T. (1989). Skill acquisition and the LISP tutor. *Cognitive Science, 13,* 467-506.

Anderson, J. R., Corbett, A. T., Koedinger, K., & Pelletier, R. (1995). Cognitive tutors: Lessons learned. *The Journal of the Learning Sciences, 4,* 167-207.

Anderson, S. J., Beveridge, M., Conway, M. A., & Dewhurst, S. A. (1999). Using computers to explore the locus of expertise in soccer players. *Cognitive Technology, 4,* 28-37.

Andrade, J. (2004). *Cognitive psychology.* Boston: Bios Scientific.

Andrzejewski, S. J., Moore, C. M., Corvette, M., & Herrmann, D. (1991). Prospective memory skills. *Bulletin of the Psychonomic Society. 29,* 304-306.

Anooshain, L.J., & Seibert, P.S. (1996). Diversity within spatial cognition: memory processes underlying place recognition. *Applied Cognitive Psychology, 10,* 281-299.

Aronson, M. K. (Ed.). (1988*). Understanding Alzheimer's disease.* New York: Scribner's Sons.

Atchison, R.,Pedersen, T.,,, Pain, J. & Wood, K. (2003). *Human Factors, 45,* p 495.

Atkinson, R. C., & Juola, J. F.. (1974). Search and decision processes in recognition memory. In D.H. Krantz, R. C. Atkinson, R. D.Luce, & P. Suppes (Eds.). *Contemporary Developments in Mathematical Psychology* (pp. 242-293). San Francisco: Freeman.

Atkinson, R. C., & Shiffrin, R. M. (1968). Human memory: A proposed system and its control processes. In K. W. Spence & J. R. Spence (Eds.), *The psychology of learning and motivation: Advances in research and theory* (Vol. 2), pp. 89-195). New York: Academic Press.

Ayres, T. J., & Wood, C. T. (1999). Cognitive technology. Memory problems for survey-based estimates of population activity. *Cognitive Technology, 4,* 4-10.

Baars, B. (1986). *The cognitive revolution in psychology.* New York: Guilford.

Bacon, F. (1905). *The philosophic works of Francis Bacon*, John M. Robertson (Ed.) (reprinted from translations by R. C. Ellis & J. Spedding). London: George Routledge and Sons.

Baddeley, A. D. (1981). The cognitive psychology of everyday life. *British Journal of Psychology, 72*, 257-269.

Baddeley, A. D. (1982). Domains of recollection. *Psychological Review, 89*, 708-729.

Baddeley, A. D. (1990). *Human memory: Theory and practice.* Boston: Allyn & Bacon.

Baddeley, A. (1993a). *Your memory: A users guide.* London: Multimedia Books.

Baddeley, A. (1993b). Holy war or wholly unnecessary? Some thoughts on the ёconflict' between laboratory studies and everyday memory. In G. M. Davies & R. H. Logie (Eds.), *Memory in everyday life.* New York: North Holland.

Baddeley, A. D. (1995). Applying psychology of memory to clinical problems. In D. Herrmann, C. McEvoy, C. Hertzog, P. Hertel, & M. Johnson, *Basic and applied memory: Theory in context.* Hillsdale, NJ: Erlbaum.

Baddeley, A., Meeks Gardner, J., Grantham-McGregor, S. (1995). Cross-cultural cognition: developing tests for developing countries. *Applied Cognitive Psychology, 9*, S173-S195.

Baddeley, A. D., Wilson, B. A., & Watts, F. N. (Eds.).(1995). *Handbook of Memory disorders.* New York: Wiley.

Baguley, T., & Landsdale, M. (2000). Memory theory and the cognitive technology of spatial methods in information retrieval systems. *Cognitive Technology, 5*, 4-19.

Bahrick, H. P. (1984). Semantic memory content in permastore: Fifty years of memory for Spanish learned in school. *Journal of Experimental Psychology: General, 113*(1), 1-29.

Bahrick, H. P., Bahrick, P. O., & Wittlinger, R. P. (1975). Fifty years of memory for names and faces: A cross-sectional approach. *Journal of Experimental Psychology: General, 104*, 54-75.

Bahrick, H. P., & Hall, L. K. (1991). Lifetime maintenance of high school mathematics content. *Journal of Experimental Psychology: General, 120*, 20-33.

Bahrick, H. P., & Phelps, E. (1987). Retention of Spanish vocabulary over 8 years. *Journal of Experimental Psychology: Learning, Memory, and Cognition, 13*, 344-349.

Bailenson, J. N., & Rips, L. J. (1996). Informal reasoning and burden of proof. *Applied Cognitive Psychology, 10*, S3-S16.

Baldi, R., A., Plude, D. J., & Schwartz, L. K. (1996). Cognitive technology new technologies for memory training with older adults. *Cognitive Technology, 1*, 25-35.

Banaji, M. R., & Crowder, R. G. (1989). The bankruptcy of everyday memory. *Americ Psychologist, 44*, 1185-1193.

Barber, D. (1988). *Applied cognitive psychology*. London: Methuen.

Barclay, R. A. (1994*). ADHD in adults*. New York: Guilford.

Barker, R. G. (1968*). Ecological Psychology*. Stanford University Press. Stanford, Calif.

Barnard, P. J., & Teasdale, J. D. (1991). Intercting cognitive subsystems: A systemic approach to cognitive-affective interaction and change. *Cognition and Emotion, 5*, 1-39.

Bartlett, F. C. (19321995). *Remembering: A study in experimental and social psychology*. Cambridge, England: Cambridge University Press.

Basden, B., Basden, D., Bryner, S. & Thomas, R. (1997). A comparison of group and individual remembering: Does collaboration disrupt retrieval strategies? *Journal of Experimental Psychologoy: Learning, Memory & Cognition, 23*, 1176-1189.

Baum, A., Cohen, L., & Hall, M. (1993). Control and intrusive memories as possible determinants of chronic stress. *Psychosomatic Medicine, 55*, 274-286.

Beach, K. (1988). The role of external mnemonic symbols in acquiring an occupation. In M. M. Gruneberg, P. E. Morris, & R. N. Sykes (Eds.), *Practical aspects of memory: Current research and issues* (Vol. 1, pp. 342-346). Chichester, England: John Wiley & Sons.

Beatty, P., & Herrmann, D. (2001). To answer or not to answer: Decision processes related to item non-response. In R. Groves, D. Dillman, J. Eltinge, & R. Little (Eds.), *Survey nonresponse*. Boston: Wiley.

Beatty, P., Herrmann, D., Puskar, C., & Kerwin, J. (1998). When people say they do not know, do they know*? Memory, 4*, 407-426.

Beck, A. T. (1976). *Cognitive therapy and the emotional disorders*. New York: International Universities Press.

Bekerian, D. A., & Dennett, J. L. (1993). The cognitive interview technique: reviving the issues. *Applied Cognitive Psychology, 7*, 275-297.

Bellezza, F. S. (1982). *Improve your memory skills*. EnglewoodCliffs, NJ: Prentice-Hall.

Bellezza, F. S., & Buck, D. K. (1988). Expert knowledge as mnemonic cues. *Applied Cognitive Psychology, 2*, 147-162.

Belli, R. F. (1998). The structure of autobiographical memory and the event history calendar: Potential improvements in the quality of retrospective reports in surveys. *Memory, 6*, 383-406.

Benbow, C. P. & Stanley, J. C. (1993). Sex differences in mathematical reasoning: More facts. *Science, 222*, 1029-1031.

Bendiksen, M., & Bendiksen, I. (1992). A multidimensional intervention program solvent injured population. *Cognitive Rehabilitation, 10*, 20-27.

References 217

Bendiksen, M., & Bendiksen, I. (1996). Multi-modal memory rehabilitation for the toxic solvent injured population. In D. Herrmann, M. Johnson, C. McEvoy, C. Hertzog, & P. Hertel (Eds.), *Basic and applied memory research: New findings.* Hillsdale, NJ: Erlbaum.

Benjafield, J.G.. (1997). *Cognition* (2nd Edition). Upper Saddle River, NJ: Prentice Hall.

Benjamin, L. T. Jr. (1988). The history of teaching machines. *American Psychologist, 43,* 713-720.

Bennett H. L. (1983). Remembering drink orders: the memory skills of cocktail waitresses. *Human Learning, 2,* 157-169.

Bentley, A. M., Kvalsvig, J., & Miller, R. (1990). The cognitive consequences of poverty: a neo-piagetian study with Zulu children. *Applied Cognitive Psychology, 4,* 451-459.

Benton, D. (1993). Blood glucose and human memory. *Psychopharmacology, 113,* 83-88.

Berger, D. E., Pezdek, K., & Banks, W. P. (1987). *Applications of cognitive psychology: Problem solving, education, and computing.* Hillsdale, N. J.: Erlbaum.

Bergman, M. M. (1998), A Proposed Resolution of the Remediation-Compensation Controversy in Brain Injury Rehabilitation. *Cognitive Technology, 3,* 45-52.

Berntsen, D. (1996). Involuntary autobiographical memories. *Applied Cognitive Psychology, 10,* 435-454.

Berry, C., Scheffler, A., & Goldstein, C. (1993). Effects of text structure on the impact of heard news. *Applied Cognitive Psychology, 7,* 381-395.

Berry, D.C. (1995). Donald Broadbent and applied cognitive psychology. *Applied Cognitive Psychology, 9,* S1-S4.

Bertrand, A., Cellier, J.-M., & Giroux, L. (1996). Expertise and strategies for the identification of the main ideas in document indexing. *Applied Cognitive Psychology, 10,* 419-433.

Best, D. (1992). The role of social interaction in memory improvement. In D. Herrmann, H. Weingartner, A. Searleman, & C. McEvoy (Eds.), *Memory improvement: Implications for memory theory* (pp. 122-149). New York: Springer Verlag.

Best, D. L., Hamlett, K. W., & Davis, S. W. (1992a). Memory complaint and memory performance in the elderly: The effects of memory-skills training and expectancy change. *Applied Cognitive Psychology, 6,* 405-416.

Bckman, L. (1981). Some distinctions between basic and applied approaches. Bickman (Ed.), *Applied social psychology* (pp. 23-44). New York: Sage.

Biederman, I. (1987). Recognition-by-components: A theory of human image understanding. *Psychological Review, 94,* 115-147.

Biederman, I., Cooper, E. E., Fox, P. W.. Fox, P. W., & Mahadevan, R. S. (1992). Unexceptional spatial memory in an exceptional memorist. *Journal of Experimental Psychology: Learning, Memory, and Cognition, 18,* 654-657.

Biel, G. A., & Carswell, C. M. (1993). Musical notation for the keyboard: an examination of stimulus-response compatibility. *Applied Cognitive Psychology, 7*, 433- 452.

Birnbaum, I. M., Taylor, T. H., Johnson, M. K., & Raye, C. L. (1987). Is event frequency encoded automaticallv? The case of alcohol intoxication. *Journal of Experimental Psychology: Learning, Memory, and Cognition, 13*, 251-258.

Bisacchi, W.F., & Starkes, J.L. (1999). A multidimensional approach to skilled perception and performance in sport. *Applied Cognitive Psychology, 13*, 1-27.

Blagrove, M., & Akehurst, L. (2000). Effect of sleep loss on confidence-accuracy relationships for reasoning and eyewitnessing memory. *Journal of Experimental Psychology-Applied, 6*, 59-73.

Blagrove, M., Alexander, C., & Home, J. A. (1995). The effects of chronic sleep reduction on the performance of cognitive tasks sensitive to sleep deprivation. *Applied Cognitive Psychology, 9*, 21-40.

Blagrove, M., Cole-Morgan, D., Lambe, H. (1994). Interrogative suggestibility: the effects of sleep deprivation and relationship with field dependence. *Applied Cognitive Psychology, 8*, 169-179.

Block, L. G., & Morwitz, V. G. (1999). Shopping lists as an external memory aid for grocery shopping: Influences on list writing and list fulfillment. *Journal of Consumer Psychology, 8*, 343-375.

Block, R. I., & Wittenborn, J. R. (1984). Marijuana effects on semantic memory: Verification of common and uncommon category members. *Psychological Reports, 55*, 503-512.

Blumenthal, J. A., & Madden, D. J. (1988). Effects of aerobic exercise training, age, & physical fitness on memory-search performance. *Psychology & Aging, 3*, 280-285.

Bohanek, J. G., Fivush, R., & Walker, E. (2005). Memories of positive and negative emotional events. *Applied Cognitive Psychology, 19*, 51-66.

Bond, G. D., & Less, A. Y. (2005). Language of lies in prison: Linguistic classification of prisoners' truthful and deceptive natural language. *Applied Cognitive Psychology, 19*, 313-344.

Boneau, A. (1994, August). A theory of the relationship between basic and applied research. Presented at the third international Practical Aspects of Memory Conference, College Park, MD.

Borgeaud, P. & Abernathy, B. (1987). Skilled perception in volleyball defense. *Journal of Sport Psychology, 9*, 400-406.

Boring, E. (1950*). A history of experimental psychology*. 2nd edition. New York: Appleton-Century-Crofts.

Bornstein, B. H. (1994). David, Goliath, and Reverend Bayes: prior beliefs about defendents' status in personal injury cases. *Applied Cognitive Psychology, 8,* 232-258.

Bornstein, B. H., Leibel, L. M., & Scarberry, N. C. (1998). Repeated testing in eyewitness memory: a means to improve recall of a negative emotional event. *Applied Cognitive Psychology, 12,* 119-131.

Bourgeois, M. (1990). Enhancing conversation skills in patients with Alzheimer's disease using a prosthetic memory aid. *Journal of Applied Behavior Analysis, 23,* 29-42.

Bourgeois, M. (1993). Effects of memory aids on the dyadic conversations of individuals with dementia. *Journal of Applied Behavior Analysis, 26,* 77-87.

Bowen, J. D., & Larson, E. B. (1993). Drug induced cognitive impairment. Defining the problem and finding solutions. *Drugs and Aging. 3,* 349-357.

Bower, G. H. (1970). Analysis of a mnemonic device. *American Scientist, 58,* 498-510.

Bower, G. H. (1981). Mood and memory. *American Psychologist, 36,* 129-148.

Bower, G. H. (1987). Commentary on mood and memory. *Behavior Research and Therapy, 25,* 443-455..

Bower, G. H., & Forgas, J. P. (2000). Affect, memory, and social cognition. In E. Eich & J. Schooler (Eds.), Cognition and memory. Mood and social memory, In J. P. Forgas (Ed.), *Handbook of affect and social cognition.* Mahwah, NJ: Erlbaum.

Bracey, O. L. (1996). *Cognitive rehabilitation: A process approach.* MarchApril, 10-11.

Bradburn, N., Rips, L. J., & Shevell, S. K. (1987). Answering autobiographical questions: The impact of memory and inference on surveys. *Science, 236,* 157-161.

Brandimonte, M., Einstein, G., & McDaniel, M. (Eds.), (1996). *Prospective memory: Theory and applications.* Hillsdale, NJ: Erlbaum.

Brandimonte, M. A., Bisiacchi, P., & Pelizzon, L. (2000). Perceptually-driven memory for intentions: A study with children and adults. *Cognitive Technology, 5,* 20-25.

Brandon, S., Boakes, J., Glaser, D., & Green, R. (1998). Recovered memories of childhood sexual abuse: Implicatins for clinical practice. *British Journal of Psychology, 172,* 296-307.

Branscomb, L. M. (1995). Public funding of scientific research. In K. Miller (Ed.), *Sigma Xi Forum: 1995 Vannvar Bush II Science for the 21st Century.* Research Triangle Park, NC: Sigma Xi.

Braun, K. A., & Loftus, E. F. (1998). Advertising's misinformation effect. *Applied Cognitive Psychology, 12,* 569-591.

Brewer, M. B. (1985). Experimental research and social policy: Must it be rigor versus relevance? *Journal of Social Issues, 41,* 159-176.

Brewer, N., Potter, R., Fisher, R. P., Bond, N., & Luszcz, M. A. (1999). Beliefs and data on the relationship between consistency and accuracy of eyewitness testimony. *Applied Cognitive Psychology, 13*, 297-313.

Brewer, W. (1994). The validity of autobiographical recall. In N. Schwarz & S. Sudman, Eds., *Autobiographical memory and the validity of retrospective reports*. New York: Springer Verlag.

Brewin, C.R. (1998). Intrusive autobiographical memories in depression and post- traumatic stress disorder. *Applied Cognitive Psychology, 12*, 359-370.

Broadbent, D. E. (1958). *Perception and communication*. Oxford: Pergamon.

Broadbent, D. E., Cooper, P. F., Fitzgerald. P., & Parks, K. R. (1982). The cognitive failures questionaire (C.F.Q.) and its correlates. *British Journal of Clinical Psychology, 21*, 1-16.

Bronfenbrenner, U. (1977). Toward an experimental ecology of human development. *American Psychologist, 32*, 513-531.

Brown, A., Jones, E. & Davis, T. (1995). Age differences in conversational source monitoring. *Psychology and Aging, 10*, 111-122.

Brown, C. & Lloyd-Jones, T. J. (2003). Verbal overshadowing of multiple face and car recognition: Effects of within- versus across category verbal descriptions. *Applied Cognitive Psychology, 17*, 183-202.

Brown, E. L., & Deffenbacher, K. A. (1988). Superior memory performance and mnemonic encoding. In L. K. Obler & D. Fein (Eds.), *The exceptional brain: Neuropsychology of talent and special abilities*. New York: Guilford.

Brown, J. D., & Larson, E. B. (1993). Drug-induced cognitive impairment: Defining the problem and finding solutions. *Drugs & Aging, 4*, 349-357.

Brown, N. R., & Schopflocher, D. (1998). Event cueing, event clusters, and the temporal distribution of autobiographical memories. *Applied Cognitive Psychology, 12*, 305-319.

Brown, R., & Kulik, J. (1977). Flashbulb memories. *Cognition, 5*, 73-99.

Bruce, D. (1985). The how and why of ecological memory. *Journal of Experimental Psychology: General, 114*, 78-90.

Bruce, D., & van Pelt, M. (1989). Memories of a bicycle tour. *Applied Cognitive Psychology, 3*, 137-156.

Bruce, V., Hanna, E., Dench, N., Healey, P., & Burton, M. (1992). The importance of 'mass' in line drawings of faces. *Applied Cognitive Psychology, 6*, 619-628.

Brunas-Wagsstaff, J. (1998). *Personality: A cognitive approach*. London: Routledge.

Bruner, J. S., Goodnow, J., & Austin, G. (1956*). A study of thinking*. New York: Wiley.

Bruning, R. H., Norby, M. M., Ronning, R. R., & Schraw, G. J., (1999). *Cognitive psychology and instruction*. Upper Saddle River, NJ: Merrill.

Brunswick, , E. (1956*). Perception and the representative design of experiments*. Berkeley: University of California Press.

Bryan, G. L. (1972). Evaluation of basic research in the context of mission orientation. *American Psychologist, 27*, 947-950.

Bryand, R. A., & Harvey, A. G. (1998). Traumatic memories and pseudomemories in posttraumatic stress disorder. *Applied Cognitive Psychology, 12*, 81-88.

Bunce, D., Hays, K., & Ping, L. (2004). Smoking attenuates regular aerobic exercise benefits to episodic free recall immediately following strenuous physical activity. *Applied Cognitive Psychology, 18*, 223-144.

Burt, C. D. B., & Forsyth, D. K. (1999.) Designing materials for efficient time management: Segmentation and planning space. *Cognitive Technology, 4*, 11-18.

Burt, C. D. B., Watt, S. C., Mitchell, D. A., & Conway, M. A. (1998). Retrieving the sequence of autobiographical event components. *Applied Cognitive Psychology, 12*, 321-338.

Buschke, H., Kuslansky, G., Katz, M., Stewart, W. F., Sliwinski, M. J., Eckholdt, H. M., & Lipton, R. B. (1999*). Neurology, 52*, 231-238.

Buschke, H., Sliwinski, M. J., & Luddy, D. (1998). Cognitive theory, experiments, applications, and cognitive impairment. *Cognitive Technology, 3*, 4-8.

Bushman, B. and Bonacci, A. (2002). Violence and sex impair memory for television ads. *Journal of Applied Psychology, 87*, 557-564.

Bushman, B. J., & Phillips, C. M. (2001). If the television program bleeds, memory for the advertisement recedes. *Current Directions Psychological Science, 10*, 43-46.

Butterfield, H. (1957). *The origins of modern science*. New York: Collier.

Cabeza, R. & Kingstrone, A. (Eds.). (2002*). Handbook of Functional Neuroimaging of Cognition*. Cambridge, MA: MIT Press.

Cacioppo, J., & Petty, R. (1982). The need for cognition. *Journal of Personality and Social Psychology, 42*, 120-121.

Camp, C. J., & Foss, J. W. (1997). Designing ecologically valid memory interventions for persons with dementia. In D. G. Payne & F. G. Conrad (Eds.*), Intersections in basic and applied memory research* (pp. 311 - 325). Mahwah, NJ: Lawrence Erlbaum Associates.

Camp, C. J., Foss, J. W., Stevens, A. B., & O'Hanlon, A. M. (1996). Improving prospective memory task performance in persons with Alzheimer's disease. In M. Brandimonte, G. Einstein, & McDaniel (Eds.*), Prospective memory: Theory and applications*. Hillsdale, NJ: Erlbaum.

Campbell, D. R., & Stanley, J. C. (1966). *Experimental and quasi-experimental designs for research.* Chicago: Rand McNally.

Campbell, R. & Conway, M. A. (Eds.).(1995*). Case Studies in Memory Impairment.* Cambridge, MA: Blackwell.

Canas, J. J. (2003). Memory issues in cognitive ergonomics. *Cognitive Technology, 8,* 4-5.

Cannon-Bowers, J. A., & Salas, E. (1998*). Making decisions under stress: Implications for individual and team training.* Hyattsville, MD: American Psychological Association.

Caprio-Prevette, M. (1999). Memory rehabilitation strategies and cognitive behavioral techniques after a brain injury. *Cognitive Technology, 4,* 39-45.

Card, S. K., Moran, T. P., & Newell, A. (1983). *The psychology of human computer interaction.* Hillsdale, NJ: Erlbaum.

Carlson, R. A. (1997). *Experienced cognition.* Mahwah: Erlbaum

Carpenter, S. K., & DeLosh, E. L. (2005). Application of the testing and spacing effects to name learning. *Applied Cognitive Psychology, 19,* 619-636.

Carroll, M., Mazzoni, G., Andrews, S., & Pocock, P. (1999). Monitoring the future: object and source memory for real and imagined events. *Applied Cognitive Psychology, 13,* 373-390.

Carswell, C. M, Bates, J. R., Pregliasco, N. R., Lonon, A., & Urban, J. (1998). Finding graphs useful: Linking preference to performance for one cognitive tool. *Cognitive Technology, 3,* 4-18.

Cavanaugh, J. C., Feldman, J. M., & Herzog, C. (1998). Memory beliefs as social cognition: A reconceptualization of what memory questionnaires assess. *Review of General Psychology, 2,* 48-65.

Cavanaugh, J. C., Feldman, J. M., & Herzog, C. (1998). Memory beliefs as social cognition: A reconceptualization of what memory questionnaires assess. *Review of General Psychology, 2,* 48-65.

Ceci, S. J., Baker, J. G., & Bronfenbrenner, U. (1988). Prospective remembering, temporal calibration, and context. In M. Gruneberg, P. Morris, & R. Sykes, Eds., *Practical aspects of memory, current research and issues,* Vol. 2. Chichester: Wiley.

Chaffin, R., & Imreh, G. (1997). Pulling teeth and torture: Musical memory and problem solving. *Thinking and Reasoning,* 3, 315-336.

Chalfonte, B. L. & Johnson, M. K. (1996). Feature memory and binding in young and older adults. *Memory & Cognition, 24,* 403-416.

Chandler, P., & Sweller, J. (1996). Cognitive load while learning to use a computer program. *Applied Cognitive Psychology, 10,* 151-170.

Channon, S., & Baker, J.E. (1996). Depression and problem-solving performance on a fault-diagnosis task. *Applied Cognitive Psychology, 10*, 327-336.

Chapanis, A. (1967). The relevance of laboratory studies to practical situations. *Ergonomics, 10*, 557-577.

Chapanis, A. (1986). A psychology for our technological society: A tale of two laboratories. In S. H. Hulse & B. F. Green (Eds.), *One hundred years of psychological research in America* (pp. 52-70). Baltimore: Johns Hopkins University Press.

Chapanis, A. (1988). Some generalizations about generalization. *Human Factors, 30*, 253-267.

Chapanis, A., & Morgan, C. (1949). *Applied experimental psychology human factors in engineering design*. New York: Wiley Publications.

Chapman, A. J., Sheehy, N. P., & Livingston, M. S. (1994). Psychology and law. In P. Spurgeoon, R. Davies, & A. J. Chapman (Eds.), *Elements of applied psychology*. Amsterdam: Harwood Academic Publishers.

Chapman, P. & Underwood, G. (2000). Forgetting near accidents: The role of severity, culpability, and experience in the poor recall of dangerous driving situations. *Applied Cognitive Psychology, 14*, 31-44..

Charness, N., & Schuletus, R. S. (1999). Knowledge and expertise. In F. Durso (Ed.), *Handbook of applied cognition*. New York: Wiley.

Chase, W. G., & Ericsson, K. A. (1981). Skilled memory. In J. R. Anderson (Ed.), *Cognitive skills and their acquisition*. Hillsdale, NJ: Erlbaum.

Chase, W. G., & Simon, H. A. (1973a). Perception in chess. *Cognitive Psychology, 4*, 55-81.

Chi, M. T. H., Feltovich, P. J., & Glosser, R. (1981). Catorization and representation of physics problems by experts and novices. *Cognitive Science, 5*, 121-152.

Chmiel, N., Totterdell, P., & Folkard, S. (1995). On adaptive control, sleep loss, and fatigue. *Applied Cognitive Psychology, 9*, S39-S53.

Chodzko_Zajko, W.J. (1991). Physical fitness, cognitive performance, and aging. *Medicine and Science in Sports and Exercise, 23*, 868-872.

Christianson, S. A. (Ed.).(1992). *The Handbook of Emotion and Memory: Research and theory*. Hillsdale, NJ: Erlbaum.

Christianson, S. A, & Hübinette, B. (1993). Hands up! A study of witnesses' emotional reactions and memories associated with bank robberies. *Applied Cognitive Psychology, 7*, 365-380.

Christianson, S., A., & Nilsson, L. (1989). Hysterical amnesia: A case of aversively motivated isolation of memory. In T. Archer & I. Nilsson (Eds.), *Aversion, avoidance, & anxiety: Perspectives on aversively motivated behavior* (pp. 289-310). Hillsdale, NJ: Erlbaum.

Cialdini, R. B. (1999). *Influence, science, and practice.* (2nd Ed.). Glenview, IL: Scorr Foresman.

Clancy Dollinger, S.M., & Hoyer, W.J. (1995). Skill differences in medical laboratory diagnostics. *Applied Cognitive Psychology, 9,* 235-247.

Clarkson-Smith, L., & Hartley, A. A. (1989). Relationships between physical exercise & cognitive abilities in older adults. *Psychology & Aging, 4,* 183-189.

Clegg, C. (1994). Psychology and information technology: The study of cognition in organizations. *British Journal of Psychology, 85,* 449-477.

Clore, G. L., Ortony, A., & Foss, M. (1987). The psychological foundations of the affective lexicon. *Journal of Personality & Social Psychology, 53,* 751-766.

Cochran, E. L. (1994). Basic versus applied research in cognitive science: A view from industry. *Ecological Psychology, 6,* 131-136.

Cockburn, J., (1996). Assessment and treatment of prospective memory deficits. In M. Brandimonte, G. Einstein, & McDaniel, Eds., *Prospective memory: Theory and applications.* Hillsdale, NJ: Erlbaum.

Cohen, G. (1989). *Memory in the real world.* Hillsdale, NJ: Erlbaum.

Cohen, G., & Java, R. (1995). Memory for medical history: accuracy of recall. *Applied Cognitive Psychology, 9,* 273-288.

Cohen, J. D. & Schooler, J. W. (Eds.), (1997). *Scientific approaches to consciousness.* Mahwah, NJ: Erlbaum.

Cole, M., & Gay, J. (1972). Culture and memory. *American Anthropologist, 74(5),* 1066-1084.

Cole, M., & Means, B. (1981). *Comparative studies of how people think.* Cambridge, MA: Harvard University Press.

Cole, M., & Scribner, S. (1974*). Culture and thought: A psychological introduction.* New York: John Wiley.

Colley, A. M., & Beech, J. R. (1989). *Acquisition and performance of cognitive skills.* New York: Wiley.

Colwell, K., Hiscock, C. K., & Menon, A. (2002). Interviewing techniques and the assessment of statement credibility. *Applied Cognitive Psychology, 17,* 287-300.

Conrad, F. G. (1997a). Basic and applied memory research: Empirical, theoretical, and metatheoretical issues. In D. G. Payne & F. G. Conrad (Eds.), *Intersections in basic and applied memory research.* Mawah, NJ: Erlbaum.

Conrad, F. G, (1997b). Using expert systems to model and improve survey classification processes. In Lyberg, Biemer, Collins, de Leeuw, Dippo, Schwarz, and Trewin (Eds). *Survey Measurement and Process Quality.* New York: Wiley.

Conway, M. A. (1993). Method and meaning in memory research. In G. M. Davies & RH. Logie (Eds.), *Memory in everyday life*. New York: North Holland.

Conway, M. A. (1995). *Flashbulb memories*. Hove, UK: Erlbaum.

Conway, M.A. (1997). *Cognitive models of memory*. New York: Bradford.

Conway, M. A. (1997b*). Cognitive models of memory*. New York: Bradford.

Conway, M. A., Collins, A. F., Gathercole, S. E., & Anderson, S. J. (1996). Recollections of true and false autobiographical memories. *Journal of Experimental Psychology: General, 125(1)*, 69-95.

Conway, M. A., & Dewhurst, S. A. (1995). The self and recollective experience. *Applied Cognitive Psychology, 9*, 1-19.

Cook, G. I., Marsch, R. L., & Hicks, J. L. (2005). Associating a time-based prospective memory task with an expected context can improve or impair intention completeion. *Applied Cognitive Psychology, 19*, 345-360.

Cook, S., & Wilding, J. (1997). Earwitness testimony: Never mind the variety, hear the length. *Applied Cognitive Psychology, 11*, 95-111.

Cooke, N. J. (1999). Knowledge elicitation. In F. Durso (Ed.), *Handbook of applied cognition*. New York: Wiley.

Cornoldi, C., & de Beni, R. (1991). Memory for discourse: loci mnemonics and the oral presentation effect. *Applied Cognitive Psychology, 5*, 511-518.

Corr, P.J., Pickering, A.D. & Gray, J. A. (1995). Sociabilityimpulsivity and caffeine-induced arousal: Critical flickerfusion frequency and procedural learning. *Personality and Individual Differences, 22*, 805-815.

Cowan, N. (2001). The magical number 4 in short-term memory: A reconsideration of mental storage capacity. *Brain & Behavioral Science, , 24*, 87-185.

Coxon, P., & Valentine, T. (1997). Effects of the age of eyewitnesses on the accuracy and suggestibility of their testimony. *Applied Cognitive Psychology, 11*, 415- 430.

Craik, F. I. M., & Lockhart, R. S. (1972). Levels of processing: A framework for memory research. *Journal of Verbal Learning and Verbal Behavior, 111*, 671-684.

Crain-Thoreson, C., (1996). Phonemic processes in children's listening and reading comprehension. *Applied Cognitive Psychology, 10*, 383-401.

Cramer, J. A., Mattson, R. H., Prevey, M. L., Scheyer, R. D., & Ouellette, V. L. (1989). How often is medication taken as prescribed? A novel assessment technique. *Journal of the American Medical Association, 261*, 3273-3277.

Crawford, M., Herrmann, D., Randal, E., Holdsworth, M., & Robbins, D. (1989). Self perception of memory performance as a function of gender. *British Journal of Psychology, 80*, 391-401

Crawford, M. & Unger, R. (2004). *Women and gender: A feminist psychology*. (4 th ed.). Boston: McGraw Hill.

Cronbach, L. J., & Meehl, P. E. (1955). Construct validity in psychological tests. *Psychological Bulletin, 52*, 281-302.

Crook III, T.H., & Longjohn, J.R. (1993). Development of treatments for memory disorders: the necessary meeting of basic and everyday memory research. *Applied Cognitive Psychology, 7*, 619-630.

Crook, T., Bartus, R. T., Ferris, S. H., Whitehouse, P., Cohen, G. D., & Gershon, S. (1986). Age-associated memory impairment: Proposed diagnostic criteria and measures of clinical change -- Report of a National Institute of Mental Health work group. *Developmental Neuropsychology, 2*, 261-276.

Crowder, R. (1993). Faith and skepticism in memory research. In G. M. Davies & R. H. Logie, (Eds.). *Memory in everyday life*. Amsterdam: North Holland.

Crundall, D., Chapman, P., France, E., Underwood, G., & Phelps, N. (2005). What attracts attention during police pursuit driving? *Applied Cognitive Psychology, 19*, 409 - 420.

Cutler, B. L., & Penrod, S. D. (1995). *Mistaken identification: The eyewitness, psychology, and the law*. New York: Cambridge University Press.

Cutler, S., & Grams, A. E. (1988). Correlates of self reported everyday memory problems. *Journal of Gerontology: Social Sciences, 43*, 582-590.

Daee, S., & Wilding, J. M. (1977). Effects of high intensity white noise on short-term memory for position in a list and sequence. *British Journal of Psychology, 68*, 335-349.

Dansereau, D. F., & Newbern, D. (1997). Using knowledge maps to enhance teaching. In W. E. Campbell & K. A. Smith (Eds.), *New paradigms for college teaching*. Edina, MN: Interaction Book Company.

Das, J. P., Kar, B. C., & Parrila, R. K. (1996). *Cognitive planning: The psychological basis of intelligent behavior*. New Deli: Sage.

Davenport, J. L., Studebaker, C. A., & Penrod, S. (1999). Perspectives on jury decision-making: Cases on pretrial publicity and cases based on eyewitness identifications. In F. Durso (Ed.), *Handbook of applied cognition*. New York: Wiley.

Davies, G. M. (1981). Face recall systems. In G. Davies, H. Ellis, & J. Shepherd (Eds.), *Perceiving and remembering faces* (pp. 227-250). London: Academic Press.

Davies, G. M., & Logie, R. H. (Eds.).(1993). *Memory in everyday life*. Amsterdam: North Holland.

Davies, G., M. & Pressley, M. (1993). Editorial. *Applied Cognitive Psychology, 7*, 95.

Davies, G. M. & Thomson, D. M. (1988). Memory in context: context in memory. Chichester: Wiley.

Davis, M. R., McMahon, M., & Greenwood, K. M. (2005). The efficacy of menomic components of the Cognitive Inteview: Towards a shortned variant for time-critical investigations. *Applied Cognitive Psychology, 19*, 75-94.

Deffenbacher, K. A. (1996). Updating the scientific validity of three key estimator variables in eyewitness testimony. In D. Herrman, C. McEvoy, C. Herzog, P. Hertel, & M. Johnson, M. K. (Eds.*), Basic and applied memory research.* Mahwah: Erlbaum.

DeGroot , A. D. (1966). Perception and memory versus thought: Some old ideas and recent findings. In B. Kleinmuntz (Ed.), *Problem Solving.* New York: Wiley.

Dekker, S. (2002). *The field guide to human error investigations.* Mahwa, N.J.; Erlbaum.

Dekle, D. J., Beal, C. R., Elliott, R., & Huneycutt, D. (1996). Children as witnesses: a comparison of lineup versus showup identification methods. *Applied Cognitive Psychology, 10*, 1-12.

Denis, M., Pazzaglia, F., Cornoldi, C., & Bertolo, L. (1999). Spatial discourse and navigation: an analysis of route directions in the city of Venice. *Applied Cognitive Psychology, 13*, 145-174.

Dennis, M. J., & Sternberg, R. J. (1999). Cognition and instruction. In F. Durso (Ed.), *Handbook of applied cognition.* New York: Wiley.

Desrochers, A., Wieland, L. D., & Coté, M. (1991). Instructional effects in the use of the mnemonic keyword method for learning German nouns and their grammatical gender. *Applied Cognitive Psychology, 5*, 19-36.

Destun, L.M. & Kuiper, N.A. (1999). Phenomenal characteristics associated with real and imagined events: the effects of event valence and absorption. *Applied Cognitive Psychology, 13*, 175-186.

Devolder, P.A., & Pressley, M. (1992). Causal attributions and strategy use in relation to memory performance differences in younger and older adults. *Applied Cognitive Psychology, 6*, 629-642.

DeWall, C., Wilson, B. & Baddeley, A. (1994). The Extended Rivermead Behavioral Memory Test: A measure of everyday memory performance in normal adults. *Memory, 2*, 149-166.

deWolff, C. J. (1993). Developments in applied psychology. *Applied Psychology: An International Review, 42*, 46-49.

Dietze, P. M., & Thomson, D. M. (1993). Mental reinstatement of context: a technique for interviewing child witnesses. *Applied Cognitive Psychology, 7*, 97-108.

Dippo, C. S. & Herrmann, D. J. (1990). The Bureau of Labor Statistics' Collection Procedures Research Laboratory: Accomplishments and Future Directions. *Seminar on Quality of Federal Data.* Washington, D.C.: Council of Professional Associations on Federal Statistics..

DiTomasso, R. A., & McDermott, P. A. (1981). Dilemma of the untreated control group in applied research: A proposed solution. *Psychological Reports, 49*, 823-828.

Doherty, E. P. (1999). Computing for the disabled using a new brain body interface. Human computer interaction. *Journal of Gerontology, 38*, 682-689.

Dollinger, S.M.C., & Hoyer, W.J. (1996). Age and skill differences in the processing demands of visual inspection. *Applied Cognitive Psychology 10*, 225-239.

Donders, F. C. (1868, republished 1969). On the speed of mental processes. In W. G. Koster (Ed. & trans), *Attention and performance II.* Amsterdam: North Holland.

Donohoe, R. T., & Benton, D. (1999). Declining blood glucose levels after a cognitively demanding task predict subsequent memory. *Nutrtional Neuroscience, 2*, 413-424.

Donovan, M. S., Bransford, J. D., & Pelligrino, J. W. (1999). *How people learn: Bridging research and practices.* Washington, DC: National Academy Press.

Driskell, J. E., & Olmsted, B. (1989). Psychology and the military: Research applications and trends. *American Psychologist, 44*, 43-54.

Dritschel, B. H. (1991). Autobiographical memory in natural discourse. A methodological note. *Applied Cognitive Psychology, 5*, 319-330.

Druckman, D. & Bjork, R. A. (1994). *Learning, Remembering, Believing: Enhancing Human Performance.* Washington, DC: National Academy Press.

Druckman, D., & Swets, J. A. (1988). *Enhancing human performance.* Washington, DC: National Academy Press.

Dubin, R. (1976). Theory building in applied areas. In M. Dunnet (Ed.), *Handbook of industrial organizational psychology.* New York: Wiley.

Dunning, D. & Peretta, S. (2002). Automaticity and eyewitness accuracy: A 10-to12-second rule for distinguishing accurate from inaccurate positive identification. *Journal of Applied Psychology, 87*, 951-962.

Durso, F. T. (Ed.). (1999). *Handbook of applied cognition.* Mahwah, NJ: Erlbaum.

Durso, F. T., & Gronlund, S. D. (1999). Situation awareness. In F. Durso (Ed.), *Handbook of applied cognition.* New York: Wiley.

Durso, F. T., Hackworth, C. A., Barile, A. L., Dougherty, M. R. P., & Ohrt, D.D. (1998). Source monitoring in face-to-face and computer-mediated environments. *Cognitive Technology, 3*, 32-38.

Eagly, A., Kulesa, P., Chen, S. & Chaiken, S. (2001). Do attitudes affect memory? Tests of congeniality hypothesis. *Current Directions in Psychological Science, 10*, 5-10.

Easterbrook, J. (1959). The effect of emotion on cue utilization and the organization of behavior. *Psychological Review, 66*, 183-201.

Ebbinghaus, H. (1885). Uber das gedachtnis: Untersuchugen zur experimentellen psychologie. Leipzig: Dunker & Humboldt. Translated by H. A. Ruger & C. E. Byssenine *as Memory: A contribution to experimental psychology*. New York: Dover, 1913.

Edwards, D., & Potter, J. (1992). The chancellor's memory: rhetoric and truth in discursive remembering. *Applied Cognitive Psychology, 6*, 187-215.

Edworthy, S., & Adams, A. (1996). *Warning design: A research perspective*. London: Taylor & Francis.

Egeth, H. E. (1993). What do we not know about eyewitness identification? *American Psychologist, 48*, 577-580.

Eich, E. & Schooler, J. (Eds.), (2000). Cognition and Memory. Mood and social memory, In J. P. Forgas (Ed.)., *Handbook of affect and social cognition*. Mahwah, NJ: Erlbaum.

Einstein, G., & McDaniel, M. (1990). Normal aging and prospective memory. *Journal of Experimental Psychology: Learning, Memory, and Cognition, 16*, 717-726.

Eisen, M.L., & Carlson, E.B. (1998). Individual differences in suggestibility: examining the influence of dissociation, absorption, and a history of childhood abuse. *Applied Cognitive Psychology, 12*, S47-S61.

Ekman, P. (2001). *Telling lies: Clues to deceit in the marketplace, politics, and marriage.* New York: W.W. Norton & Co.

Elaad, E. (2003). Effects of feedback on the overestimated capacity to detect lies and the underestimated ability to tell lies. *Applied Cognitive Psychology, 17*, 349-364.

Ellis, C. J. & Beaton A. (1993).Factors affecting the learning of foreign language vocabulary: Imagery keyword mnemonics and phonological short term memory. *Quarterly Journal of Experimental Psychology 46A*, 553-568

Ellis, J. A., (1988). Memory for future intentions: Investigating pulses and steps. In M. M. Gruneberg, P. E. Morris, & R. N. Sykes, Eds., *Practical aspects of memory: Current research and issues* (Vol. 1, pp. 371-376). Chichester, England: Wiley

Ellis, J., (1996). Prospective memory or the realization of delayed intentions. In M.
    Brandimonte, G. Einstein, & McDaniel, Eds., *Prospective memory: Theory and
    applications*. Hillsdale, NJ: Erlbaum.

Ellis, J., A., & Jones, D. (1994). Applied cognitive psychology. In P. Spurgeoon, R. Davies,
    & A. J. Chapman (Eds.), *Elements of applied psychology*. Amsterdam:
    Harwood Academic Publishers.

Embretson, S. E. (1999). Cognitive psychology applied to testing. In F. Durso *Handbook
    of Applied Cognition*, Mahwah, NJ: Erlbaum.

Emery, C. F., & Gatz, M. (1990). Psychological & cognitive effects of an exercise program
    for community-residing older adults. *The Gerontologist, 30*, 184-188.

Engel, S. (1999). *Context is everything: The nature of memory*. New York: Freeman.

Engle, P.L., & Lumpkin, J.B. (1992). How accurate are time-use reports? Effects of
    cognitive enhancement and cultural differences on recall accuracy. *Applied
    Cognitive Psychology, 6*, 141-159.

Eley, M.G. (1993). The differential susceptibility of topographic map interpretation to
    influence from training. *Applied Cognitive Psychology, 7*, 23-42.

Ellis, H., Ottaway, S., Varner, L., Becker, A., & Moore, B. (1997). Emotion, motivation, and
    text comprehension: The detection of contradictions in passages. *Journal of
    Experimental Psychology: General, 126*, 131-146.

Erdelyi, M. H. (1996). *The recovery of unconscious memories: Hypermnesia and
    reminiscence*. Chicago: University of Chicago Press.

Ericsson, K. A. (1985). Memory skill. *Canadian Journal of Psychology, 39*, 188-231.

Ericsson. K. A. (2005). Recent advances in expertise research: A commentary on the
    contributions to the special issue. *Applied Cognitive Psychology, 19*, 233-241.

Ericsson, K. A., & Polson, P. G. (1988). An experimental analysis of the mechanisms of a
    memory skill. *Journal of Experimental Psychology: Learning, Memory, and
    Cognition, 14(2)*, 305-316.

Ericsson, K. A., & Simon, H. A. (1993). *Protocol analysis: Verbal reports as data* (Rev. ed).
    Cambridge, MA: MIT Press.

Esgate, A., & Groome, D. et al. (2005). *An introduction to applied cognitive psychology*.
    New York: Psycholoogy Press.

Etnier, J. L., Salazar, W., Landers, D. M., Petruzzello, S. J., Han, M., & Nowell, P. (1997).
    The influence of physical-fitness and exercise upon cognitive functioning - A
    metaanalysis. *Journal of Sport & Exercise Psychology, 19*, 249-277.

Evers, S. M. A. A., Stevens, F. C. J., Diederiks, J. P. M., Ponds, R. W. H. M., Kaplan, C.,
    Drop, M. J., Metsemakers, J. F. M., & Jolles, J. (1997). Age-related differences
    in cognition. *European Journal of Public Health, 8*, 133-139.

Everson, M. D., & Boat, B. W. (1997). Anatomical dolls in child sexual abuse assessments: a call for forensically relevant research. *Applied Cognitive Psychology, 11,* S55-S74.

Eysenck, M. W. (1982). *Attention and arousal: Cognition and performance.* Berlin: Springer.

Eysenck, M. W. (2001). *Principles of cognitive psychology.* London: Taylor & Francis.

Fabrigar, L. R., Smith, S. M., & Brannon, L. A. (1999). Applications of social cognition: Attitudes on cognitive structures. In F. Durso (Ed.), *Handbook of applied cognition.* New York: Wiley.

Fagan, T. K., & VandenBos, G. R. (Eds.). (1993*). Exploring applied psychology: Origins and critical analyses.* Washington, DC: American Psychological Association.

Farley, F., & Null, C. N. (1987). *Using psychological science: Making the public case.* Washington, DC: The Federation of Behavioral, Psychological and Cognitive Sciences.

Featherman, D. L. (1991). Mission-oriented basic research. Items*: Social Science Research Council, 45,* 75-77.

Fiedler, K. (1991). On the task, the measures and the mood in research on affect and social cognition. In J. P. Forgas (Ed.), *Emotion and social judgments* (pp. 83-104). Oxford: Pergamon.

Fiore. S. M., Jentsch, F., & Rubinstein, J. (2004). Science and security: Human-centered research for keeping our nation safe. *Cognitive Technology, 9,* 20-21.

Fiore, S. M., Rubinstein, J., Jentsch, F. (2004). Considering science and security from a broader research perspective. *Cognitive Technology, 9,* 40-42.

Fischoff, B. (1990). Psychology and public policy: Tool or toolmaker? *American Psychologist, 45,* 647-653.

Fisher, R. P., & Geiselman, R. E. (1992). *Memory enhancing techniques for investigating interviewing.* Springfield: Thomas.

Fleishman, E. A., Quaintance, M. K., & Broedling, L. A. (1984). *Taxonomies of human performance.* New York: Academic Press.

Folkard, S. (1979). Time of day and level of processing. *Memory & Cognition, 7,* 247-252.

Folkard, S., & Monk, T. H. (1980). Circadian rhythms in human memory. *British Journal of Psychology, 71,* 295-307.

Folstein, M. F., Folstein, S. E., & McHugh, P. R. (1975). A practical method for grading the cognitive sate of patients for the clinician. *Journal of Psychiatric Research, 12,* 189-198.

Forgas, J. P., & Moylan, S. J.(1987). After the movies. The effects of transient mood states on social judgments. *Personality and Social Psychology Bulletin, 13,* 478-489.

ForsterLee, L., & Horowitz, I. A. (1997). Enhancing juror competence in a complex trial. *Applied Cognitive Psychology, 11*, 305-319.

Forsyth, B. H., & Lessler, J. T. (1991). Cognitive laboratory methods: A taxonomy. In P. P. Biemer, R. Groves, L. E. Lyberg, N. A. Mathiowetz, & S. Sudman. *Measurement errors in surveys.* New York: Wiley.

Foster, J. K., Lidder, P. G., & Sunram, S. I. (1998). Glucose and memory: Fractionation of enhancement effects? *Psychopharmacology, 137*, 259-270.

Foster, R. A., Libkuman, Goldsmith T. M., Schooler, J. W., & Loftus, E. F. (1994). Consequentiality and eyewitness person identification. *Applied Cognitive Psychology, 8*, 107-121.

Fotuhi, M. (2003). *The memory cure: How to protect your brain against memory loss and Alzheimer's disease.* New York: McGraw Hill.

Fowler, R., Hart, J. & Sheehan, M. (1972). A prosthetic memory: An application of the prosthetic environment concept. *Rehabilitation Counseling Bulletin, 15*, 80-85.

Fowles, D. C. (1988). Psychophysiology and pathology: A motivational approach. *Psychophysiology. 25*, 373-391.

Freud, S. (i960). *The psychopathology of everyday life.* In J. Strachey (Ed. and Trans.), The standard edition of the complete psychological works of Sigmund Freud (Vol. 6, pp. 1-289). London: Hogarth Press. (Original work published 1901.)

Friedman, W. J. (1993). Memory for the time of past events. *Psychological Bulletin, 113*, 44-66.

Friendly, M. (1999). Visualizing categorical data. In M. Sirken, D. Herrmann, S. Schecter, N. Schwarz, J. Tanur, & R. Tourangeau, (Eds.*), Cognition and survey research.* Boston: Wiley.

Galotti, K. M. (1995). Memories of a 'decision-map': recall of a real-life decision. *Applied Cognitive Psychology, 9*, 307-319.

Galotti, K. M. (2003). *Cognitive psychology: In and out of the laboratory*, 2nd ed. Belmont, CA: BrooksCole and Wadsworth.

Gardiner, H. (1985). *The mind's new science.* New York: Basic Books.

Gardner, H., Kornhaber, M. L., & Wake, W. K. (1996). *Intelligence: Multiple perspectives.* Fort Worth: Harcourt Brace.

Garner, W. R. (1962). *Uncertainty and structure as psychological concepts.* New York: Wiley.

Garry, M., & Polaschek, D. L. L. (2000). Imagination and memory. Current Directions in *Psychological Science, 9*, 6-9.

Gates S. J., & Colborn, D. K. (1976). Lowering appointment failures in a neighborhood health center. *Medical Care, 14*, 263-267.

Gathercole, S. E., Service, E., Hitch, G. J., Adams, A.M., & Martin, A. J. (1999). Phonological short-term memory and vocabulary development: further evidence on the nature of the relationship. *Applied Cognitive Psychology, 13,* 65-77.

Geiselman, R. E., & Fisher, R. P. (1997). Ten years of cognitive interviewing. In D. G. Payne & F. G. Conrad (Eds.), *Intersections of basic and applied research.* Mahwah: Erlbaum.

Gelzheiser, L. M. (1991). Learning soundsymbol correspondences: transfer effects of pattern detection and phonics instruction. *Applied Cognitive Psychology, 5,* 361-371.

Gentry, M., & Herrmann, D. J. (1990). Memory contrivances in everyday life. *Personality and Social Psychology Bulletin, 18,* 241-253.

Gernsbacher, M. A. (Ed.). (1994). *Handbook of psycholinguistics.* San Diego, CA: Academic Press.

Gianutsos, R. (1991). Cognitive rehabilitation: A neuropsychological specialty comes of age. *Brain Injury, 5,* 353-368.

Gifford, D. R., & Cummings, J. L. (1999). Evaluating dementia screening tests: Methodologic standards to rate their performance. *Neurology, 52,* 224-227.

Gilbert, D. T. (1993). The assent of man: Mental representation and the control of belief. In D. M. Wegner and J. W. Pennebaker (Eds). *Handbook of mental control.* Englewood Cliffs, NJ: Prentice Hall.

Gilbert, D. T., Fiske, S. T., & Lindzey, G. (Eds.). (1998). *The handbook of social psychology.* Oxford: Oxford University Press.

Gilhooly, K. J. (1990). Cognitive psychology and medical diagnosis. *Applied Cognitive Psychology, 4,* 261-272.

Gillan, D. J., & Schvaneveldt, R. W. (1999). Applying cognitive psychology: Bridging the gulf between basic research and cognitive artifacts. In F. Durso (Ed.), *Handbook of applied cognition.* New York: Wiley.

Gilland, S. W., & Day, D. V. (1999). Business management. In F. Durso (Ed.), *Handbook of applied cognition.* New York: Wiley.

Glass, A. L., & Waterman, D. (1988). Predictions of movie entertainment value and the representativeness heuristic. *Applied Cognitive Psychology, 2,* 173-179.

Gluck, M. A., & Myers, C. E. (2000). Gateway to Memory*: An Introduction to Neural Network Modelling of the Hippocampus and Learning.* Cambridge, MA: Bradford.

Gold, P. E. (1986). Glucose modulation of memory storage processing. *Behavioral and Neural Biology, 45,* 342-349.

Gold, P. E., & Greenough, W. T. (Eds.).(2001). *Memory Consolidation.* Washington, DC: APA.

Goldman, S. R., Petrosino, A. J., & Cognition and Technology Group at Vanderbilt. Design principles for instruction in content domains: Lessons from expertise and learning. In F. Durso (Ed.), *Handbook of applied cognition.* New York: Wiley.

Goldstein, E. B. (2004). *Cognitive psychology: Connecting mind, research and everyday experience.* Belmont, CA: Wadsworth.

Goleman, D. (1995). *Emotional intelligence.* New York: Bantam.

Gonder-Frederick, L., Hall, J. L., Vogt, J., Cox, D. J., Green, J. & Gold, P. E. (1987). Memory enhancement in elderly humans: Effects of glucose ingestion. *Physiology & Behavior, 41,* 503-504.

Goodman, G. S., & Schaef, J. M. (1997). Over a decade of research on children's eyewitness testimony: What have we learned? Where do we go from here? *Applied Cognitive Psychology, 11,* S5-S20.

Gorayska, B., Cox, K., Ho, J., & Roberts, T. (1998), Utilising human cognitive resources in browsing face recall systems: an exercise in human computer integration. *Cognitive Technology, 3,* 13-23

Goschke, T. & Kuhl, J. (1996). Remembering what to do: explicit and implicit memory for intentions. In M. Brandimonte, G. Einstein, & McDaniel (Eds.). *Prospective memory: Theory and applications.* Hillsdale, N. J.: Erlbaum.

Graesser, A. C., Baggett, W., & Williams, K. (1996). Question-driven explanatory reasoning. *Applied Cognitive Psychology, 10,* S17-S31.

Graesser, A. C., Person, N. K., & Magliano, J. P. (1995). Collaborative dialogue patterns in naturalistic one-to-one tutoring. *Applied Cognitive Psychology, 9,* 495-522.

Green, D., & Loveluck, V. (1994). Understanding a corporate symbol. *Applied Cognitive Psychology, 8,* 37-47.

Green, D. M., & Swets, J.A. (1966). *Signal-detection theory and psychophysics.* New York: Wiley.

Green, J. P., Lynn, S. J., & Malinoski, P. (1998). Hypnotic pseudomemories, prehypnotic warnings, and the malleability of suggested memories. *Applied Cognitive Psychology, 12,* 431-444.

Greene, E., & Loftus, E. F. (1998). Psycholegal research on jury damage awards. *Current Directions in Psychological Science, 7,* 50-54.

Greene, E., & Wade, R. (1988). Of private talk and public print: general pre-trial publicity and juror decision-making. *Applied Cognitive Psychology, 2,* 123-135.

Greenstock, J, & Pipe, M. E. (1997). Are two heads better than one? Peer support and children's eyewitness reports. *Applied Cognitive Psychology, 11,* 461-483.

Greenwald, A. G. (1980). The totalitarian ego. *American Psychologist, 35*, 603-618.

Greenwald, A. G. (1981). Self and memory. In G. H. Bower (Ed.), *The psychology of learning and motivation* (Vol. 15, pp. 201-236). New York: Academic Press.

Groeger, J.A., & Chapman, P.R. (1996). Judgment of traffic scenes: the role of danger and difficulty. *Applied Cognitive Psychology, 10*, 349-364.

Groeger, J. A. (2000). *Understanding driving: Applying cognitive psychology to a complex everyday task.* . London: Routledge.

Groninger, L. D. (2000). Face-name mediated learning and lont-term retention: The role of images and imagery processes. *American Journal of Psychology, 113*, 199-219.

Grosofsky, A., Payne, D. G., & Campbell, K. D. (1994). Does the generation effect depend upon selective displaced rehearsal? *American Journal of Psychology, 107*, 53-68.

Gruneberg, M. M. (1985). *Computer Linkword: French, German, Spanish, Italian, Greek, Russian, Dutch, Portuguese, Hebrew.* Penfield, NY: Artworx.

Gruneberg, M. M. (1987). *Linkword: French, German, Spanish, Italian, Greek, Russian, Dutch, Portuguese.* London: Corgi Books.

Gruneberg, M. M. (1992). The practical application of memory aids: Knowing how, knowing, when, and knowing when not. In M. M. Gruneberg & P. Morris (Eds.), *Aspects of memory.* London: .

Gruneberg, M. M., & Mathieson, S. (1997). The perceived value of mind maps (spider diagrams) as learning and memory aids. *Cognitive Technology, 2*, 21-24.

Gruneberg, M. M. & Morris, P. (Eds.). (1992a*). Aspects of Memory, Vol. 1, & 2*, 2nd edition. London: Routledge.

Gruneberg, M. M., & Morris, P. E. (1992b). Applying memory research. In M. M. Gruneberg & P. E. Morris (Eds.), *Aspects of memory, Vol. 1*, pp 1-17.

Gruneberg, M. M., Morris, P. E., & Sykes, R. N. (Eds.). (1978). *Practical aspects of memory.* London: Academic Press.

Gruneberg, M. M., Morris, P. E., & Sykes, R. N. (Eds.). (1988). *Practical aspects of memory.* Chichester: Wiley.

Gruneberg, M. M., Morris, P. E., & Sykes, R. N. (1991). The obituary on everyday memory and its practical applications is premature. *American Psychologist, 46*, 74-76.

Gruneberg, M. M., Morris, P. E., Sykes, R. N., & Herrmann, D. J. (1996). The practical application of memory research: Practical problems in the relationship between theory and practice. In D. J. Herrmann, M. Johnson, C. McEvoy, C. Hertzog, & P. Hertel (Eds.), *Basic and applied memory: Theory in context, Vol. 1.* Hillsdale, NJ: Erlbaum.

Gruneberg, M. M., & Sykes, R. N. (1993). The generalizability of confidence-accuracy studies in eyewitnessing. *Memory, 1*, 185-190.

Guadagno, M. A., & Herrmann, D. (1998). Further consideration of the role of socio-economic status in memory performance. *Applied Cognitive Psychology, 12*, 611-616.

Gudjonsson, G. H. (1991). The 'notice to detained persons', PACE codes, and reading ease. *Applied Cognitive Psychology, 5*, 89-95.

Gudjonsson, G. H., & Sigurdsson, J. F. (1996). The relationship of confabulation to the memory, intelligence, suggestibility and personality of prison inmates. *Applied Cognitive Psychology, 10*, 85-92.

Guenther, R.K. (1998). *Human Cognition.* Prentice-Hall, Incorporated: Upper Saddle River, New Jersey.Guilford, J. (1967).

Guilford, J. (1967). *The nature of human intelligence.* New York: McGraw-Hill.

Gunter, B. (1987). *Poor reception: Misunderstanding and forgetting broadcast news.* Hillsdale, NJ: Erlbaum.

Gwyer, P., & Clifford, B. R. (1997). The effects of the cognitive interview on recall, identification, confidence and the confidenceaccuracy relationship. *Applied Cognitive Psychology, 11*, 121-145.

Haberandt, K. (1997). *Cognitive Psychology.* Allyn & Bacon: Needham Heights, MA.

Hagman, J. D., & Rose, A. M. (1983). Retention of military tasks: A review. *Human Factors, 25(2)*, 199-213.

Hall, R. A., & Hall, M. B. (1964) *A brief history of science.* New York: Signet.

Halpern, D. F. (1996). *Thought and knowledge: An introduction to critical thinking.* Mahwah: Erlbaum.

Halpern, D. F. (2002). *Sex differences in cognitive abilities.* Mahwah: Erlbaum.

Halpern, D. F., Blackman, S., & Salzman, B. (1989). Using statistical risk information to assess oral contraceptive safety. *Applied Cognitive Psychology, 3*, 251-260.

Hamid, M. S., Garner, R., & Parente, R. (1996). Improving reading rate and reading comprehension with iconic memory training. *Cognitive Technology, 1*, 19-24.

Hamilton, C. & Parker, C. (1992). *Communicating for results.* Belmont, CA: Wadsworth.

Hammand, K. R. (2000). *Judgements under stress.* New York: Oxford University Press.

Harrell, M., Parente, F., Bellingrath, E. G., & Lisicia, K. A. (1992). *Cognitive rehabilitation of memory: A practical guide.* Rockville: Apen Publishers.

Harris, D., (2001). Engineering psychology and cognitive ergonomics. Burlington, VT: Ashgate.

Harris, J. E. (1980a). Memory aids people use: Two interview studies. *Memory and Cognition, 8*, 31-38.

Harris, J. E., (1980b, May). We have ways of helping you to remember. *Journal of the British Association for Service to the Elderly, 17*, 21-27.

Harris, J. E. (1984). Methods of improving memory. In B. A. Wilson & N. Moffatt (Eds.), *Clinical management of memory problems*. Croon Helm: Beckenham.

Harris, J. E. (1984). Remembering to do things: A forgotten topic. In J. E. Harris & P. E. Morris, Eds., *Everyday memory, actions, and absentmindedness*. Academic Press: London.

Harris, J. E., & Wilkins, A.J. (1982). Remembering to do things: A theoretical framework and an illustrative experiment. *Human Learning, 1*, 123-136.

Harris, R. J. (2004*). A cognitive psychology of mass communication.* Mawah:Erlbaum.

Hartley, L. R. , Lyons, D., & Dunne, M. (1987). Memory and menstrual cycle. *Ergonomics, 30*, 111-120.

Hartley, T. A. (1995). *The psychology of language: From data to theory*. East Sussex, England: Erlbaum.

Hasher, L. & Zacks, R. T. (1979).Automatic and effortful processes in memory. *Journal of Experimental Psychology: General*, 108, 356-388.

Hashtroudi, S., & Parker, E. S. (1986). Acute alcohol amnesia: What is remembered and what is forgotten. In H. D. Cappell, F. B. Glaser, Y. Israel, H. Kalant, W. Schmidt, E. Sellers, & R. C. Smart (Eds*.), Research advances in alcohol and drug problems* (pp. I7cr209). New York: Plenum.

Hashtroudi, S., Johnson, M. K., Vnek, N. & Ferguson, S. A. (1994). Aging and the effects of affective and factual focus on source monitoring and recall. *Psychology and Aging, 9*, 160-170.

Hastie, R. (1993). *Inside the juror: The psychology of juror decision making*. New York, NY: Cambridge University Press. (Excerpts only).

Hastie, R., Hammerle, O., Kerwin, J., Croner, C., & Herrmann, D. (1996). Human performance reading statistical maps. *Journal of Experimental Psychology: Applied, 2*, 3-16.

Hastie, R., & Pennington, N. (1991). Cognitive and social processes in decision making. In L. B. Resnick, J. M. Levine et al. (Eds.), *Perspectives on socially shared cognition* (pp. 308-327). Washington, DC, USA:

Hawkes, G. R. (1973). Strategy for the basic-applied research interaction. *American Psychologist, 28*, 269.

Healy, A. F. (2004). *Experimental cognitive psychology and its applications.* Washington, D. D.: American Psychological Association.

Healy, A. F. & Bourne, L. E., Jr. (1995). *Learning and memory of knowledge and skills: Durability and specificity*. Thousand Oaks: Sage.

Hedge, A. (1994). Environmental psychology. In P. Spurgeoon, R. Davies, & A. J. Chapman (Eds.), *Elements of applied psychology*. Amsterdam: Harwood Academic Publishers.

Hedrick, T. E., Bickman, L., & Rog, D. J. (1993). *Applied research design: A practical guide*. Applied social research methods series, Vol. 32.Thousands Oaks, CA: Sage Publications.

Hekkanen, S. T., & McEvoy, C. (2001). False memories and source-monitoring problems: Criterion differences. *Applied Cognition Psychology, 16*, 73-86.

Helsen, W.F., & Starkes, J.L. (1999). A multidimensional approach to skilled perception and performance in sport. *Applied Cognitive Psychology, 13*, 1-27.

Hempel, C. G. (1966). Philosophy of natural science. Englewood Cliffs, NJ: Prentice Hall.

Hergenhahn, B. R. (1986). *An introduction to the history of psychology*. Belmont, CA: Wadsworth.

Herrmann, D. J. (1990). The representational bias of acquired memory processes. *Zeitschrift fur Psychologie, 198*, 265-281.

Herrmann, D. (1994). The validity of retrospective reports as a function of the directness of retrieval processes. In N. Schwarz & S. Sudman, Eds., *Autobiographical memory and the validity of retrospective reports*. New York: Springer Verlag.

Herrmann, D. J. (1995). Applied cognitive psychology versus applicable cognitive psychology (a review of *Cognitive PsychologyApplied* edited by Chizuko Izawa*). Applied Cognitive Psychology, 9*, 448-449.

Herrmann, D. (1996). Improving prospective memory. In M. Brandimonte, G. Einstein, & McDaniel, Eds., *Prospective memory: Theory and applications*. Hillsdale, NJ: Erlbaum.

Herrmann, D. (1997a). Rewards of public service: Research psychologists in the government. In R. J. Sternberg (Ed.), *Career paths in psychology: Where your degree can take you*. Washington, DC: American Psychological Association.

Herrmann, D. J. (1997b). The relationship between basic research and applied research in memory and cognition. In C. P. Thompson, D. J. Herrmann, D. Bruce, D. G. Payne, J. D. Read, & M. P. Toglia (Eds.), *Event memory: Papers from the first SARMAC Conference*. Hillsdale, NJ: Erlbaum.

Herrmann, D., Brubaker, B., Yoder, C., Sheets, V., & Tio, A. (1999). Devices that remind. In F. Durso (Ed.), *Handbook of applied cognition*. Mahwah, NJ: Erlbaum.

Herrmann, D. & Cadwallader, T. (2000). Societal benefits for treating IQ tests as Measures of Competence. *The General Psychologist, 5*, 1-5.

Herrmann, D. J., & Chaffin, R. (1988*). Memory in historical perspectives: The literature on memory before Ebbinghaus*. New York: Springer Verlag.

Herrmann, D. J., Crawford, M., & Holdsworth, M. (1992). Gender linked differences in everyday memory performance. *British Journal of Psychology, 83*, 221-231.

Herrmann, D. J., & Gruneberg, M. M. (1993). The need to expand the horizons of the practical aspects of memory. *Applied Cognitive Psychology, 7*, 553-566.

Herrmann, D. J. & Gruneberg, M. M. (1999). *How to cure your memory failures.* London: Blandford. Press.

Herrmann, D. & Gruneberg, M. (in press). The Causes and Consequences of Memory Failures in the Workplace and in Everyday Life. In W. Karwowski (Ed.) *International Encyclopedia of Ergonomics and Human Factors.* (2nd edition). Boca Raton, FL: CRC Press.

Herrmann, D., & Guadagno, M. A. (1997). Memory performance and socio-economic status. *Applied Cognitive Psychology, 11*, 113-120.

Herrmann, D. J., & Neisser, U. (1978). An inventory of memory experiences. In M. M. Gruneberg, P. E. Morris, & R. N. Sykes (Eds.), *Practical aspects of memory: The proceedings of an international conference.* New York: Academic Press.

Herrmann, D., & Parente', R. (1994). The multi-modal approach to cognitive rehabilitation. *Journal of Head Trauma Rehabilitation, 4*, 133-142.

Herrmann, D. J., & Petro, S. (1990). Commercial memory aids. *Applied Cognitive Psychology, 4*, 439-450.

Herrmann, D., & Pickle, L.. W. (1996). A cognitive subtask model of the of statistical map reading. *Visual Cognition, 3*, 165-190.

Herrmann, D., & Raybeck, D. (1997). The relationship between basic and applied research cultures. In D. G. Payne & F. G. Conrad (Eds.*), Intersections in basic and applied memory research.* Mawah, NJ: Erlbaum.

Herrmann, D. J. & Rubenfeld, L. (1985). Lexical properties of fact and opinion words. *Journal of Psycholinguistic Research, 14*, 81-95.

Herrmann, D. J., & Searleman, A. (1990). A multi-modal approach to memory Improvement. In G. H. Bower (Ed.), *Advances in learning and motivation* (pp. 147-206). New York: Academic Press.

Herrmann, D., & Yoder, C. (1998). Cognitive technology. In M. Intons-Peterson & D. Best (Eds.), *Distortion in memory.* Mahwah, NJ: Erlbaum.

Herrmann, D., Raybeck, D., & Gruneberg, M. (1998). *A clash between scientific cultures: The relationship between basic and applied research.* Terre Haute, IN: Indiana State University Press.

Herrmann, D. J., Raybeck, D., & Gruneberg, M. (2002). *Improving memory and study skills.* Toronto: Hogrefe & Huber.

Herrmann, D., Gruneberg, M., Fiore, S., Schooler, J. & Torres, R. (in press). Accuracy of Reports of Memory Failures in Everyday Life. In L. Nilson & N. Ohta (Eds)., *Memory & Society*, London: Psychology Press.

Herrmann, D., Plude, D., Yoder, C., & Mullin, P. (1999). Cognitive processing and extrinsic psychological systems: A holistic model of cognition. *Zeitschrift fur Psychologie, 207*, 123-147.

Herrmann, D. Weingartner, H., Searleman, A., & McEvoy, C. (Eds.). (1992*). Memory improvement: Implications for memory theory.* New York: Springer Verlag.

Herrmann, D., Yoder, C., Parente, R., & Schooler, J. (Eds.).(1997). *The first American Cognitive Technology Conference.* Terre Haute: Psychology Department of Indiana State University.

Herrmann, D., Gruneberg, M., Fiore, S., Schooler, J. & Torres, R. (in press). Accuracy of Reports of Memory Failures in Everyday Life. In L. Nilson & N. Ohta (Eds)., *Memory & Society,* London: Psychology Press.

Herrmann, D., McEvoy, C., Hertzog, C., Hertel, P., & Johnson, M. (Eds.). (1996). *Basic and applied memory: Vol. 1. Theory in context.* Mahwah, NJ: Erlbaum.

Herrmann, D., McEvoy, C., Hertzog, C., Hertel, P., & Johnson, M. (Eds.). (1996). *Basic and applied memory: Vol. 2. New Findings.* Mahwah, NJ: Erlbaum.

Herrmann, D., Raybeck, D., Gruneberg, M., Grant, R., & Yoder, C. (1998). The importance of applied research to demonstrating the utility of basic findings and theories: Commentary on Buschke, Sliwinski, and Luddy. *Cognitive Technology, 3*, 9-12.

Herrmann, D., Schooler, C., Caplan, L. J., Darby-Lipman, P., Grafman, J., Schoenbach, C., Schwab, K., & Johnson, M. L. (2001). The latent structure of memory: A confirmatory factor-analytic study of memory distinctions. *Multivariate Behavioral Research, 36,* 29-51

Hersh, N. A., & Treadgold, L. G. (1994). Neuropage: The rehabilitation of memory dysfunction by prosthetic memory and cueing. *NeuroRehabilitation, 4*, 187-197.

Hertel, G., & Fielder, K. (1994). Affective and cognitive influences in a social dilemma game. *European Journal of Social Psychology, 24*, 131-146.

Hertel, P. T. (1988). Monitoring external memory. In M. Gruneberg, P. Morris, & R. Sykes (Eds.), *Practical aspects of memory: Current research and issues, Vol. 2.* Chichester: Wiley.

Hertel, P. T. (1993). Implications of external memory for investigations of mind. *Applied Cognitive Psychology, 7*, 665-674.

Hertel, P. T. (1996). Practical aspects of emotion and memory. In D. J. Herrmann, M. Johnson, C. McEvoy, C. Hertzog, & P. Hertel (Eds.). *Basic and applied memory: Theory in context, Vol. 1.* Hillsdale, NJ: Erlbaum.

Hertzog, C., Park, D. C., Morrell, R. W., & Martin, M. (2000). Ask and ye shall receive: Behavioral specificity in the accuracy of subjective memory complaints. *Applied Cognitive Psychology, 14*, 257-275.

Higbee, K. L. (1988a). *Your memory* (2nd ed.). Englewood Cliffs, NJ: Prentice-Hall.

Higbee, K. L. (1988b). Students' perceptions and reported use of their memories after a memory-improvement course. *Psychological Reports, 86*, 622-628.

Higbee, K. L. (1999). 25 years of memory Improvement: The evolution of a memory-skills course. *Cognitive Technology, 4*, 38-42.

Hill, B., Long, J., Smith, W., & Whitefield, A. (1995). A model of medical reception – the planning and control of multiple task work. *Applied Cognitive Psychology, 9*, S81- S114.

Hintzman, D. L. (1990). *Human learning and memory: Connections and dissociations.* Palo Alto: Annual Reviews.

Hippler, H. J., Schwarz, N., & Sudman, S. (Eds.). (1987). *Social information processing and survey methodology.* New York: Springer Verlag.

Hirshman, E., & Lanning, K. (1999). Is there a special association between self judgements and conscious recollection? *Applied Cognitive Psychology, 13*, 29-42.

Hirt, E. R., Lynn, S. J., Payne, D. G., Krackow, E., & McCrea, S. M. (1999). Expectancies and memory: Inferring the past from what must have been. In I. Kirsch (Ed.), *How expectancies shape experiences.* Washington, DC, American Psychological Association.

Hockey, R. (1983). *Stress and fatigue in human performance.* Chichester: Wiley.

Hockey. R. (1984). Varieties of attentional state: The effects of environment. In R. Parasuraman and D. R. Davies (Eds.), *Varieties of Attention*, New York: Academic Press.

Hoffman, R. R. (1997). How to doom yourself to repeat the past: Some reflections on the history of cognitive technology. *Cognitive Technology, 2*, 4-15.

Hoffman, R. R., & Deffenbacher, K. A. (1992). A brief history of applied cognitive psychology. *Applied Cognitive Psychology, 6*, 1-48.

Hoffman, R. R., & Deffenbacher, K. A. (1993). An ecological sortie into the relations of basic and applied science: Recent turf wars in human factors and applied cognitive psychology. *Ecological Psychology, 5*, 315-352.

Hoffman, R. R., Shadbolt, N. R., Burton, A., & Klein, G. (1995). Eliciting knowledge from experts: A methodological analysis. *Organizational Behavior and Human Decision Processes, 62,* 129-158.

Holland, J. (1994). *The Occupations Finder.* Odessa, FL:PAR Inc.

Holland, C.A., & Rabbitt, P.M.A. (1992). People's awareness of their age-related sensory and cognitive deficits and the implications for road safety. *Applied Cognitive Psychology, 6,* 217-231.

Hollands, J. G., & Spence, I. (1998). Judging proportion with graphs: the summation model. *Applied Cognitive Psychology, 12,* 173-190.

Holley, P.E., & McEvoy, C.L. (1996). Aging and inhibition of unconsciously processed Information: no apparent deficit. *Applied Cognitive Psychology, 10,* 241-256.

Hollingsworth, H. L., & Poffenberger, A. T. (1929). *Applied psychology.* New York: D. Appleton.

Holyoak, K. J., & Thagard, P. (1994). *Mental leaps: Analogy in Creative Thought.* New York: Bradford.

Honeycutt, J.M. & Cantril, J.G. (2000). *Cognition, communication and romantic relations.* New York: Erlbaum.

Horawitz, I. & Bordens, R. (2002). The effects of jury size, evidence complexity, and note-taking on jury process and performance in a civil trial. *Journal of Applied Psychology, 87,* 121-130.

Hovland, C. I., Janis,I. L. & Kelly H. H. (1953). *Communication and persuasion: Psychological Studies of Opinion Change.* New Haven, CT: Yale University   Press.

Huff, D. (1954). *How to lie with statistics.* New York: Norton.

Humphreys, M. S., & Revelle, W., (1984). Personality, motivation, and performance: A theory of the relationship between individual differences and information processing., *Psychological Review, 91,* 153-184.

Hunt, R. R., & Ellis, H. C. (2004). *Fundamentals of cognitive psychology.* Boston: McGraw Hill.

Humphreys, M. S., & Revelle, W., (1984). Personality, motivation, and performance: A theory of the relationship between individual differences and information processing. *Psychological Review, 91,* 153-184.

Hutchins, E. (1995). *Cognition in the wild.* Cambridge, MA: MIT Press.

Huttenlocher, J., Hedges, L. V. & Bradburn, N. M. (1990). Reports of elapsed time; Bounding and rounding processes in estimation. *Journal of learning, memory and cognition, 16,* 196-213.

Huttenlocher, J., Hedges, L. V. & Prohaska, V. (1988). Hierarchical organization in ordered domains: Estimating dates of events. *Psychological Review, 95,* 471-484.

Hux, K., Reid, R., & Lugert, M. (1994). Self-instruction training following neurological injury. *Applied Cognitive Psychology, 8,* 259-271.

Hyde, J.S. & Linn, M. C. (1988). Gender differences in verbal ability: A meta-analysis. *Psychological Bulletin, 104,* 53-69.

Hyman, Jr., I.E., Gilstrap, L.L., Decker, K., & Wilkinson, C. (1998). Manipulating remember and know judgements of autobiographical memories: an investigation of false memory creation. *Applied Cognitive Psychology, 12,* 371-386.

Idzikowski, C. (1984). Sleep and memory. *British Journal of Psychology, 75,* 439-449.

Intons-Peterson, M. J. (1997). How basic and applied research inform each other. In D. G. Payne and F. G. Conrad (Eds.) Intersections in basic and applied memory resaerch. Mawah, N.J.: Erlbaum.

Intons-Peterson, M. J. & Newsome, G. L. III (1992). External memory aids: Effects and effectiveness. In D. Herrmann, H. Weingartner, A., Searleman, C. *Memory Improvement.* New York: Springer Verlag.

Isen, A.M. (1987). Positive affect, cognitive processes, and social behavior. In L. Berkowitz (Ed.). *Advances in experimental social psychology* (vol. 20, pp. 203-253): New York: Academic Press.

Izawa, C. (1993). *Cognitive Psychology Applied.* Hillsdale, N.J.: Lawrence Erbaum.

Jabine, T. B., Straf, M. L., Tanur, J. M., & Tourangeau, R. (1984).*Cognitive aspects of survey methodology: Building a bridge between disciplines.* Washington, D. C.: National Academy Press.

Jacoby, L., Lindsay, D. & Toth, J. (1992). Unconscious influences revealed: Attention, awareness, and control. *American Psychologist, 37,* 802-809.

Jahnke, J.C. & Nowaczyk, R. H. (1998). *Cognition.* Prentice-Hall: Upper Saddle River, NJ.

Jelsma, O., & Pieters, J.M. (1989). Practice schedule and cognitive style interaction in learning a maze task. *Applied Cognitive Psychology, 3,* 73-83.

Jennings, J. R. (1986a) Bodily changes during attending. In M. G. H. Coles, E. Donchin, and S. W. Porges (Eds.) *Psychophysiology: Systems, Processes, and Applications.* New York: Guilford.

Jennings, J. R. (1986b) Memory, thought, and bodily response. In M. G. H. Coles, E. Donchin, and S. W. Porges (Eds.) *Psychophysiology: Systems, Processes, and Applications.* New York: Guilford.

Jentsch, F. , Barnett, J., Bowers, C. A., & Salas, E. (1999). Who is flying this plane anyway? What mishaps tell us about crew member role assignment and air crew situation awareness. *Human Factors, 41,* 1-14.

Jobe, J. B., & Herrmann, D. (1996). Comparison of survey cognition and models of memory. In D. Herrmann, C. McEvoy, C. Hertzog, P. Hertel, & M. Johnson (Eds.), *Basic and applied memory research: New findings.* Hillsdale, NJ: Erlbaum.

Jobe, J. B., & Mingay, D. J. (1991). Cognition and survey measurement: History and overview. *Applied Cognitive Psychology, 5,* 173-175.

Jobe, J. B., Tourangeau, R., & Smith, A. F. (1993). Contributions of survey research to the understanding of memory. *Applied Cognitive Psychology, 7,* 567-584.

Johansson, O., Andersson, J. & Ronnberg, J. (2000). Do elderly couples have a better prospective memory than other elderly people when they collaborate? *Applied Cognitive Psychology, 14,* 121-133.

Johnson, D., & Field, D. R. (1981). Applied and basic social research: A difference in social context. *Leisure Sciences, 4,* 269-279.

Johnson, M. K. (1996). Fact, fastasy, and public policy. In D. J. Herrmann, M. Johnson, C. McEvoy, C. Hertzog, & P. Hertel (Eds.), *Basic and applied memory: Theory in context,* Vol. 1. Hillsdale, NJ: Erlbaum.

Johnson, M.K. (1997). Identifying the origin of mental experience. In M.S. Myslobodsky (Ed.), Mythomanias: *The nature of deception and self-deception* (pp. 133-180). Hillsdale, NJ: Erlbaum.

Johnson, M. K., Hashtroudi, S. & Lindsay, D.S. (1993). Source monitoring. *Psychological Bulletin, 114,* 3-28.

Johnson, M. H., & Magaro, P. A. (1987). Effects of mood and severity on memory processes in depression and mania. *Psychological Bulletin, 89,* 28-40.

Johnson, M. K., & Raye, C. L. (1981). Reality monitoring. *Psychological Review, 88,* 67-85.

Jones, G. & Adam, J. (1979). Towards a prosthetic memory. *Bulletin of the British Psychological Society, 32,* 165-167.

Kahl, B., & Woloshyn, V. E. (1994). Using elaborative interrogation to facilitate acquisition of factual information in cooperative learning settings: one good strategy deserves another. *Applied Cognitive Psychology, 8,* 465-478.

Kahneman, D., Slovic, P., & Tversky, A. (1982). *Judgment under uncertainty: Heuristics and biases.* Cambridge, U: Cambridge University Press.

Kalyuga, S., Chandler, P., & Sweller, J. (1999). Managing split-attention and redundancy in multimedia instruction. *Applied Cognitive Psychology, 13,* 351-371.

Kapur, N. (1988). *Memory disorders in clinical practice.* London: Butterworth.

Kasper, L. F., & Glass, A. L. (1988). An extension of the keyword method facilitates the acquisition of simple Spanish sentences. *Applied Cognitive Psychology, 2,* 137-146.

Kaufmann, G., & Vosburg, S. (1999). "Paradoxical" mood effects on creative problem-solving. *Cognition & Emotion, 11*, 151-170.

Keane, M. T. (2005). *Cognitive Psychology.* Hove: Psychology Press.

Kearns, K. P. (1986). Flexibility of single-subject experimental designs; II. Design selection and arrangement of experimental phases. *Journal of Speech and Hearing Disorders, 51*, 204-214.

Kellog, R. T. (2002). *Cognitive psychology.* Thousand Oaks: Sage.

Keogh, L., & Markham, R. (1998). Judgements of other people's memory reports: differences in reports as a function of imagery vividness. *Applied Cognitive Psychology, 12*, 159-171.

Kernaghan, K., & Woloshyn, V. E. (1995). Providing grade one students with multiple spelling strategies: comparisons between strategy instruction, strategy instruction with metacognitive information, and traditional language arts. *Applied Cognitive Psychology, 9*, 157-166.

Khan, A. U. (1986). *Clinical Disorders of Memory.* New York: Plenum.

Kiewra, K. (1989). A Review of note-taking: The Encoding-storage paradigm and beyond. *Educational Psychology Review, 1*, 147-172.

Kiewra, K., Dubois, N., Christian, D., McShane, A., Meyerhoffer, M. & Roshkelley, D. (1991). Note-taking functions and techniques. *Journal of Educational Psychology, 83*, 240-245.

Kim, H. J., Burke, D. T., Dowds, M. M. Jr., Boone, K. A., & Park, G. J. (2000). Electronic memory aids for out patient brain injury: Followup findings. *Brain Injury, 14*, 187-196.

King, A. (1991). Improving lecture comprehension: effects of a metacognitive strategy. *Applied Cognitive Psychology, 5*, 331-346.

Kintsch, W. (1974). *The representation of meaning in memory.* Hillsdale, NJ: Erlbaum.

Klatzky, R. L. (1984) *Memory and Awareness.* New York: W. H. Freeman.

Klein, G. (1997). *Sources of power: How people make decisions.* London: Bradford.

Kleinsmith, L. J. & Kaplan, S. (1963). Paired associate learning as a function of arousal and interperlated interval. *Journal of Experimental Psychology, 66*, 190-196.

Klix, F. (1980). On the structure and function of semantic memory. In F. Klix, J. Hoffman, & E. van der Meer (Eds*), Cognitive research in psychology.* Amsterdam: North Holland.

Kobasa, S. C. (1979). Stressful life events, personality, and health: An inquiry into hardiness. *Journal of Personality and Social Psychology, 37*, 1-11.

Kohn, L. T., Corrigan, J. M., & Donaldson, M. S. (Eds). (2000). *To err is human: Building a safer health system.* Washington, DC: National Academy Press.

Kolakowsky, S. A, (1997). Improving Cognition through the Use of Nutrients, Drugs, and other Cognitive-Enhancing Substances. *Cognitive Technology, 2,* 44-54.

Koriat, A. (1993). How do we know that we know? The accessibility account of the feeling of knowing. *Psychological Review, 100,* 609-639.

Koriat, A. (1994). Memory's knowledge of its own knowledge: The accessibility account of the feeling of knowing. In J. Metcalfe & A. P. Shimamura (Eds.), *Metacognition* (pp. 115-136).

Koriat, A. & Fischhoff, B. (1974). What day is today? An inquiry into the process of time orientation. *Memory and Cognition, 2,* 201-205.

Koriat, A., & Goldsmith, M. (1996). Memory metaphors and the laboratoryreal life controversy: Correspondence versus storehouse views of memory. *Brain and Behavior, 19,* 167-228.

Kosslyn, S. M. (1989) Understanding charts and graphs. *Applied Cognitive Psychology, 3,* 185-226.

Kosslyn, S. M. (1995). Mental imagery. In S. M. Kosslyn & D. N. Osherson (Eds.), *Visual cognition: An introduction to cognitive science.* Cambridge, MA: MIT Press.

Kovera, M. B., & Borgida, E. (1997). Expert testimony in child sexual abuse trials: the admissibility of psychological science. *Applied Cognitive Psychology, 11,* S105- S129.

Kramer, A.F., Hahn, S., Cohen, N.J., Banich, M.T., McAuley, E., Harrison, C.R., Chason, J., Vakil, E., Bardell, L., Boileau, R.A., & Colcombe, A. (1999). Ageing, fitness and neurocognitive function. *Nature, 400,* 418-419.

Kreutzer, J. S., & Wehman, P. H. (1991). *Cognitive rehabilitation for persons with traumatic brain injury: A functional approach.* Baltimore: Paul H. Brookes.

Krishnan, H. S., & Shapiro, S. (1996). Comparing implicit and explicit memory for brand names from advertisements. *Journal of Experimental Psychology: Applied, 2,* 147-163.

Krosnick, J. A. (1991). Response strategies for coping with the cognitive demands of attitude measures in surveys. *Applied Cognitive Psychology, 5,* 213-236.

Kruysse, H.W. (1992). How slips result in traffic conflicts and accidents. *Applied Cognitive Psychology, 6,* 607-618.

Kuhn, T. S. (1962). *The structure of scientific revolutions.* Chicago: University of Chicago Press.

Kurlychek, R. T. (1983). Use of a digital alarm chronograph as a memory aid in early dementia. *Clinical Gerontologist,1,* 93-94.

Kvavilashvili, L. (1998). Remembering intentions: testing a new method of investigation. *Applied Cognitive Psychology, 12,* 533-554.

LaBerge, D. (1995). *Attentional processing: The brains art of mindfulness*. Cambridge, MA: Harvard University Press.

Lachman, R., Lachman, J. L., & Butterfield, E. C. (1979). *Cognitive psychology and information processing: An introduction*. Hillsdale, NJ: Erlbaum.

Lambiotte, J. G., Skaggs, L. P., & Dansereau, D. F. (1993). Learning from lectures: effects of knowledge maps and cooperative review strategies. *Applied Cognitive Psychology, 7*, 483-497.

Lampinen, J. M., Neuschatz, J. S., & Payne, D. G. (1997). Memory illusions and consciousness: Exploring the phenomenology of true and false memories. *Current Psychology, 16*, 181-224.

Lampinen, J. M., Neuschatz, J. S., & Payne, D. G. (1999). Source attributions and false memories: A test of the demand characteristics account. *Psychonomic Bulletin and Review, 6*, 130-135.

Landauer, T. K. (1996). *The trouble with computers*. Cambridge, MA: MIT Press.

Landauer, T. K., & Ross, B. H. (1977). Can simple instructions to used spaced practice improve ability to remember a fact?: An experimental test using telephone numbers. *Bulletin of the Psychonomic Society, 10*, 215-218.

Landy, F. J. (1993). Basic applied psychology: Which is the cart and which is the horse. *Applied Psychology: An International Review, 42*, 49-51.

Lansdale, M., & Cotes, E. (1999). Analysing uncertainty in location memory: issues in the design of spatial database systems. *Applied Cognitive Psychology, 13*, 237-256.

Larigauderie, P., Gaomac'h, D., & Lacroix, N. (1998). Working memory and error detection in texts: What are the roles of the central executive and the phonological loop? *Applied Cognitive Psychology, 12*, 505-527.

Larrabee, G. J., & Crook, T. H. (1989). A computerized battery for assessment of memory. In R. L. West & J. D. Sinnot (Eds.), *Everyday memory and aging: Current research and methodology*. New York: Springer Verlag.

Larson, G.E., & Perry, Z.A. (1999). Visual capture and human error. *Applied Cognitive Psychology, 13*, 227-236.

Lave, J. (1988). *Cognition in practice: Mind, mathematics, and culture in everyday life*. Cambridge, MA: Cambridge University Press.

Leahley, T. H., & Harris, R.J. (1997). *Learning and cognition* (fourth edition). Upper Saddle River, NJ: Prentice-Hall, Inc.

Leirer, V.O., Decker Tanke, E., & Morrow, D.G. (1993). Commercial cognitivememory systems. *Applied Cognitive Psychology, 7*, 675-689.

Leirer, V. O., Morrow, D. G., & Tanke, E. D. (1994, August). Moving off the campus and into the community: The relation between basic and applied research. Presented at the third international Practical Aspects of Memory Conference, College Park, MD.

Leirer, V. O., Morrow, D. G., Pariante, G. M., & Sheikh, J. I. (1991). Elder's nonadherence, its assessment and computer assisted instruction for medication recall training. *Journal of the American Gerontological Society, 36*, 877-884.

Leirer, V. O., Morrow, D. G., Tanke, E., & Pariante, G. M., (1991). Elder's nonadherence: Its assessment and medication reminding by voice mail. *Gerontology, 31*, 514-520.

Leirer, V. O, Tanke, E. D., Morrow, D. G., & Kahn, J. (1997). 10-minute interventions for remembering peoples' names, directions to places, and household objects' locations: Computerized memory training for older adults. *Cognitive Technology, 2*, 25-39.

Lens, W. (1987). Theoretical research should be useful and used. *International Journal of Psychology, 22*, 453-461.

Lessler, J., Tourangeau, R., & Salter, W. (1989). Questionnaire design in the cognitive research laboratory. *Vital and Health Statistics, Series 6*, Number 1, Washington, DC: U.S. Government Printing Office

Levi, A. M., & Almog, J. (2000). Cognitive technology and criminal justice: The police composite. *Cognitive Technology, 5*, 26-34.

Levine, J. M., & Murphy, G. (1943). The learning and forgetting of controversial material. *Journal of Abnormal and Social Psychology, 38*, 507-517.

Levy, J. & Heller, W. (1992). Gender differences in human neuropsychological function. In A.A. Gerall, H. Moltz & I. L. Ward (Eds.), *Handbook of behavioral neurobiology* (Vol. 11, pp245-274). New York: Plenum Press.

Levy-Leboyer, C. (1993). The chicken and the egg: Which came first. *Applied Psychology: An International Review, 42*, 52-54.

Lewandowsky, S. (1999). Statistical graphs and maps: Higher level cognitive processes. In M. Sirken, D. Herrmann, S. Schecter, N. Schwarz, J. Tanur, & R. Tourangeau (Eds.), *Cognition and survey research*. Boston: Wiley.

Lewandowsky, S. & Behrens, J. (1999). Statistical graphs and maps. In F. T. Durso (Ed.), *Handbook of Applied Cognition*. New York: Wiley.

Lewandowsky, S., Herrmann, D. J., Behrens, J. T, Li, S,C., Pickle, L, & Jobe, J. B. (1993). Perception of clusters in statistical maps. *Applied Cognitive Psychology, 7*, 533- 531.

Lewkowicz, S. S., &, Whitton, J. L. (1995). The new inventory for exploring neuropsychological change resulting from brain injury. *Cognitive Rehabilitation, 1*, 8-20.

Lindholm, T., Christianson, S,A., & Karlsson, I. (1997). Police officers and civilians as witnesses: intergroup biases and memory performance. *Applied Cognitive Psychology, 11*, 431-444.

Lindsay, D. S., & Read, J. D. (1994). Psychotherapy and memories of childhood sexual abuse: A cognitive perspective. Special Issue: Recovery of memories of childhood sexual abuse. *Applied Cognitive Psychology, 8*, 281-338.

Lindsay, R. C. L. (1999). Applying applied research: selling the sequential line-up. *Applied Cognitive Psychology, 13*, 219-225.

Linton, M. (1975). Memory for real-world events. In D. A. Norman & D. E. Rumelhart (Eds.), *Explorations in cognition* (pp. 376-404). San Francisco: Freeman.

Linton, M. (1986). Ways of searching and the contents of memory. In D. Rubin *autobiographical memory* (pp. 50-67). New York: Cambridge University Press.

Linton, M. (2000). Transformations of memory in everyday life. In U. Neisser & J. I. E. Hyman (Eds.), *Memory observed: Remembering in natural contexts* (2nd ed.). New York: Worth Publishers.

Lipman, P. D., Caplan, L. J., Schooler, C., & Lee, J. (1995). Inside and outside the mind: The effects of age, organization, and access to external sources on retrieval of life events. *Applied Cognitive Psychology, 9*, 289-306.

Loftus, E. F. (1979). *Eyewitness testimony*. Cambridge, MA: Harvard University Press.

Loftus, E. F. (1991). The glitter of everyday memory .... And the gold. *American Psychologist, 46*, 16-18.

Loftus, E. F. (1997). Creating childhood memories. *Applied Cognitive Psychology, 11*, S75-S86.

Loftus, E. F., & Ketcham, K. (1994). *The myth of repressed memory: False memories and allegations of sexual abuse*. New York: St. Martins Press.

Loftus, E. F., & Marburger, W. (1983). Since the eruption of Mt. St. Helens, has anyone beaten you up? Improving the accuracy of retrospective reports with landmark events. *Memory & Cognition, 11*, 114-120.

Loftus, E. F., & Palmer, J.C. (1974). Reconstruction of automobile destruction: An example of the interaction between memory and language. *Journal of Verbal Learning and Verbal Behavior, 13*, 585-589

Loftus, E. F., Fienberg, S. E., & Tanur, J. M. (1985). Cognitive psychology meet that national survey. *American Psychologist, 40*, 175-180.

Loftus, E.F., Levidow, B., & Duensing, S. (1992). Who remembers best? Individual differences in memory for events that occurred in a science museum. *Applied Cognitive Psychology, 6*, 93-107.

Loftus, E. F., Loftus, G. R., & Messo, J. (1987). Some facts about "weapon focus." *Law and Human Behavior, 11*, 55-62.

Loftus, E. F., Miller, D.G., & Burns, H. J. (1978). Semantic integration of verbal information into visual memory. *Journal of Experimental Psychology: Human Learning and Memory, 4*, 19-31

Loftus, E. F., Banaji, M. R., Schooler, J. W., & Foster, R. A. (1987). Who shall remember? Gender differences in memory. *Michigan Quarterly Review, 26*, 64-85.

Logan, K., Maybery, M., & Fletcher, J. (1996). The short-term memory of profoundly deaf people for words, signs, and abstract spatial stimuli. *Applied Cognitive Psychology, 10*, 105-119.

Logie, R.H., & Bruce, D. (1990). Developments and directions in applying cognitive psychology. *Applied Cognitive Psychology, 4*, 349-358.

Logie, R., Wright, R. & Decker, S. (1992). Recognition memory performance and residential burglary. *Applied Cognitive Psychology, 6*, 109-123.

Loisette, A. (1896). *Assimilative memory or how to attend and never forget.* New York: Funk & Wagnalls.

Long, J., (!995). Commemorating Donald Broadbent's contribution to the field of applied cognitive psychology: a discussion of the special issue papers. Applied *Cognitive Psychology, 9*, S197-S215

Loring-Meier, S. & Halpern, D. F. (1999). Sex differences in visuospatial working memory: Components of cognitive processing. *Psychonomic Bulletin and Review, 6*, 464-471.

Luh, C. W. (1922). The conditions of retention. *Psychological Monographs, 31* (3, Whole No. 142).

Luria, A. R. (1973a). *Restoration of function after brain injury.* New York: McMillan.

Luria, A. R. (1973b). *Higher cortical functions in man.* New York: Basic Books.

Lynch, W. J. (1995). You must remember this: Assistive devices for memory impairment. *Journal of Head Trauma Rehabilitation, 10*, 94-97.

Lynn, S. J., & Payne, D. G. (1997). Memory as the theater of the past: The psychology of false memories. *Current Directions in Psychological Science, 6*, 55-60.

Lynn, S. J., Lock, T., Myers, B., & Payne, D. G. (1997). Recalling the unrecallable: Should hypnosis be used for memory recovery in psychotherapy? *Current Directions in Psychological Science, 6*, 79-83.

Mace, J. H. (2004). Involuntary autobiographical memories are highly dependent on abstract cuing: The Proustian view is incorrect. *Applied Cognitive Psychology, 18*, 332-356.

Mackie, D., & Worth, L. (1991). Feeling good, but not thinking straight: The impact of positive mood on persuasion. In J. P. Forgas (Ed.), *Emotion and social judgments* (pp. 201-220). Oxford: Pergamon.

MacLachlan, J. (1986). Psychologically based techniques for improving learning within computerized tutorials. *Journal of Computer Based Instruction, 13(3)*, 65-70.

MacLeod, C. (1992). Individual differences in learning and memory. In L. Squire (Ed.), *Encyclopedia of learning and memory*. New York: Macmillan.

Maher, R. (1995). A history of the influence of statistical maps on public policy. In L. Pickle & D. Herrmann (Eds.), *Cognitive Aspects of Statistical Mapping* (pp. 13-20). National Center for Health Statistics, Working Paper Series, No. 18

Mandler, G. (1985). *Cognitive psychology: An essay in cognitive science*. Hillsdale, NJ: Erlbaum.

Manning, C. A., Stone, W. S., Korol, D. L., & Gold, P. E. (1998). Glucose enhancement of 24-h memory retrieval in healthy elderly humans. *Behavioural Brain Research, 93(1-2)*, 71-76.

Mantyla, T. (1994). Remembering to remember: Adult age differences in prospective memory. *Journal of Gerontology, 49*, 276-282.

Mark, V. H. & Mark, J. P. (1992). *Reversing memory loss*. Boston: Houghton Mifflin.

Marsh, E. J., & Bower, G. H. (1999). Applied aspects of source monitoring. *Cognitive Technology, 4*, 4-17.

Marsh, E. J. & Tversky, B. (2004). Spinning stories of our lives. *Applied Cognitive Psychology, 18*, 491-504.

Marsh, E. J., Tversky, B., & Hutton, M. (2005). How eyewitnesses talk about events. *Applied Cognitive Psychology, 19*, 531-544.

Martin K.A., Moritz, S.E. & Hall, C.R. (1999). Imagery use in sport: A literature review and applied model. *The Sport Psychologist, 13*, 245-268.

Martin, L. L., Ward, D. W., Achee, J. W., & Wyer, R. S. (1993). Mood as input: People have to interpret the motivational implications of their moods. *Journal of Personality and Social Psychology, 64*, 317-326.

Martin, M., & Jones, G.V. (1997). Memory for orientation in the natural environment. *Applied Cognitive Psychology, 11*, 279-288.

Marx, M. H., & Hillix, W. A. (1963). *Systems and theories in psychology*. New York: McGraw Hill.

Masson, M. E. J., & Waldron, M. A. (1994). Comprehension of legal contracts by non-
    experts: effectiveness of plain language redrafting. *Applied Cognitive
    Psychology, 8,* 67-85.

Mathews, G., Davies, R. D., Westerman, S. J., & Stammers, R. B. (2000). *Human
    performance: Cognition, stress, and individual differences.* Philadelphia:
    Psychology Press.

Matlin, M. W. (2005). *Cognition* (6th Ed.). Hoboken, NJ: Wiley.

Mayer, J., & Salovey, P. (1997). What is emotional intelligence? In P. Salovey & D. Sluyter
    (Eds.*), Emotional development, emotional literacy, and emotional intelligence.*
    New York: Basic Books.

Mayer, R. E. (1999a). Instructional technology. In F. Durso (Ed.), *Handbook of applied
    cognition.* New York: Wiley.

Mayer, R. E. (1999b). *The promise of educational psychology.* Upper Saddle River, NJ:
    Merrill.

Maylor, E. A. (1990). Age and prospective memory. *Quarterly Journal of Psychology, 42a,*
    471-493.

Mazzoni, G., Conoldi, C., Tomat, L., & Vecchi, T. (1997). Remembering the grocery
    shopping list: a study on metacognitive biases. *Applied Cognitive Psychology,
    11,* 253-267.

McAdams, D. P. (2001). The psychologies of life stories. *General Psychology, 5,* 100-122.

McAlliarwe, H. A., Bearden, J. N., Kohlmaier, J. R., & Warner, M. D. (1997). Computerized
    mug books: Does adding multimedia help? *Applied Psychology, 82,* 688-698.

McCarthy, R. A., & Warrington, E. K. (1990). *Cognitive neuropsychology: A clinical
    introduction.* San Diego, CA: Academic Press.

McDaniel, M. A., & Einstein, G. O. (1993). The importance of cue familiarity and cue
    distinctiveness in prospective memory. *Memory, 1,* 23-41.

McDaniel, M. A., & Einstein, G. O. (2000). Strategic and automatic processes in prospective
    memory retrieval: A multiprocess framework. *Applied Cognitive Psychoology,
    14,* S127-144.

McEvoy, C. L. (1992). Memory improvement in context: Implications for the development of
    memory improvement theory. In D. Herrmann, H. Weingartner, A. Searleman,
    & C. McEvoy (Eds.), *Memory improvement: Implications for memory theory*
    (pp. 210-231). New York: Springer Verlag.

McGaugh, J. (1992). Affect, neuromodulatory systems and memory storage. In S.A.
    Christinason (Eds.), *The handbook of emotion and memory: Research and
    theory* (pp. 245-268). Hillsdale, NJ: Erlbaum.

McGuire, W. J. (1964). Inducing resistance to persuasion: Some contemporary approaches. In L. Berkowitz (Ed.).*Advances in experimental social psychology* (Vol. 1, pp 191-229). San Diego, CA: Academic Press.

McIntire, S. A., & Miller, L. A. (2000). *Foundations of psychological testing*. Boston: McGraw Hill.

McKenna, F.P. (1990). Learning implications of field dependence-independence: cognitive style versus cognitive ability. *Applied Cognitive Psychology, 4*, 425-437.

McLaughlin, J. P., Dunckle, J., Brown, S. (1999). The role of memory in aesthetic responses. *Cognitive Technology 4*, 26-28.

McLaughlin Cook, N. (1989). The applicability of verbal mnemonics for different populations: a review. *Applied Cognitive Psychology, 3*, 3-22.

Meacham, J. A., & Kushner, S. (1980). Anxiety, prospective remembering, and performance of planned actions. *Journal of General Psychology, 103*, 203-209.

Meacham, J. A., & Leiman, B. (1982). Remembering to perform future actions. In U. Neisser (Ed.), *Memory observed: Remembering in natural contexts* (pp. 327-336). San Francisco: Freeman.

Meacham, J. A., & Singer, J. (1977). Incentive effects in prospective remembering. *Journal of Psychology, 97*, 191-197.

Means, B., & Loftus, E. F. (1991). When personal history repeats itself: decomposing memories for recurring events. *Applied Cognitive Psychology, 5*, 297-318.

Means, B., Habina, K., Swan, G. E., & Jack, L. (1992). Cognitive research on response error in survey questions on smoking. *Vital and Health Statistics, Series 6, No. 5* (DHHS Publication No. PHS 92-1080). Washington, DC: U.S. Government Printing Office.

Means, B., Nigam, A., Zarrow, M., Loftus, E.F., & Donaldson, M.S. (1989). Autobiographical memory for health-related events: Enhanced memory for recurring incidents. *Vital and Health Statistics, Series 6, No. 2* (DHHS Publication No. PHS 89-1077). Washington, DC: U.S. Government Printing Office.

Medin, D. L. Ross, B.H., & Maarkman, A. B. (2004). *Cognitive Psychology*. New York: Wiley.

Meissner, C. A., Brigham, J. C., & Butz, D. A. (2005). How to refer to 'diabetes'? Language in online health advice. *Applied Cognitive Psychology, 19*, 569-586.

Memon, A., Holley, A., Wark, L., Bull, R., & Köhnken, G. (1996). Reducing suggestibility in child witness interviews. *Applied Cognitive Psychology, 10*, 503-518.

Metz, S. M., & Hoffman, B. (1997). Mind operated devices. *Cognitive Technology, 2*, 69-74.

Meudell, P. R., Hitch, G. J., & Kirby, P. (1992). Are two heads better than one? Experimental investigations of the social facilitation of memory. *Applied Cognitive Psychology, 6*, 525-543.

Meyer, J., Shamo, M. K., & Gopher, D. (1999). Information structure and the relative efficacy of tables and graphs. *Human Factors, 41*, 570-587.

Migueles, M., & Garcia-Bajos, E. (1999). Recall, recognition, and confidence patterns in eyewitness testimony. *Applied Cognitive Psychology, 13*, 257-268.

Miller, E., & Karoni, P. (1996). The cognitive psychology of delusions: a review. *Applied Cognitive Psychology, 10*, 487-502.

Miller, G. A. (1956). The magical number seven, plus or minus two: Some limits on our capacity for processing information. *Psychological Review, 101(2)*, 343-352.

Miller, G. A. (1969). Psychology as a means of promoting human welfare. *American Psychologist, 24*, 1063-1075.

Miller, G. A., Galanter, E., & Pribram, K. H. (1960). *Plans and the structure of behavior.* New York: H. Holt.

Miller, K. (1995). Why should federal dollars be spent to support scientific research? *Sigma Xi forum: 1995 Vannevar Bush II Science for the 21st Century.* Research Triangle Park, NC: Sigma Xi.

Miller, L. (1998). Brain injury and violent crime: Clinical, neuropsychological, and forensic considerations. *Cognitive Rehabilitation, 16*, 12-25.

Miller, L. A., & Herrmann, D. (1998). Improving survey design: The linguistic complexity of survey responses and the quality of responses. *Cognitive Technology, 2*, 31-40.

Moray, N. (1999). The cognitive psychology and cognitive engineering of industrial systems. In F. Durso (Ed.), *Handbook of applied cognition.* New York: Wiley.

Morgan, C. H., Lilley, J. D., & Boreham, N. C. (1988). Learning from lectures: the effect of varying the detail in lecture handouts on note-taking and recall. *Applied Cognitive Psychology, 2*, 115-122.

Morrell, R. W. (1997). The application of cognitive theory in aging research. *Cognitive Technology, 2*, 44-47.

Morreell, R. W., Mayhorn, C. B., & Bennett, J. (2000). A surey of world wide web use in middle-aged and older adults. *Human Factors, 42*, 175-182.

Morris, P. E. (1984). The validity of subjective reports on memory. In J. E. Harris & P. E. Morris (Eds.), *Everyday memory, actions and absentmindedness* (pp. 153-172). London: Academic Press.

Morris, P. E. (1992). Prospective memory: Remembering to do things. *Aspects of memory* (Vol. 1, pp. 196-222). London: Metheun.

Morris, W. N. (1992). A functional analysis of the role of mood in affective systems. *Review of personality and social psychology* ,11, 256-293).

Mullin, P., Herrmann, D. J., & Searleman, A. (1993). Forgotten variables in memory research. *Memory, 15*, 43.

Munsterberg, H. (1908). *On the witness stand*. New York: Clark Boardman

Munsterberg, H. (1913). *Psychology and industrial efficiency*. Boston: Houghton Mifflin.

Munsterberg, H. (1914). *Hugo Munsterberg: His life and work*. New York: Appleton.

Munsterberg, M. (1922). *Psychology: General and applied*. New York: Appleton.

Murphy, M. J. (2000). Computer technology for office-based psychological practice: Applications and factors affecting adoption. *Cognitive Technology, 5*, 35-41.

Narby, D. J., Cutler, B. L., & Penrod, S. D. (1996). The effects of witness, target and situational factors on eyewitness identifications. In S. L. Sporer, R. S. Malpass, & G. Koehnken (Eds.), *Psychological issues in eyewitness identification* (pp. 23-52). Mahwah: L.E.A.

National Science Foundation. (1994). *Characteristics of doctoral scientists and engineers in the United States*:1991. NSF 94-307, Arlington, VA.

Natter, H. M. & Berry, D. C. (2005). Efects of active information processing on the understandind of risk information. *Applied Cognitive Psychology, 19*, 123-136.

Naugle, R., Prevey, M., Naugle, C., & Delaney, R. (1988). New digital watch as a compensatory device for memory dysfunction. *Cognitive Rehabilitation, 6*, 22-23.

Naveh-Benjamin, M., McKeachie, W. J., Lin, Y.G., & Lavi, H. (1997). Individual differences in students' retention of knowledge and conceptual structures learned in university and high school courses: the case of test anxiety. *Applied Cognitive Psychology, 11*, 507-526.

Neath, I., & Surprenant, A. M. (2003). *Human Memory* (2nd Edition). Belmont, CA: WadsworthThomson Learning.

Neisser, U. (1967*). Cognitive psychology*. New York: Appleton Century Crofts.

Neisser, U. (1976). *Cognition and reality: Principles and implications of cognitive psychology*. San Francisco, CA: Freeman.

Neisser, U. (1978). Memory: what are the important questions. In M. M. Gruneberg, P. E. Morris, & R. N. Sykes (Eds.), *Practical aspects of memory*. London: Academic Press.

Neisser, U. (1982). *Memory observed: Remembering in natural contexts*. San Francisco: Freeman.

Neisser, U. (1992). The development of consciousness and the acquisition of skill. In F. S. Kessel, P. M. Cole, & D. L. Johnson (Eds.), *Self and consciousness: Multiple perspectives* (pp. 1-18). Hillsdale, NJ: Erlbaum.

Neisser, U., & Becklin, R. (1975). Selective looking: Attending to visually significant events. *Cognitive Psychology, 7*, 480-494.

Neisser, U., & Harsch, N. (1992). Phanthom flashbulbs: False recollections of hearing the news about Challenger. In E. Winograd & U. Neisser (Eds.), *Affect and accuracy in recall: Studies of flashbulb memories*. Cambridge: Cambridge University Press.

Neisser, U., & Winograd, E. (Eds.). (1988*). Remembering reconsidered: Ecological and traditional approaches to the study of memory*. Cambridge, England: Cambridge University Press.

Nelson, T.O. (1996). Gamma is a measure of the accuracy of predicting performance on one item relative to another item, not of the absolute performance on an individual item. Comments on Schraw (1995*). Applied Cognitive Psychology, 10*, 257-260.

Neuhoff, J. (2000). Classroom demonstrations in perception and cognition using presentation software. *Teaching of Psychology, 27*, 142-144.

Neuschatz, J. S., Payne, D. G, Lampinen, J. M., & Toglia, M. P. (2001). Assessing the phenomenological characteristics of false memories. *Memory 9*, 53-71.

Newell, A. (1990*). Unified theories of cognition*. Cambridge, MA: Harvard University Press.

Newlands, A., Anderson, A.H., & Mullin, J. (2003). Adapting communicative strategies to computer-mediated communication: An analysis of task performance and dialogue structure. *Applied Cognitive Psychology, 17*, 325-348.

Niccaise, M. (1998). Cognitive research, learning theory & software design: The virtual library. *Journal of Educational Computing Research. 18*, 105-121.

Nickerson, R. S. (1992). *Looking ahead: Human factors challenges in a changing world*. Hillsdale, NJ: Erlbaum.

Nickerson, R. S. (1997). Cognitive technology: Reflections on a long history and promising future. *Cognitive Technology, 2*, 6-20.

Nickerson, R. S. (1999). The natural environment: Dealing with the threat of detrimental change. In F. Durso (Ed.), *Handbook of applied cognition*. New York: Wiley.

Niederehe, G., & Yoder, C. Y. (1989). Metamemory perceptions in depression of young and older adults. *Journal of Nervous and Mental Disease, 177*, 4-14.

Niedzwienska, A. (2003). Distortion of autobiographical memories. *Applied Cognitive Psychology, 17*, 81-92.

Nilsson, L. G., & Markowitsch, G. (Eds.). (1999). *Cognitive neuroscience of memory*. Toronto: Hogrefe and Huber.

Nisbett, R. E., & Wilson, T. D. (1977). Telling more than we can know: Verbal reports on
    mental processes. *Psychological Review, 84*, 231-259.

Noice, H., Noice, T., Perrig-Chiello, P., & Perrig, W. (1999). Improving memory in older
    adults by instructing them in professional actors' learning strategies. *Applied
    Cognitive Psychology, 13*, 315-328.

Noice, T., & Noice, H. (2002). Very long-term recall and recognition of well-learned
    material. *Applied Cognitive Psychology, 16*, 259-272.

Noice, T., & Noice, H. (2004). A cognitive learning principle derived from the role of
    acquisition strategies of professional actors. *Cognitive Technology, 9*, 34-39.

Nolan, J., & Markham, R. (1998). The accuracy-confidence relationship in an eyewitness
    task: anxiety as a modifier. *Applied Cognitive Psychology, 12*, 43-54.

Norman, D. A. (1968). Toward a theory of memory and attention. *Psychological Review, 75*,
    522-536.

Norman, D. A. (1981). Categorization of action slips. *Psychological Review, 88 (1)*, 1-15.

Norman, D. A. (1988*). The psychology of everyday things*. New York: Basic Books.

Norman, D. (1993). *Things that make us smart: Defending human attributes in the age of
    the machine*. NY: Addison-Wesley.

Norman, D. A. (1998). *The invisible computer*. Cambridge, MA: MIT Press.

Norman, D., & Fisher, D. (1982). Why alphabetic keyboards are not easy to use:
    Keyboard layout doesn't much matter. *Human Factors, 24*, 509-519.

Norman, D. A. & Shallice, T. (1986). Attrntion to action: Willed and automatic control
    of behavior. In R. J. Davidson, G. E. Schwartz, and D. Shapiro (Eds.),
    Consciousness and self regulation (Vol. 4; pp. 1-18). New York: Plenum.

Norman, K. L., (1997). Cognitive impact of graphical user interfaces. *Cognitive Technology,
    2*, 22-30.

Norris, C. E., & Colman, A. M. (1996). Context effects of radio programming on cognitive
    processing of embedded advertisements. *Applied Cognitive Psychology, 10*,
    473-486.

Nyberg, L. (1994). A structural equation modeling approach to the multiple memory system
    question. *Journal of Experimental Psychology: Learning, Memory, and
    Cognition, 20*, 484-491.

O'Hare, D., Wiggins, M., Batt, R., & Morrison, D. (1994). Cognitive failure analysis for
    aircraft accident investigation. *Ergonomics, 7*, 1855-1869.

Oaksford, M., & Chater, N. (2001). The probabilistic approach to human reasoning. *Trends
    in Cognitive Sciences, 5*, 349-357.

Olson, J. S., & Olson, G. M. (1999). Computer supported cooperative work. In F. Durso (Ed.), Handbook of applied cognition. Mahwah, NJ: Erlbaum. In F. Durso (Ed.), *Handbook of applied cognition.* New York: Wiley.

Ornstein, P. A., Baker-Ward, L., Gordon, B. N., & Merritt, K. A. (1997). Children's memory for medical experiences: implications for testimony. *Applied Cognitive Psychology, 11,* S87-S104.

Paddock, J.R., Joseph, A.L., Chan, F.M., Terranova, S., Manning, C., & Loftus, E.F. (1998). When guided visualization procedures may backfire: imagination inflation and predicting individual differences in suggestibility. *Applied Cognitive Psychology, 12,* S63- S75.

Palmer, E. J., & Hollin, C. R. (1999). Social competence and sociomoral reasoning in young offenders. *Applied Cognitive Psychology, 13,* 79-87.

Panzarella, C., Alloy, L. B., Abramson, L. Y., Klein, K. (1999). Cognitive contributions to mental illness and mental health. In F. Durso (Ed.). *Handbook of Applied Cognition,* New York: Wiley.

Parente', R. (1998), Retraining rehearsal after traumatic brain injury. *Cognitive Technology, 3,* 33-38.

Parente', R. (2000). Memory works CDs. *Cognitive Technology, 5,* 45-47.

Parente,' R., & Anderson-Parente,' J. (1991). *Retraining memory: Techniques and applications.* Houston, TX: CSY Publishing.

Parente,' R. & Herrmann, D.,(1996; second edition, 2003). *Retraining Cognition.* Gaithersburg: Aspen.

Park, D. C., & Kidder, D. P. (1996). Prospective memory and medication adherence. In M. Brandimonte, G. Einstein, & McDaniel (Eds.), *Prospective memory: Theory and applications.* Hillsdale, NJ: Erlbaum.

Park, D. C., Smith, A. D., & Cavenaugh, J. C. (1990). Metamemories of memory researchers. *Memory and Cognition, 18,* 321-327.

Parker, A., & Gellatly, A. (1997). Moveable cues: a practical method for reducing context-dependent forgetting. *Applied Cognitive Psychology, 11,* 163-173.

Parkes, K.R. (1995). The effects of objective workload on cognitive performance in a field setting: a two-period cross-over trial. *Applied Cognitive Psychology, 9,* S153- S171.

Parkin, A. J. (1993). *Memory.* Oxford: Blackwell.

Parkin, A. J. (2000). *Essential cognitive psychology.* London: Psychology Press.

Pashler, H. E. (1998). *The psychology of attention.* Cambridge, MA: MIT Press.

Patel, V. L., Arocha, J. F., & Kaufman, D. R. (1999). Medical cognition. In F. Durso (Ed.), *Handbook of applied cognition.* New York: Wiley.

Patel, V. L., Groen, G. J., & Frederiksen, C. H. (1986). Differences between medical students and doctors in memory for clinical cases. *Medical Education, 20*, 3-9.

Patrick, J. (1994). Training. In P. Spurgeoon, R. Davies, & A. J. Chapman (Eds.), *Elements of applied psychology.* Amsterdam: Harwood Academic Publishers.

Patton, G. W. R., D'Agaro, W. R., & Gaudette, M. D. (1991). The effect of subject-generated and experimenter-supplied code words on the phonetic mnemonic system. *Applied Cognitive Psychology, 5*, 135-148.

Payne, D. G. (1991). Selective auditory-visual interference effects in a dual-task paradigm: Implications for assessing individual differences. *Proceedings of the Human Factors Society 35th Annual Meeting*, 622-626.

Payne, D. G. (2001). Windows on Ulric Neisser's contributions to psychology. (Review of *Ecological approaches to cognition: Essays in honor of Ulric Neisser*. E. Winograd, R. Fivush, & W. Hirst, W. (Eds.), Lawrence Erlbaum Associates, Mahwah, NJ.), *Applied cognitive psychology, 15*, 694-695.

Payne, D. G., & Blackwell, J. M. (1997). Toward a valid view of human factors research: Response to Vicente , *Human Factors, 39*, 329-331.

Payne, D. G., & Blackwell, J. M. (1998). Truth in memory: Caveat emptor. In S. J. Lynn & K. M. McConkey (Eds.), *Truth in memory.* New York: Guilford Press.

Payne, D. G., & Conrad, F. G. (1997). *Intersections in basic and applied memory research.* Mahwah, NJ: Lawrence Erlbaum Associates.

Payne, D. G., & Wenger, M. J. (1992). Improving memory through practice. In D. Herrmann, H. Weingartner, A. Searleman, & C. McEvoy (Eds.), *Memory improvement: Implications for memory theory* (pp. 205-229). New York: Springer-Verlag.

Payne, D. G., & Wenger, M. J. (1995). Practice effects in memory: Data, theory, and unanswered questions. In D. Herrmann, M. K. Johnson, C. McEvoy, C. Hertzog, & P. Hertel (Eds.), *Basic and applied memory: Research on practical aspects of memory.* Hillsdale, NJ: Erlbaum.

Payne, D. G., & Wenger, M. J. (1998). *Cognitive psychology.* New York, NY: Houghton Mifflin Company.

Payne, D. G., Cohen, M. S. & Pastore, R. E. (1992). Computer-based task analysis: A methodology for improving system design. *Interacting with Computers, 4*, 267-288.

Payne, D. G., Conrad, F. G., & Hager, D. R. (1997). Basic and applied memory research: Empirical, theoretical, and metatheoretical issues. In D.G. Payne & F. G. Conrad (Eds.), *Intersections in basic and applied memory research.* Hillsdale, NJ: Lawrence Erlbaum.

Payne, D. G., Lang, V. A., & Blackwell, J. M. (1995). Mixed versus pure display format in integration and nonintegration visual display monitoring tasks. *Human Factors, 37*, 507-527.

Payne, D. G., Wenger, M. J., & Cohen, M. S. (1993). Cognitive processing and hypermedia comprehension: A preliminary synthesis. In G. Salvendy & M. J. Smith (Eds.), *Human-computer interaction: Software and hardware interfaces*. New York: Elsevier.

Payne, D. G., Elie, C. J., Blackwell, J. M., & Neuschatz, J. S. (1996). Memory illusions: recalling, recognizing and recollecting events that never occurred. *Journal of Memory and Language, 35*, 261-285.

Payne, D. G., Klin, C. M., Lampinen, J. M., Neuschatz, J. S., & Lindsay, D. S. (1999). Memory applied. In F. T. Durso, R. Nickerson, R. W. Schvaneveldt, S. T. Dumais, D. S. Lindsay, & M.T.H. Chi (Eds.), *The handbook of applied cognition* (83-113). New York: John Wiley and Sons.

Payne, D. G., Neuschatz, J. S., Lampinen, J. M., & Lynn, S. J. (1997). Compelling memory illusions: The phenomenological qualities of false memories. *Current Directions in Psychological Science, 6*, 56-60.

Pedhazur, E. J., & Schmelkin, L. P. (1991). *Measurement, design, and analysis: An integrated approach*. Hillsdale, NJ: Erlbaum.

Perfect, T. J., & Hollins, T. S. (1996). Predictive feeling of knowing judgements and postdictive confidence judgements in eyewitness memory and general knowledge. *Applied Cognitive Psychology, 10*, 371-382.

Perfect, T. J. & Schwartz, B. L. (2002). *Applied Metacognition* (pp. 39-7=67). Cambridge, England: Cambridge University Press.

Perner, J. (1997). Children's competency in understanding the role of a witness: truth, lies, and moral ties. *Applied Cognitive Psychology, 11*, S21-S35.

Peters, G. A., & Peters, B. J. (1999). *Warnings, instructions, and technical communications*. Tucson: Lawyers and Judges Publishing.

Peterson, N. G., Mumford, M. D., Borman, W. C., Jeanneret, P. R., & Fleishman, E. A. (1999). *An occupational information system for the 21st century: The development of O'NET*. Hyattsville, MD: American Psychological Association.

Petro, S., Herrmann, D., Burrows, D., & Moore, C. (1991). Usefulness of commercial memory aids as a function of age. International *Journal of Aging and Human Development, 33*, 295-309.

Petros, T., Beckwith, B. E., Erickson, G., Arnold, M. E., & Sternhagen, S. (1987). The effects of caffeineee on the efficience of working memory. Presented at the annual meeting of APA, New York.

Petroski, H. (1994). *The evolution of useful things*. New York: Vintage Books.

Phillips, R.J., Coe, B., Kono, E., Knapp, J., Barrett, S., Wiseman, G., & Eveleigh, P. (1990). An experimental approach to the design of cartographic symbols. *Applied Cognitive Psychology, 4*, 485-497.

Pickle, L. W., & Herrmann, D. J. (Eds.). (1995). Cognitive aspects of statistical mapping. *NCHS Working Paper Series Report, No. 18*. Hyattsville, MD: National Center for Health Statistics.

Pickle, L., Mason, T., Howard, N., Hoover, R., & Fraumeni, J (1987). *Atlas of US Cancer Mortality among Whites: 1950-1980*. Washington, DC: National Institutes of Health.

Pillemer, D. B. (2001). Momentous events and life story. *General Psychology, 5*, 123-134.

Pillemer, D. B. & Goldsmith, L. R. (1988).Very long-term memories of the first year in college. *Journal of Experimental Psychology: Learning, Memory, and Cognition, 14*, 709-715.

Pinker, S. (1997). *How the mind works*. New York: W. W. Norton & Co.

Piolat, A., Olive, T., & Kellog, R. T. (2005). Cognitive effort during note taking. *Applied Cognitive Psychology, 19*, 291-312.

Pirolli, P. (1999). Cognitive engineering models and cognitive architectures in human-computer interaction. In F. Durso (Ed.), *Handbook of applied cognition*. New York: Wiley.

Platt, J. R. (1964). Strong inference. *Science, 146*, 347-353.

Platt, R.D., Lacey, S.C., Iobst, A.D., & Finkelman, D. (1998). Absorption, dissociation, and fantasy-proneness as predictors of memory distortion in autobiographical and laboratory-generated memories. *Applied Cognitive Psychology, 12*, S77- S89.

Plude, D. J., & Schwartz, L. K. (1996a). The promise of Compact Disc-interactive memory training with the elderly. *Educational Gerontology. , 22*, 507-521.

Plude, D. J., & Schwartz, L. K. (1996b). The promise of Compact Disc-interactive technology for memory training with th*.), Basic and applied memory: New findings on the practical aspects of memory* e elderly. In D. Herrmann, C. McEvoy, C. Hertzog, P. Hertel, & M. Johnson (Eds. Englewood Cliffs, NJ: Erlbaum.

Podd, J. (1990). The effects of memory load and delay on facial recognition. *Applied Cognitive Psychology, 4*, 47-59.

Poffenberger, A. T. (1929). *Applied psychology: Its principles and its methods*. New York: D. Appleton.

Polusny, M. A., &, Follette, V. M. (1996). Remembering childhood sexual abuse: A national survey of psychologists, clinical practice, beliefs, and personal experiences. *Journal of Professional Psychology, 27,* 41-52.

Poon, L.W. (1980). A systems approach for the assessment and treatment   of   memory problems. In J.M. Ferguson & C.B. Taylor (Eds.) *The Comprehensive Handbood of Behavior Medicine, Vol 1,* 191-212.

Poon, L. W. (Ed.). (1986). *Clinical memory assessment of older adults.* Washington, DC: American Psychological Association.

Poon, L. W., Rubin, D. C., & Wilson, B. A. (Eds.). (1988). *Everyday cognition in adult and late life (The Fifth Talland Conference).* New York: Cambridge University Press

Poon, L. W., Crook, T., Davies, K. L., Eisdorfer, C., Gurland, B. J., Kaszniak, A. W., & Thompson, L. W. (Eds.). (1986). *Handbook clinical cognitive assessment of older adults.* Hyattsville, MD: American Psychological Association.

Pope, K. S. (1996). Memory abuse and science: Questioning claims about the false memory syndrome. *American Psychologist, 51,* 957-974.

Pope, K. S., & Brown, L. S. (1996*). Recovered memories of abuse: Assessment, therapy, forensics.* Washington, DC: American Psychological Association.

Popper, K. R. (1959). *The logic of scientific discovery.* London: Hutchinson.

Posner, M. I. (1984). Selective attention and the storage of information. In G. Lynch, J. L. McGaugh, and N. M. Weinberger (Eds.). *Neurobiology of Learning and Memory,* New York: Guilford.

Posner, M. I. (1992). Attention as a cognitive and neural system. *Current directions in psychological science.* Cambridge, MA: MIT Press.

Posner, M. I., & Raichle, M. E. (1994). *Images of the mind.* New York: Scientific American Library.

Powell, E. (1974). Psychological effects of exercise therapy upon institutionalized geriatric mental patients. *Journal of Gerontology, 29,* 157-161.

Pressley, M. (1996). Personal reflections on the study of practical memory in the mid-1990s: The complete cognitive researcher. In D. Herrmann, C. McEvoy, C. Herzog, P. Hertel, & M. Johnson (Eds*.), Basic and applied memory: New findings.* Mawah, NJ: Erlbaum.

Proshansky, H. M. (1981). Uses and abuses of theory in applied research. In L. Bickman (Ed.), *Applied social psychology annual 2* (pp. 97-135). Newbury Park, CA: Sage.

Pylyshyn Z. W. (1973). What the mind's eye tells the mind's brain: A critique of mental imagery. *Psychological Bulletin, 80,* 1-24.

Pylyshyn Z. W. (2003). Return of the mental image: are there pictures in the brain? *Trends in Cognitive Science, 7,* 113-118.

Rabbitt, P. (1990). Applied cognitive gerontology: some problems, methodologies and data. *Applied Cognitive Psychology, 4,* 225-246.

Rabbitt, P. M. A., & Abson, V.(1990). Lost and found: the search for mislaid objects and some limitations on what self rating questionnaires can tell us about the effects of old age and I.Q. on everyday competence. *British Journal of Psychology, 81,* 1-16.

Rabbitt, P., Maylor, E., McInnes, L., Bent, N., & Moore, B. (1995). What goods can self- assessment questionnaires deliver for cognitive gerontology? *Applied Cognitive Psychology, 9,* S127-S152.

Rabins, P.V. (Ed.) (2003). Memory boosters. *The Johns Hopkins Memory Bulletin.* New York: Medletter Associates.

Rankin, J. L., Bruning, R. H., & Timme, V. L. (1994). The development of beliefs about spelling and their relationship to spelling performance, *Applied Cognitive Psychology, 8,* 213-232.

Rasinski, K., Willis, G., Baldwin, A., Yeh, W. & Lee, L. (1999). Methods of data collection, perceptions of risks and losses, and motivation to give truthful answers to sensitive survey questions. *Applied Cognitive Psychology, 13,* 465-484.

Raugh, M. R., & Atkinson, R. C. (1975). A mnemonic method for learning a second language vocabulary. *Journal of Educational Psychology, 67,* 1-16.

Read, J. D. (2001). Introduction to the Special Issue: Trauma, stress and autobiographical memory. *Applied Cognitive Psychology. 15,* S1-S6.-56.

Read, J.D., & Winograd, E. (1998). Introduction. *Applied Cognitive Psychology, 12,* S1-S4.

Read J. D., Lindsay D. S., & Nicholls, T. (1998). The relationship between confidence and accuracy in eyewitness identification studies: Is the conclusion changing? In C. P. Thompson, D. J. Herrmann, J. D. Read, D., Bruce, D. G.,Payne, & M. P. Toglia (Eds.), *Eyewitness memory.* Mahwah: L.E.A.

Read, J. D., Hammersley, R., Cross-Calvert, S., & McFadzen, E. (1989). Rehearsal of faces and details in action events. *Applied Cognitive Psychology, 3,* 295-311.

Reagan, M. D. (1967). Basic and applied research: A meaningful distinction. *Science, 155,* 1383-1386.

Reason, J. T., (1988). Stress and cognitive failure. In S. Fisher & J. T. Reason (Eds.), *Handbook of life stress, cognition and health.* New York: Wiley.

Reason, J. (1990). *Error.* Cambridge: Cambridge University Press.

Reason, J. (1998). How necessary steps in a task get omitted: Revising old ideas to combat a persistent problem. *Cognitive Technology, 3,* 24-32.

Reason, J. T. & Lucas, D. (1984). Absentmindedness in shops: Its correlates and consequences. *British Journal of Clinical Psychology, 23,* 121-131.

Reason, J., & MyCielska, M. (1983). *Absentmindedness.* Hillsdale, NJ: Prentice-Hall.

Rebok, G. W., & Folstein, M. F. (1993). Dementia. *Journal of Neuropsychiatry and Clinical Neurosciences, 5,* 265-276.

Rebok, G. W., Rasmussson, D. X., & Brandt, J. (1996). Prospects for computerized memory training in normal elderly: effects of practice on explicit and implicit memory tasks. *Applied Cognitive Psychology, 10,* 211-223.

Reder, L. M. (1987). Strategy-selection in question answering. *Cognitive Psychology, 19,* 90-134.

Reder L. M. (1988). Strategic control of retrieval processes. In G. Bower (Ed.), *The psychology of learning and motivation, Vol. 22.* San Diego: Academic Press.

Reisberg, D. (1997). *Cognition: Exploring the science of the mind.* New York, NY: W. W. Norton and Company.

Reitan, R. M. (1955). An investigation of Halstead's measures of biological intelligence. *Archives of Neurology and Psychiatry, 73,* 28-35.

Revelle, W., Humphreys, M. S., Simon, L. & Gilliland, K., 1980. The interactive effect of personality, time of day, and caffeine: A test of the arousal model. *Journal of Experimental Psychology: General, 109,* 1-31.

Reynolds, J. K., & Pezdek, K. (1992). Face recognition memory: the effects of exposure duration and encoding instruction. *Applied Cognitive Psychology, 6,* 279-292.

Richardson, J. T. E. (1991). Social class limitations on the efficacy on the efficacy of imagery mnemonic instructions. *British Journal of Psychology, 78,* 65-77.

Richardson, J. T. E. (1999). *Imagery.* Hove: Taylor Francis.

Rikers, R. M. J. P., & Pass, F. (2005). Recent advances in expertise research. *Applied Cognitive Psychology, 19,* 145-149.

Rinck, M. (1999). Memory for everyday objects: Where are the digits on numerical keypads? *Applied Cognitive Psychology, 13,* 329-350.

Roberts, K. P., & Blades, M. (1998). The effects of interacting in repeated events on children's eyewitness memory and source monitoring. *Applied Cognitive Psychology, 12,* 489-503.

Robinson-Riegler, G., & Robinson-Riegler, B., (2004). *Cognitive psychology: Applying the science of the mind.* Boston: Pearson.

Roebuck, R., & Wilding, J. (1993). Effects of vowel variety and sample on identification of a speaker in a line-up. *Applied Cognitive Psychology, 7,* 475-481.

Roediger, H. L. lll, & Guynn, M. J. (1996). Retrieval processes. In E. L. Bjork & R. A. Bjork (Eds.), *Memory* (pp. 197-236). San Diego, CA: Academic Press.

Roediger, H. L. III, & McDermott, K. B. (2000). Tricks of memory. *Current Directions in Psychological Science, 9,* 123-127.

Roediger, H. L. III, Nairne, J. S., Neath, I., & Surprenant, A. M. (Eds.).(2001). *The Nature of Remembering.* Washington,DC: APA.

Rogers, W. A., Rousseau, G. K., & Fisk, A. D. (1999). Applications of attention research. In F. Durso (Ed.), *Handbook of applied cognition.* New York: Wiley.

Rohrbaugh, C. C., & Shanteau, J. (1999). Context, process and experience: Research on judgement and decision making. In F. Durso (Ed.), *Handbook of applied cognition.* New York: Wiley.

Rohrer, D., Taylor, K., Pashler, H., Wixted, J. T., & Cepeda, N. J. (2005). The effect of overlearning on long-term retention. *Applied Cognitive Psychology, 19,* 361-374.

Rosenzweig, M. R. (1998). Introduction to the symposium on drug improvement of memory. *International Journal of Psychology, 33,* 81-85.

\Rozeboom, W. W. (1997). Good science is abductive, not hypothetico-deductive. In L. L. Harlow, S. A. Mulaik, & J. H. Steiger (Eds), *What if there were no significance tests?* Mahwah, NJ: Erlbaum.

Rubenstein, T., & Mason, A. F. (1979, November). The accident that shouldn't have happened: An analysis of Three Mile Island. *IEEE Spectrum,* 33-57.

Rubin, D. C. (Ed.), (1986). *Autobiographical memory.* Cambridge, MA: Cambridge University Press.

Rupert, T. J., & Wartick, M. L. (1997). Facilitating performance with cued working: an examination of reasoning in the tax content. *Applied Cognitive Psychology, 11,* 321-337.

Rutherford & Fernie, G. (2005). The accuracy of footballer's frequency estimates of their own football heading. *Applied Cognitive Psychology, 19,* 455-476..

Rybash, J.M. (1996). Memory aging research: real-life and laboratory relationships. *Applied Cognitive Psychology, 10,* 187-191.

Rybash, J. M. (1998). Cognitive Technology Memory Works: A CD-i memory training program for older adults. *Cognitive Technology, 3,* 39-41.

Safer, M. A. (1998). Memory bias in the assessment and recall of pre-exam anxiety: How anxious was I? *Applied Cognitive Psychology, 12,* S127-S137.

Safer, M. A., Christianson, S. A., Autry, M., & Osterlund, K. (1995). Tunnel memory for traumatic events. *Applied Cognitive Psychology, 12,* 99-117.

Sanders, M. S., & Mc Cormick, E. J. (1993). *Human factors in engineering and design.* New York: McGraw Hill.

Sandler, A. B. & Harris, J. L., (1991). Use of external aids with a head injured patient. *The American Journal of Occupational Therapy, 46,* 163-166.

Sarapata, M., Herrmann, D., Johnson, T., & Aycock, R. (1998). The role of head injury in cognitive functioning and criminal behavior. *Brain Injury, 12,* 821-842.

Sarter. N. B., & Amalberti, R. R. (Eds.). (2000). *Cognitive engineering in the aviation domain.* Mahwah: Erlbaum.

Saunders, J., & MacLeod, M. D. (2002). New evidence on the suggestibility of memory: The role of retrieval-induced forgetting in misinformation effects. *Journal of Experimental Psychology, 8,* 127-142.

Schacter, D. L. (1984). Toward the multidisciplinary study of memory: Ontogeny, phylogeny, and pathology of memory systems. In L. R. Squire and N. Butters (Eds.). *Neuropsychology of Memory,* New York: Guilford.

Schacter, D, L, (Eds.).(1995). *Memory Distortions.* Cambridge: Harvard University Press.

Schacter, D. L. (2001*). The seven sins of memory: How the mind forgets and remembers.* Boston: Houghlin Mifflin.

Schacter, D. L., & Gilsky, E. L. (1986). Memory remediation: Restoration alleviation, and the acquisition of domain-specific knowledge. In B. Uzzell & Y. Gross (Eds.) *Clinical neuropsychology of intervention.* (pp. 257-282). Boston: Martibus Nijolf.

Schmidt, J. A., McLaughlin, J. P., & Leighten, P. (1989). Novice strategies for understanding paintings. *Applied Cognitive Psychology, 3,* 65-72.

Schmolck, H., Buffalo, E. A., & Squire, L. R. (2000). Memory distortions develop over time: Recollections of the O. J. Simpson trial verdict after 15 and 32 months. *Psychological Science, 11,* 39-45.

Schneiderman, B. (1987). *Designing the user interface: Strategies for effective human-computer interaction.* New York: Addison Wesley.

Schoenfeld, A. H. & Herrmann, D. J. (1982). Problem perception and knowledge structure in expert and novice mathematical problem solvers. *Journal of Experimental Psychology: Human Learning, Memory,and Cognitive, 8,* 484-494.

Schonflug, W. (1986). The trade-off between internal and external information storage. *Journal of Memory and Language, 25,* 657-675.

Schonflug, W. (1993a). Practical and theoretical psychology: Singles with wedding rings? *Applied Psychology: An International Review, 42,* 58-60.

Schonflug, W. (1993b). Applied psychology: Newcomer with a long tradition. Applied Psychology: *An International Review, 42*, 5-30.

Schooler, C. (1989a). Levels and proof in cross-disciplinary research. In D. Kertzer, J. Meyer, and K. W. Schaie (Eds*.), Social Structure and Aging: Comparative Perspectives on Age Structuring in Modern Societies.* Hillsdale, N. J.: Erlbaum.

Schooler, C. (1989b). Social structural effects and experimental situations: Mutual lessons of cognitive and social science. In K. W. Schaie and C. Schooler (Eds.), *Social Structure and Aging:_Psychological Processes.* Hillsdale, N. J.: Erlbaum.

Schooler, J. W., & Engstler-Schooler, T. Y. (1990). Verbal overshadowing of visual memories: Some things are better left unsaid. *Cognitive Psychology, 17*, 36-71.

Schooler, J., & Herrmann, D. J. (1992). There is more to episodic memory than just episodes, and more to autobiographical memory than can be revealed by standard memory measures. In M. A. Conway, D. Rubin, H. Spinnler, & W. Wagenaar (Eds.), *Theoretical perspectives on autobiographical memory.* Boston: Kluwer.

Schooler, J. W., Gerhard, D., & Loftus, E. (1986). Qualities of the unreal. Journal of *Experimental Psychology: Learning, Memory, and Cognition, 12*, 171-181.

Schraw, G. J. (1995). Measures of feeling-of-knowing accuracy: a new look at an old problem. *Applied Cognitive Psychology, 9*, 321-332.

Schraw, G.,J., Dunkle, M. E., & Bendixen, L. D. (1995). Cognitive processes in well-defined and ill-defined problem solving. *Applied Cognitive Psychology, 9*, 523-538.

Schultz, D. P. (1979). *Psychology in use: An introduction to applied psychology.* New York: Macmillan.

Schvaneveldt, R. W., Reid, G. B., Gomez, R. L., & Rice, S. (1998). Modeling mental workload. *Cognitive Technology, 3*, 19-31.

Schwartz, N. (1996*). Cognition and communication: Judgmental biases, research methods and the logic of conversation.* Hillsdale, NJ: Erlbaum.

Schwartz, N. (1999). Self-reports: How the questions shape the answers. *American Psychologist, 54*, 93-105.

Schwartz, N., & Sudman, S. (Eds.). (1994). *Autobiographical memory and the validity of retrospective reports.* New York: Springer-Verlag.

Schwartz, R. H. (1991). Heavy marijuana use and recent memory impairment. *Psychiatric Annals, 21*, 80-82.

Scribner, S., & Beach, K. (1993). An activity theory approach to memory. *Applied Cognitive Psychology, 7*, 185-190.

Seabrook, R., Brown, G. D. A., & Solity, J. E. (2005). Distributed and massed practice: From the laboratory to the classroom. *Applied Cognitive Psychology, 19*, 107-122.

Searleman, A., & Gaydusek, K. A. (1996). Relationship between prospective memory ability and selective personality varialbes. In D. Herrmann, C. McEvoy, C. Herzog, P. Hertel, & M. Johnson (Eds.), *Basic and applied memory,* Mawah: Erlbaum.

Searleman, A., & Herrmann, D. (1994). *Memory from a broader perspective.* New York: McGraw Hill.

Sears, D. O. (1987). Implications of the life-span approach for research on attitudes of social cognition. In R. P. Ables (Ed.). *Life-span Perspectives and Social Psychology.* Hillsdale, New Jersey: Erlbaum.

Sellen, A. J. (1994). Detection of everyday errors. *Applied Psychology: An International Review, 143*, 475-498

Semmer, N. (1993). Differentiation between social groups: The case of basic and applied psychology. *Applied Psychology: An International Review, 42*, 40-46.

Senders, J., & Moray, N. (1991). *Human error: Cause prediction and reduction.* Hillsdale, NJ: Erlbaum.

Shohov, S. (2005). *Leading edge research in cognitive psychology.* Orlando: Nova.

Shallice, T. (1979). Case study approach in neuropsychological research. *Journal of Clinical Neuropsychology, 1*, 183-211.

Sherman, S. J., & McConnell, A. R. (1996). The role of counterfactual thinking in reasoning. *Applied Cognitive Psychology, 10*, S113-S124.

Shiffrin, R. M., & Schneider, W. (1977). Controlled and automatic human information processing: II. Perceptual learning, automatic attending, and a general theory. *Psychological Review, 84*, 127-190.

Shrimpton, S, Oates, K., & Hayes, S. (1998). Children's memory of events: effects of stress, age, time delay and location of interview. *Applied Cognitive Psychology, 12*, 133-143.

Sidman, M. (1960). *Tactics of scientific research Evaluating Experimental Data in Psychology*: New York: Basic Books.

Sigma Xi (1991). *Honor in science.* Research Triangle Park, NC: Sigma Xi, The Scientific Research Society.

Singh, J., Dwivedi, K. & Saxena, V. B. (1987) Memory and subjective symptoms in automobile painters. *Indian Psychological Review, 32*, 5-12.

Simon, H. A. (1980). Cognitive science: The newest science of the artificial. *Cognitive Science, 4*, 33-46.

Simon, H. A., & Barenfeld, M. (1969). Information processing analysis of perceptual processes in problem solving. *Psychological Review, 76*, 473-483.

Simpson, S. A., & Gilhooly, K. J. (1997). Diagnostic thinking processes: evidence from a constructive interaction study of electrocardiogram (EGG) interpretation. *Applied Cognitive Psychology, 11*, 543-554.

Singer, E., Thurn, D. R. V., & Miller, E. R. (1995). Confidentiality assurances and response. *Public Opinion Quarterly, 59*, 59-66.

Singer, J. A. & Salovey, P. (1988). Mood and memory: evaluating the network theory of affect. *Clinical Psychology Review, 8*, 211-251.

Sirken, M., Herrmann, D., Schecter, S., Schwarz, N., Tanur, J., & Tourangeau, R. (1999). *Cognition and survey research.* Boston: Wiley.

Skilbeck, C. (1984). Computer assistance in the management of memory and cognitive impairment. In B. A. Wilson & N. Moffat (Eds.), *Clinical management of memory problems.* Rockville, MD: Aspen Systems.

Smart, R. (1964). The importance of negative results in psychological research. *Canadian Psychologist, 5*, 225-232.

Smith, A. (1988). Effects of meals on memory and attention. In M. M. Gruneberg, P. E. Morris, & R. N. Sykes (Eds.), *Practical aspects of memory: Current research and issues* (Vol. 2, pp. 477-482). Chichester, England: John Wiley & Sons.

Smith, A. P. (1992). Colds, influenza and performance. In A. P. Smith & D. M. Jones (Eds.), *Handbook of human performance, Vol. 2: Health and performance.* London: Academic Press.

Smith, A.P., Chappelow, J., & Belyavin, A. (1995). Cognitive failures, focused attention, and categoric search. *Applied Cognitive Psychology, 9*, S115-S126.

Smith, E. E., Shoben, E. J., & Rips, L. J. (1974). Structure and process in semantic memory: A feature model for semantic decisions. *Psychological Review, 81*, 214-241.

Smith, W., Randell, M., Lewandowsky, S., Kirsner, K., & Dunn, J. (1996). Collaborative research into cognitive technology: The role of shared commitment, problem coherence, and domain knowledge. *Cognitive Technology, 1*, 9-18.

Smyth, M.M., & Waller, A. (1998). Movement imagery in rock climbing: patterns of interference from visual, spatial and kinaesthetic secondary tasks. *Applied Cognitive Psychology, 12*, 145-157.

Smyth, M. M., Collins, A. F., Morris, P. E., & Levy, P. (1994*). Cognition in action*, 2nd edition. Hove: Erlbaum.

Solberg, M., & Mateer, C. (2001). *Introduction to cognitive rehabilitation*. New York: Guilford
    Press, 1989.

Solomon, P. R., Goethals, G. R. Kelley, C. M. and Stephens, B. R. (Eds.). (1987). *Memory:
    Interdisciplinary Approaches*, New York: Springer Verlag.

Solso, R. L. (2001). *Cognitive psychology*, fifth edition. Needham Heights, MA: Allyn &
    Bacon.

Spanos, N. P., Burgess, C. A., Burgess, M. F., Samuels, C., & Blois, W. O. (1999). Creating
    false memories of infancy with hypnotic and non-hypnotic procedures. *Applied
    Cognitive Psychology, 13*, 201-218.

Spelke, E., Hirst, W. & Neisser, U. (1976). Skills of divided attention. *Cognition, 4*, 215-230.

Spence, I., & Lewandowsky, S. (1991). Displaying proportions and percentages. *Applied
    Cognitive Psychology, 5*, 61-77.

Speth, C., & Brown, R. (1990). Effects of college students' learning styles and gender on
    their test preparation strategies. *Applied Cognitive Psychology, 4*, 189-202.

Sporer, S. L. (1997). The less travelled road to truth: verbal cues in deception detection
    in accounts of fabricated and self-experienced events. *Applied Cognitive
    Psychology, 11*, 373-397.

Sprock, J., & Herrmann, D. (2004). The focus on cognition in the psychopathology
    literature: A bibliographic analysis, *Cognitive Technology, 9*, 4-19.

Spurgeon, P., Davies, R. & Chapman, T. (1994*). Elements of applied psychology*.
    Amsterdam: Harwood.

Squire, L. R. (1987). *Memory and Brain*. New York: Oxford University Press.

Squire, L. R. (Ed.).(1992). *Encyclopedia of Learning and Memory*. New York: Macmillan.

Squire, L. R., Knowlton, B., & Musen, G. (1993). The structure and organization of
    memory. In L. W. Porter & M. R. Rosenzweig (Eds.), *Annual Review of
    Psychology* (Vol. 44, pp. 453-495).Palo Alto, CA: Annual Review Inc.

Stamford, B. A., Hambacher, W. & Fallica, A. (1974). Effects of daily exercise on the
    psychiatric state of institutionalized geriatric mental patients. *Research
    Quarterly, 45*, 35-41.

Stanovich, K. E. & West, R. F. (2000). Individual differences in reasoning:
    Implicaitons for the rationality debate? *Behavioral and Brain Sciences, 23*,
    645-726.

Stelmack, R. M. (1990). Biological bases of extraversion: Psychophysiological evidence.
    Journal of Personality, 58, 293-311.

Ste-Marie, D.M. (1999). Expert-novice differences in gymnastic judging: an
    information-processing perspective. *Applied Cognitive Psychology, 13*, 269-
    281.

Stephenson, G. M., & Wagner, W. (1989). Origins of the misplaced confidence effect in collaborative recall. *Applied Cognitive Psychology, 3*, 227-236

Sternberg, R. J., (1986). *Intelligence applied: Understanding and increasing your intellectual skills.* San Diego: Harcourt Brace Jovanovich.

Sternberg, R. J., (2005). *Cognitive Psychology.* Belmont, CA: Brooks Cole and Wadsworth.

Sternberg, S. (1975). Memory scanning: New findings and current controversies. *Quarterly Journal of Experimental Psychology, 27*, 1-32.

Stevens, J. (1993). An observational study of skilled memory in waitresses. *Applied Cognitive Psychology, 7*, 205-217.

Stigsdotter, A., & Backman, L. (1989). Multifactorial memory training with older adults: How to foster maintenance of improved performance. *Gerontology, 35*, 260-267.

Stigsdotter-Neely, A., & Backman, L. (1993a). Maintenance of gains following multifactorial and unifactorial memory training in late adulthood. *Educational Gerontology, 19*, 105-117.

Stollery, B. (1988). Neurotoxic exposure and memory function. In M. M. Gruneberg, P. E. Morris, & R. N. Sykes, (Eds.), *Practical aspects of memory: Current research and issues Vol. 2,* (pp 242-247). Chichester, England: John Wiley & Sons.

Stolte, J. F. (1994). The context of satisficing in vignette research. *The Journal of Social Psychology, 134*, 727-733.

Stone, A. A., Turkkan, J. S., Bachrach, C. A., Jobe, J., Kurtzman, H. S., & Cain, V. S. (2000). *The science of self report: Implications for research and practice.* Mahwah, NJ: Erlbaum.

Strauch, B. (2001*). Investigating human error in incidents and accidents.* Burlington, VT: Ashgate.

Strayer, D. L., & Johnston, W. A. (2001). Driven to distraction: Dual-task studies of simulated driving and conversing on a cellular phone . *Psychological Science, 12*, 462-466.

Strayer, D. L., Drews, F. A., & Johnston, W. A. (2003). Cell phone induced failures of visual attention during simulated driving. *Journal of Experimental Psychology: Applied, 9*, 23-52.

Strayer, D. L, Drews, F. A.,. Crouch, D. J. & Johnston, W. A. (2004). Why Do Cell Phone Conversations Interfere With Driving? In R. Walker and D. Herrmann (EDs). *Cognitive Technology,* Jefferson, North Carolina: McFarland.

Steyvers, F.J.J.M., Dekker, K., Brookhuis, K.A., & Jackson, A.E., (1994). The experience of road environments under two lighting and traffic conditions: application of a road environment construct list. *Applied Cognitive Psychology, 8*, 497-511.

Suchman, L., & Jordan, B. (1990). Interactional troubles in face-to-face survey interviews. *Journal of the American Statistical Association, 85,* 232-241, 252-253.

Suigman, T. (1993). Applied and basic psychology: Towards a dynamic, bi-directional relationship. *Applied Psychology: An International Review, 42,* 37-40.

Sullivan, E. B. (1927). Attitude in relation to learning. *Psychological Monographs, 36,* 1-149.

Sunderland, A., Beech, J.R., Sheehan, E. (1996). The current orientation test: a study of speed and consistency of retrieval of recent everyday memories by old and young subjects. *Applied Cognitive Psychology, 10,* 337-347.

Sutherland, E. (2003). *Cognitive psychology.* London: Learning Matters Limited.

Sweller, J. (1989). Cognitive psychology: Some procedures for facilitating learning and problem solving in mathematics and science. *Journal of Educational Psychology, 81,* 457-466.\

Swets, J. A., Dawes, R. M., & Monahan, J. (2000). Psychological science can improve diagnostic decisions. *Psychological Science, 1,* 1-26.

Teasdale, J. D., Dritschel, B. H., Taylor, M. J., Proctor, L., Lloyd, C. A., Nimmo-Smith, I., & Baddeley, A. D. (1995). Stimulus-independent thought depends on central executive resources. *Memory and Cognition, 23,* 551-559.

Teigen , K. H., & Jorgensen, M. (2005). When 90% confidence intervals are 50% certain: On the credibility of credible intervals. *Applied Cognitive Psychology, 19,* 455-476.

Tenenbaum, G., Tehan, G., Stewart, G. & Christensen, S. (1999). Recalling a floor routine: the effects of skill and age on memory for order. *Applied Cognitive Psychology, 13,* 101-123.

Terry, R. D., Katzman, R., Bick, K. L., & Sisodia, S. S. (Eds). (1999). *Alzheimer disease, second edition.* New York: Lippincott, Williams, and Wilkins.

Thagard, P. (1992). *Conceptual revolutions.* Princeton, N. J.: Princeton University Press.

Theeuwes, J., & Alferdinck, J. W. A. M. (1995). Rear light arrangements for cars equipped with a center high-mounted stop lamp. *Human Factors, 37(2),* 371-380.

Thomas, J.W., Bol, L., Warkentin, R.W., Wilson, M., Strage, A., & Rohwer, Jr., W.D. (1993). Interrelationships among students' study activities, self-concept of academic ability, and achievement as a function of characteristics of high-school biology courses. *Applied Cognitive Psychology, 7,* 499-532.

Thompson, C. P., Cowan, T., Frieman, J., Mahadeeran, R. S., & Vogl, R. J. (1991). Rajan: A study of a memorist. *Journal of Memory and Language, 30,* 702-724.

Thompson, C. P., Herrmann, D. J., Bruce, D., Payne, D. G., Read, J. D., & Toglia, M. P. (1997a*). Autobiographical memory.* Hillsdale, NJ: Erlbaum.

Thompson, C. P., Herrmann, D. J., Bruce, D., Payne, D. G., Read, J. D., & Toglia, M. P. (1997b). *Eyewitness memory*. Hillsdale, NJ: Erlbaum.

Thompson, R. F. & Madigan, S. A. (2005). *Memory : The key to consciousness*. Washington, D.C.: Joseph Henry Press.

Thorndike, E. L., & Woodworth, R. S. (1901). The influence of improvement in one mental function upon the efficiency of other functions. *Psychological Review, 8,* 247-261, 384-395, 553-564

Tiedemann, J. (1987). Measures of cognitive styles: A Critical review,. *Educational Psychologist, 24,* 261-275.

Tilley, A. & Statham, D. (1989). The effect of prior sleep on retrieval. *Acta Psychologica, 70,* 199-203.

Tomes, J. L., & Katz, A. N. (1997). Habitual susceptibility to misinformation and individual differences in eyewitness memory. *Psychology Applied Cognitive, 11,* 233-251.

Tourangeau, R. (1984). Cognitive sciences and survey methods. In T. B. J abine, M. L. Straf, J. M. Tanur, & R. Tourangeau (Eds.), *Cognitive aspects of survey methodology: Building a bridge between disciplines* (pp. 73-101). Washington, DC: National Academy Press.

Treadway, M., & McCloskey, M. (1989). Effects of racial stereotypes on eyewitness performance: implications of the real and the rumoured Allport and Postman studies. *Applied Cognitive Psychology, 3,* 53-63.

Tulving, E. (1972). Episodic and semantic memory. In E. Tulving & W. Donaldson (Eds.), *Organization of memory*. Academic Press: New York.

Tulving, E. (1983). *Elements of episodic memory*. Oxford: Oxford University Press.

Tulving, E., & Craik, F. M. (2000). *The Oxford handbook of memory*. Oxford: Oxford University Press.

Underwood, B. J., Baruch, R. F., & Malmi, R. A. (1978). Composition of episodic memory. *Journal of Experimental Psychology: General, 107,* 393-419.

Underwood, G., & Milton, H. (1993). Collusion after a collision: witnesses' reports of a road accident with and without discussion. *Applied Cognitive Psychology, 7,* 11-22.

Van der Linden, D., Frese, M. & Meigman, T. (2003). Mental fatigue and the control of cognitive processes: Effects on perseveration and planning. *Acta Psychological, 113,* 45-65.

Vandermaas, M. O., Hess, T. M., & Baker-Ward, L. (1993). Does anxiety affect children's reports of memory for an event? *Applied Cognitive Psychology, 7,* 109-127.

Vick, O. & Jackson, D. (1976). Cognitive styles in the schematizing process: A critical evaluation. *Educational and Psychological Measurement, 27,* 267-286.

Vincente, K. J. (1994). A pragmatic conception of basic and applied research: Commentary on Hoffman and Deffenbacher (1993). *Ecological Psychology, 6*, 65-81.

Vitkovitch, M., & Barber, P. (1996). Visible speech as a function of image quality: effects of display parameters on lip reading ability. *Applied Cognitive Psychology, 10*, 121-140.

Voevodsky, J. (1974). Evaluation of a deceleration warning light for reducing rear-end automobile collisions. *Journal of Applied Psychology, 59(3)*, 270-273.

von Gorp, W. G., Hull, J., Wilkins, J. N., Hinkin, C. H., Plotkin, D., Moore, L. H., & Horner, M. D. (2000). Declarative and procedural memory function in abstinent cocaine abusers. *Archives of General Psychiatry, 57*, 512-513.

Vortac, O. U., Barile, A. L., Albright, C. A., Truitt, T. R., Manning, C. A., & Bain, D. (1996). Automation of flight data in air traffic control. In D. Herrmann, C. McEvoy, C. Hertzog, P. Hertel, & M. Johnson (Eds.). (1996). *Basic and applied memory: Theory in context, Vol. 1.* Mahwah, NJ: Erlbaum.

Vosburg, S. (1998). The effects of positive and negative mood on divergent-thinking performance. *Creativity Research Journal, 11*, 165-172.

Wagenaar, W. A., (1986). My memory: A study of autobiographical memory over six years. *Cognitive Psychology, 18*, 225-252.

Wagenaar, W. A., & Groeneweg, J. (1990). The memory of concentration camp survivors. *Applied Cognitive Psychology, 4*, 77-87.

Wagenaar, W. A., Hudson, P. T. W., & Reason, J. T. (1990). *Cognitive failures and accidents. 4*, 273-294

Walbaum, S. D. (1997). Marking time: the effect of timing on appointment keeping. *Applied Cognitive Psychology, 11*, 361-368.

Walker, R. W., & Andrews, R. Y. (2005). Training college students to use personal data assistants. In R. W. Walker and mD. Herrmann (Eds), *Cognitive Technology.* Jefferson, N.C.: McFarland.

Walker, R. W., & Andrews, R. Y. (2001). External memory aids and the use of personal data assistants in improving everyday memory, *Cognitive Technology, 6*, 15-25.

Walker, W. R., & Herrmann, D. J. (2005). *Cognitive technology.* Wintons Salem, NC: McFarland Publishers.

Walker, W. R., Skowronski, J. J., & Thompson, C. P. (2003). Life is pleasant and Memory helps to keep it that way. *Review of General Psychology, 7*, 203-210.

Walker, W.R., Vogl, R.J., & Thompson, C.P. (1997). Autobiographical memory: unpleasantness fades faster than pleasantness over time. *Applied Cognitive Psychology, 11*, 399-413.

Wang, A. Y., & Thomas, M. H. (1999). In defence of keyword experiments: a reply to Gruneberg's commentary. *Applied Cognitive Psychology, 13*, 283-287.

Ward, G., & Carroll, M. (1997). Reality monitoring for sexual abuse memories. *Applied Cognitive Psychology, 11*, 293-304.

Watson, F. L., & Brown, G. D. A. (1992). Single-word reading in college dyslexics. *Applied Cognitive Psychology, 6*, 263-272.

Weber, N. & Brewer, N. (2003). Expert memory: The interaction of stimulus structure, attention, and expertise. *Applied Cognitive Psychology, 17*, 295-308.

Wechsler, D. (1945). A standardized memory scale for clinical use. *Journal of Psychology, 19*, 87-95.

Weil, M. M., & Rosen, L. D. (1994). The psychological impact of technology from a global perspective: A study of technological sophistication and technophobia in university students from twenty-three countries. *Human Behavior, 11*, 95-133.

Wells, G. L., & Bradfield, A. L. (1998). "Good, you identified the suspect": Feedback to eyewitnesses distorts their reports of the witnessing experience. *Journal of Applied Psychology, 83*, 360-376.

Wells, G. L. & Olson, E. A. (2003). Eyewitness testimony. *Annual Review of Psychology, 54*, 277-295.

Wells, G. L., Malpass, R. S., Lindsay, R. C. L., Fisher, R. P., Turtle, J. W., & Fulero, S. M. (2000). Mistakes in eyewitness identification that are caused by known factors. Collaboration between criminal justice experts and research psychologists may lower the number of errors. *American Psychologist, 55*, 581-598.

Wenger, E. (1987). *Artificial intelligence and tutoring systems.* Lost Altos, CA: Morgan Kaufman.

Wells, G. L., Seelau, E. P., Rydell, S. M., & Luus, C. A. (1994). Recommendations for properly conducted lineup identification tests. In D. F. Ross, J.D. Read, & M. Toglia (Eds.), *Adult eyewitness testimony* (pp. 223-244). New York: Cambridge University Press.

Wenger, E. (1987). *Artificial intelligence and tutoring systems.* LosAltos, CA: Morgan Kaufman.

Wenger, M. J., & Payne, D. G. (1995). On the acquisition of mnemonic skill: Applications of skilled memory theory. *Journal of Experimental Psychology: Applied, 1*, 194-215.

Wentzel, K. R. (1995). Does interest justify further research? Comments on Tang and Hall. *Applied Cognitive Psychology, 9*, 405-409.

West, R. (1985). *Memory fitness over 40.* Gainesville, FL: Triad Publishing Company.

West, R. (1988). Prospective memory and aging. In M. Gruneberg, P. Morris, & R. Sykes
(Eds.), *Practical aspects of memory: Current research and issues, Vol. 2.*
Chichester: Wiley.

West, R. L., & Crook, T. H. (1992). Video training of imagery for mature adults. *Applied Cognitive Psychology, 6,* 307-320.

West, R. L., Yassuda, M. S., & Welch, D. C. (1997). Imagery training via videotape:
Progress and potential for older adults. *Cognitive Technology, 2,* 16-21.

Whimbey, A., & Lockhead, J. (1999). *Problem solving and comprehension,* sixth edition.
Mahwah, NJ: Erlbaum.

White, N. M. (1998). Cognitive enhancement: An everyday event. *International Journal of Psychology, 33,* 95-105.

White, R. T. (1982). Memory for personal events. *Human Learning, 1,* 171-183.

White, R. T. (1989). Recall of autobiographical events. *Applied Cognitive Psychology, 3,*
127-135.

White, T. L., Leichtman, M. D., & Ceci, S. J. (1997). The good, the bad, and the ugly:
accuracy, inaccuracy, and elaboration in preschoolers' reports about a past
event. *Applied Cognitive Psychology, 11,* S37-S54.

Whitehouse, W. G., Orne, E. C., Orne, M. T., & Dinges, D. F. (1991). Distinguishing the
source of memories reported during prior waking and hypnotic recall attempts.
Applied Cognitive Psychology, 5, 51-59.

Wichman, H., & Oyasato, A. (1983). Effects of locus of control and task complexity on
prospective remembering. *Human Factors, 25,* 583-591.

Wickens, C. D. (1999). Cognitive factors in aviation. In F. Durso (Ed.), *Handbook of applied cognition.* New York: Wiley.

Wierda, M., &. Brookhuis, K.A. (1991). Analysis of cycling skill: a cognitive approach.
Applied Cognitive Psychology, 5, 113-122.

Wilding, J., & Hayes, S. (1992). Relations between approaches to studying and note-taking
behaviour in lectures. *Applied Cognitive Psychology, 6,* 233-246.

Wilding, J., & Valentine, E. (1992). Factors predicting success and failure in the first-year
examinations of medical and dental courses. *Applied Cognitive Psychology, 6,*
247-261.

Wilding, J., & Valentine, E. (1996). Memory expertise. In J. Wilding & S. Hayes (1992),
Relations between approaches to studying and note-taking behavior in
lectures. *Applied Cognitive Psychology, 6,* 233-246.

Wilding, J., & Valentine, E. (1997). *Superior memory.* Hove: Psychology Press.

Wilkins, A. J., & Baddeley, A. D. (1978). Remembering to recall in everyday life: An
approach to absent-mindedness. In M. M. Gruneberg, P. E. Morris, & R. N.

Sykes (Eds.), *Practical aspects of memory*. London: Academic Press.

Wilkinson, C., & Hyman Jr, I.E. (1998). Individual differences related to two types of memory errors: Word lists may not generalize to autobiographical memory. *Applied Cognitive Psychology, 12*, S29-S46.

Williams, A. M., Ward, P., Knowles, J. M., & Smeeton, N. J. (2002). Anticipation skill in a real-world task: Measurement, training, and transfer in tennis. *Journal of Experimental Psychology, 8*, 259-270.

Williams, J. M. G. & Dritschel, B. H. (1992). Categoric and extended autobiographical memories. In M. A. Conway, D. C. Rubin, H. Spinler, and W. A. Wagenaar (Eds.). *Theoretical perspectives on autobiographical memory* (pp. 391-412). The Netherlands: Khuwer.

Williams, J. M. G. & Scott, J. (1988). Autobiographical memories in depression. *Psychological Medicine, 18*, 689-695.

Williams, L. (1994). Recall of childhood trauma: A prospective study of women's memories of child sexual abuse. *Journal of Consulting & Clinical Psychology, 62*, 1167-1176.

Willingham, D. T. (2004). *Cognition: The Thinking Animal* (2nd ed.). Upper Saddle River, NJ: Pearson Education, Inc.

Willis, G. B., Royston, P. N., & Bercini, D. (1991). The use of verbal report methods in the applied cognitive laboratory. *Applied Cognitive Psychology, 5*, 251-267.

Willis, L., Yeo, R. A., Thomas, P., & Garry, P. J.(1988) Differential declines in cognitive function with aging. The possible role of healoth status. Developmental Neurospyhchology, 4, 23-28.

Wilson, B. A. (1987). *Rehabilitation of memory*. New York: Guilford.

Wilson, B. & Moffat, N. (1984). *Clinical Management of Memory Problems*. Rockville, Maryland: Aspen Systems.

Wilson, B. & Moffat, N. (1992). *Clinical Management of Memory Problems*. Second edition. Rockville, Maryland: Aspen Systems.

Wilson, B., & Patterson, K. (1990). Rehabilitation for cognitive impairment: Does cognitive psychology apply? *Applied Cognitive Psychology, 4*, 247-260.

Winograd, E., & Neisser, U. (Eds.). (1992). *Affect and accuracy in recall: Studies of flashbulb memories*. Cambridge: Cambridge University Press.

Winograd, E., Fivush, R., & Hirst, W. (Eds.) (1996). *Ecological approaches to cognition: Essays in honor of Ulric Neisser*. Mahwah, NJ: Erlbaum.

Witkin, A. P., & Tenenbaum, J. M. (1983). On the role of structure in vision. In J. Beck, B. Hope, & A. Rosenfield (Eds.), *Human and machine vision*. New York: Academic Press.

Witus, G. & Ellis, R.D. (2003. Computational modeling of foveal target detection. *Human Factors, 45,* 47-60.

Wolfe, D. (Ed.). (1959). *Symposium on basic research.* Washington, DC: American Association for the Advancement of Science.

Woloshyn, V. E., Wood, E., & Willoughby, T. (1994). Considering prior knowledge when using elaborative interrogation. *Applied Cognitive Psychology, 8,* 25-36.

Wood, E., Fler, C. , & Willoughby, T. (1992). Elaborative interrogation applied to small and large group contexts. *Applied Cognitive Psychology, 6,* 361-366.

Woods, D. D., & Cook, R. I. (1999). Perspectives on human error: Hindsight biases and local rationality. In F. Durso (Ed.), *Handbook of applied cognition.* New York: Wiley.

Woodworth, R. S. (1938). *Experimental psychology.* London: Methuen.

Woodworth, R. S. & Scholsberg, F. 1954). *Experimental psychology.* London: Methuen.

World Book Encyclopedia (1995). Chicago: Scott Fetzer Company.

Wortham, S. (2001). Interactionally situated cognition: A classroom example. *Cognitive Science, 25,* 37-66.

Wright, D. B. (1993a). Misinformation and warnings in eyewitness testimony: A new testing procedure to differentiate explanations. *Memory, 1,* 153-166.

Wright, D. B. (1993b). Recall of the Hillsborough disaster over time: systematic biases of 'flashbulb' memories. *Applied Cognitive Psychology, 7,* 129-138.

Wright, D. B. (1997). Methodological issues for naturalistic event memory research. In D. G. Payne & F. G. Conrad (Eds.), *Intersections in basic and applied memory research.* Mawah, NJ: Erlbaum.

Wright, D. B. (1998). Modelling clustered data in autobiographical memory research: the multilevel approach. *Applied Cognitive Psychology, 12,* 339-357.

Wright, D. B., & Davies, G. M. (1999). Eyewitness testimony. In F. Durso (Ed.), *Handbook of applied cognition.* New York: Wiley.

Wright, D. B., & McDaid, A. T. (1996). Comparing system and estimator variables using data from real line-ups. *Applied Cognitive Psychology, 10,* 75-84.

Wright, P. (1978). Feeding the information eaters: Suggestions for integrating pure and applied research on language comprehension. *Instructional Science, 7,* 249-312.

Wright, P. (1999). Designing healthcare advice for the public. In F. Durso (Ed.). *Handbook of Applied Cognition,* New York: Wiley.

Wright, P., & Hull, A.J. (1999). How people give verbal instructions. *Applied Cognitive Psychology, 4,* 153-174.

Wulf, F. (1922). Uber die veranderung von vorstellungen Gedactnis und gestalt. *Psychologie Forsh, 1*, 333-373.

Wyer, R. S., & Srull, T. K. (1986). Human cognition in its social context. *Psychological Review, 93*, 322-359.

Wynn, V. E., & Logie, R. H. (1998). The veracity of long-term memories – did Bartlett get it right? *Applied Cognitive Psychology, 12*, 1-20.

Wyon, D.P., Andersen, B., & Lundqvist, G.R. (1979). The effects of moderate heat stress on mental performance. *Scandanavian Journal of Work Environment and Health, 5*, 352-361.

Yamagishi, K. (1997). When a 12.86% mortality is more dangerous than 24.14%: implications for risk communication. *Applied Cognitive Psychology, 11*, 495-506.

Yarmey, A. D. (1988). Victims and witnessses to deadly force. *Canadian Police College Journal, 12*, 99-109.

Yarmey, A. D. (1993). Stereotypes and recognition memory for faces and voices of good guys and bad guys. *Applied Cognitive Psychology, 7*, 419-431.

Yarmey, A. D., Yarmey, A. L., & Yarmey, M. J. (1994). Face and voice identification in showups and lineups. *Applied Cognitive Psychology, 8*, 453-464.

Yates, F. (1966). *The arts of memory*. Chicago: Chicago University Press.

Yerkes, R. M., & Dodson, J. D. (1908). The relation of strength of stimulus to rapidity of habit formation. *Journal of Comparative and Neurological Psychology, 18*, 459-482.

Yin, R. K. (1994*). Case Study Research Design and Methods*, Second Edition, Applied Social Research Methods Series, Volume 5. Thousand Oaks, CA: Sage.

Yoder, C .Y. (1984) Clinical issues and applications in late life adjustment. *Experimental Aging Research, 10*, 237-238.

Yoder, C. Y. & Elias, J. W. (1987). Age, affect and memory for pictorial story sequences. *British Journal of Psychology, 78*, 545-549.

Yoder, C .Y., & Elias, J. W. (1991). The role of affect in memory. In R. L. West & J. P. Sinnott (Eds.*), Everyday memory and aging: Current research methodology*. New York: Springer-Verlag

Yoder, C. & Herrmann, D. (2004). Individual differences in external aid use. In R. W. Walker and D. Herrmann (Eds.*). Cognitive Technology: Transforming Thought and Society*. Jefferson, N.C.: McFarland.

Yoder, C. Y., & Murray, M. C. (1989). Adjustment and aging: Some influences and implications of personality and cognitive style. *The Southwestern, 5*, 12-23.

Yuille, J. C. (1993). We must study forensic eyewitnesses to know about them. *American Psychologist, 48*, 572- 573.

Yuille, J. C., & Cutshall, J. L. (1986). A case study of eyewitness memory of a crime. *Journal of Applied Psychology, 71(2)*, 291-301.

Yuille, N., & Oakhill, J. (1988). Effects of inference awareness training on poor reading comprehension. *Applied Cognitive Psychology, 2*, 33-45.

Zacks, R. T., & Hasher, L. (1992). Memory in life, lab, and clinic: Implications for memory theory. In D. Herrmann, H. Weingartner, A. Searleman, & C. McEvoy (Eds.). *Memory Improvement: Implications for memory theory.* (pp. 232-248). New York: Springer Verlag.

Zaragoza, M. S., McCloskey, M., & Jamis, M. (1987). Misleading post-event information and recall of the original event: Further evidence against the memory impairment hypotheseis. *Journal of Experimental Psychology: Learning, Memory and Cognition, 13*, 36-44.

Zeitz, C.M., & Spoehr, K.T. (1989). Knowledge organization and the acquisition of procedural expertise. *Applied Cognitive Psychology, 3*, 313-336.

Author Index

Subject Index

#0254 - 130115 - C0 - 229/152/17 - PB